AT THE BORDER
CALLED HOPE

AT THE BORDER
CALLED HOPE

WHERE REFUGEES ARE
NEIGHBOURS

Mary Jo Leddy

A Phyllis Bruce Book

HarperPerennial

HarperCollins*Publishers*Ltd

All of these stories are true. Some of the names and details have been changed to protect those whose lives are still at risk.

http://www.harpercollins.com/canada

First published in hardcover by HarperCollins Publishers Ltd: 1997
First HarperPerennial edition: 1998

HarperCollins books may be purchased for educational, business, or sales promotional use. For information please write: Special Markets Department, HarperCollins Canada, 55 Avenue Road, Suite 2900, Toronto, Ontario M5R 3L2.

Canadian Cataloguing in Publication Data

Leddy, Mary Joanna, 1946–
At the border called hope : where refugees are neighbours

1st HarperPerennial ed.
"A Phyllis Bruce book".
ISBN 0-00-638646-6

1. Romero House (Toronto, Ont.). 2. Refugees - Ontario - Toronto.
3. Refugees - Services for - Ontario - Toronto. I. Title.

HV640.4.C3L44 1998   362.87'85'09713541   C97-932317-7

98 99 00 v HC 10 9 8 7 6 5 4 3 2 1

Printed and bound in the United States

for those who call Romero House their community

for the members of the Church of the Holy Trinity
Sanctuary Group

for June Callwood and Wilber Sutherland

Do not oppress the stranger, for you know the feeling of the stranger, because you yourselves once were strangers.
—Exodus 23: 9

Love your neighbour as yourself . . . but someone who wanted to justify himself asked Jesus, "Who is my neighbour?"
—Luke 10: 26–29

CONTENTS

POINTS OF DEPARTURE

IT WAS NEVER MY INTENTION to live with refugees. It was not, as they say, part of my game plan. I was in between jobs, perhaps even in between lives. A friend asked me to take her place as a night manager in a house for refugees until a more permanent replacement could be found.

"What would be involved?" I asked.

"Just living with them."

The simplicity of the request felt like a summoning. I said yes immediately and moved into a dilapidated old house near Keele and Bloor in Toronto. It was only to be for a few months. There were other things I had planned to do, other books I had intended to write. Life, I have learned, is what happens when you are busy planning something else.

I had entered a world of strangers and together we discovered how to become neighbours. Within weeks I realized that I liked these people, enjoyed being with them. It was a realization shared by other friends who came to visit the house and were introduced to the people living there. It was a way of being we wanted to continue because we had seen what happened when people related to one another as good neighbours rather than as landlords and tenants, social workers and clients or advocates and cases. We began to talk, to pray, to dream and to scheme.

Thus, Romero House was born about five years ago and grew somewhat like Topsy until there are now, in fact, three houses in the area which lies a little north of High Park and slightly south of "the Junction" in the west end of Toronto.

Although each of the houses receives a government subsidy to ensure that all the rent is geared to a refugee's income, almost all of the settlement work is done on a voluntary basis by people, usually young people, who live in the houses with the refugees. Their remarkable generosity, unique sense of humour and chutzpah have given us all reason to hope.

This community of people trying to live as good neighbours is named after Archbishop Oscar Romero of El Salvador, the church leader martyred for his outspoken defence of the poor in his country. At any one time, there are ten to thirteen refugees living in a house together with one or two volunteers. Many other refugees simply show up on our doorstep for various kinds of assistance. There are about 150 people who continue to think of themselves as part of the Romero community even after they have left the houses.

I cannot imagine living anywhere else. Where you live determines what you see. The people you listen to influence what you hear. In the course of these five years, how I write and what I write about and for whom has been transformed. My words became stripped down, to the point. To speak with my neighbours I had to do so carefully. I had to say it with my hands and eyes. You are welcome here. Please sit. Have tea. I listened more carefully, learned how to read eyes and smell fear.

I write many things for my neighbours: personal information forms for refugee hearings, letters to immigration officials, humanitarian requests, faxes to politicians, memos to lawyers, complaints to the law society, briefs to political forums, sponsorship forms, applications for minister's permits, requests to embassies and consulates, applications for work permits, jobs and day care. And letters. Endless letters.

Recommendations, supplications: Please, help.

I hear many stories or parts of stories. This book is an effort to communicate the blessing and the burden of what I have heard. It seemed imperative to tell these stories, however fragmentary and unfinished they may be. Some day, when their future feels more secure, some of these refugees will tell their own stories in their own way and with their own voices. For now they remain reluctant to speak, prefer to remain invisible.

The stories I can and must tell are partial but true accounts of what has happened between us as we have lived together as neighbours. We have eaten together, rubbed shoulders daily and hung out our laundry on the same line. This is my point of departure in this book.

Refugees are no longer a statistic for me, or an occasional issue that flames across the front pages of the newspapers. Such abstractions are ultimately dehumanizing and demoralizing for all concerned. In my experience, there are less than a hundred people in Canada who can discuss the issues of immigration and refugee policy in the terms with which they have been defined. I am not unaware of such discussion. The language is specialized, the policies obscure and the system almost Byzantine. Many immigration officers themselves have told me the system has changed so often that it is impossible to know what is going on or why. For ordinary Canadians, this can be daunting; for refugees, it is almost defeating.

The structure of this book reflects the experience of what happens when human beings encounter one another. You learn each other's names and begin to hear each other's stories. This is the reach of mercy and within it the desire for justice is borne. I believe that human beings long to be recognized and to have someone speak their name and understand their story. Many people today, even those who are not refugees, know what it means to be defaced and rendered of no account by vast impersonal systems. The great global economic imperative of downsizing has diminished us all as human beings.

To remain life-size in a time of moral diminishment—this is the challenge for all of us today. It is my experience that when Canadians meet people called refugees or when they hear their stories, they are usually impressed by their courage, imagination and enduring capacity for joy. They begin to see Canada through the eyes of a refugee. Chapter IV, Mirrors, reflects some of the insights that arise from this perspective, for the refugee sees a country that is better than we think and worse than we know.

Canadians who have never met refugees often confuse their status with that of immigrants. The confusion is understandable because the term "refugee" is relatively recent and once a refugee claim is accepted by Canada, the person may apply for landed immigrant status. However, the distinction is important, a matter of life and death importance.

Immigrants, by definition, come to this country to be reunited with their family, to work at a specific job or to invest in some business in Canada. The process is initiated at a Canadian immigration office outside of Canada and may take up to two years.

Refugees seldom have time to apply through the normal immigration process. They usually do not have time to liquidate their assets and may be prevented from doing so by the laws and practices of the country they are fleeing. And there may not be a Canadian visa officer in the vicinity. However, through gritty determination and in an act of desperate hope, people make their way to Canada to seek protection. The protection of human beings who are in danger of arbitrary torture, detention or death is something Canada is supposedly committed to. After the Second World War, Canada signed a series of international agreements that were put in place to assure that never again would people fleeing for their lives be denied protection.*

The refugees whom I have begun to know have come to Canada for one reason and one reason only: they want to live and they want to be free. Living in Canada usually means accepting a much lower economic and social status and the loss of much of their personal identity and prestige. However, these refugees know that Canada has offered them hope. They hope in this country more than we, who are already citizens, do at times.

There is an ongoing public discussion about the economic benefits and/or liabilities that refugees represent. What such a debate overlooks is the incalculable gift of hope that many a refugee brings to the spiritual geography of this time and place.

---

* See Appendix 2 for a sampling of the international guarantees that Canada has promised to uphold.

*   *   *

After refugee children arrive at our house, I know that within a month they will be singing an old familiar tune. The words sound a little strange but these kids sing the national anthem at the top of their lungs. "O Canada" is the first song they learn at school and they sing it with all their hearts. In their playful wisdom they know that this is a song about their future and the hope of their parents. Unlike those of us who have lived here all or most of our lives, they cannot afford not to hope.

One Canada Day, I took a group of children to see the evening fireworks at Ontario Place. I was not sure this was a good idea, worried about what memories the noise and flashes would awaken. They sat very still on the grass overlooking Lake Ontario, entranced. On the way back to the car one of the little girls grabbed my hand and said, "Oh, Mary Jo, today I see flowers in sky."

Yet, their hope is sometimes surely tested—as mine has been. I have seen a face and a smile folded into a file and sent to a "removals" unit. It shocked me to learn that crucial information proving a person's life was in danger was dismissed as "irrelevant" or lost in a flurry of bureaucratic paperwork. It was a side of this country that I had never experienced so profoundly. The sense that I was walking in a shadow land led me to join with others to form a Sanctuary Group in southern Ontario. Chapter V, Files and Numbers, details some of our four-year history together, which began in an act of solidarity with innocent refugees whose lives were at stake.

Chapter VI, Neighbours, testifies to the fact that there are good neighbours, that there is a wellspring of decency in this country that continues to bubble up through the cracks in any system and in the midst of our own human fragility. Even in difficult economic times, most Canadians know there is a world of difference between being out of a job or in danger of losing your life. This book is an act of faith and hope that ignorance and intolerance are not the last word about us as human beings and as a nation. We have been, we are, much better than this.

*　　*　　*

As I write these words, a small canary is singing at the top of his lungs in the living room of our house. He came in a birthday card. I had casually mentioned to some friends that I thought it would be good to have something in the house that would sing of joy and hope. I felt the need for such a song because so much anxiety and fear condition the air at Romero House. The birthday card said that I could go to Universal Pet Shop and choose a canary for the house.

The next day I went to the shop and told the owner I would like a healthy canary which sang. Could she pick one out for me? "No," she replied, "you have to choose it yourself. You have to feel a sense of bonding with the bird." I was at a loss—there were 120 chirping canaries in the store!

I walked around the room for a few minutes and then I heard one bird singing a long sustained note of hope.

"That's the one," I said.

"It's not for sale."

I presumed it was extremely valuable but I asked anyway, "Why not?"

"Because it's handicapped."

As I looked more closely I could see that the bird had only one foot. The other was a stump. But such a song! Was it because of, or in spite of, its handicap?

"But this is just the right bird for our house," I pleaded. Although she could not comprehend my insistence, she gave the canary to me for half the price of the others.

"I don't know what you see in this one," she said as she added up the bill.

"It's what I heard," I replied.

We brought the bird home and made special perches for it, flat on the top so the stump could rest easily and support the rest of its body. And now the rooms are filled with the sound of pure joy.

His name is Hopi. Hope on one foot.

AT THE BORDERS

I

FACES

The blur of a face comes to the door, the face of a stranger. I try not to look too closely, to question with my eyes. This will not become a checkpoint, another place of interrogation.

"Please. Come in. You are welcome here."

The face does not move. So, once again I summon up the language of my hands, drawing the face from out of the door frame towards the closest chair in the front room. The face moves forward and lowers itself.

"Tea? Water?" I cup the invisible liquid in my hand and bring it to my lips. The head swings slowly upwards and then bows.

This means yes or I remember tea or if it pleases you or I don't know any more or it doesn't matter or that would be lovely.

I go to the kitchen and take the old chipped teapot from the cupboard. As I place the pot under the tap, I try to stop the flow of questions in my mind. Who are you? Where are you from? Why are you here?

Stop. You must wonder who I am, where I am from and why I am here.

I wait until the questions settle and bring the tea tray into the front room. We sip our tea together, the silence broken only by the clinking of spoons.

And then I look at the face, the landscape of one particular history.

It usually begins like this. Face after face fills the frame of my mind and then slowly comes into focus.

The face of a woman drooping with fatigue whose eyes flutter over her five sleeping children until they come to rest on the cup of tea. And then she looks at me and smiles upon me, steadily and sure.

And there are others.

A man as though in a face guard, his eyes darting out and around the room. Under surveillance.

The bronze face in a billow of white cotton, her chin like the prow of a boat ready to set sail.

The gleaming olive face of a young woman who grins ear to ear and giggles whenever I look at her.

The porcelain face of a little boy with a blue haze hovering over his skin.

There are as yet no names or at least none that I can pronounce. But we are no longer strangers.

II

NAMES

SEMIRA

The woman who had smiled upon me took off the worn beige coat and the red wool toque she had been wearing and fell asleep in the old chair as we were having tea. Her long black hair had tumbled down around her shoulders as she sat slumbering and resplendent in a long gold and green robe. As her face relaxed, I saw her beauty surface. The chair itself seemed transformed by her presence into the throne of a queen of ancient grace.

I left her there for a few hours with her five children fast asleep in one inseparable clump on the couch. I used the time to prepare a space for the six of them as they had arrived quite unexpectedly from the border crossing between Buffalo and Fort Erie. Lynn Hannigan, the director of Casa El Norte, a church-based refugee shelter located near the Peace Bridge in Fort Erie, had called asking us to take an Eritrean woman and her children.

"Where is Eritrea?" I asked.

"You'll soon find out," she laughed. Lynn had prophesied the course of the next five years of my life.

I told Lynn that the only space we could offer at the time was a room with two beds and a kitchenette.

When the woman awoke, I beckoned her with my hands to follow me up the stairs. As the children unfurled and stumbled from the couch, I looked in the hallway for their luggage.

"Luggage? Suitcase? Valise?" I drew a square with my index fingers and leaned to pull it up with my hand. The woman held up a small overnight case which she had let fall beside her throne.

"That's all?"

But she was already heading up the stairs with two small children in her arms and the other three in a close, silent formation behind her. I nattered on saying how sorry we were that there wasn't more room, that we felt badly because it was so small and we didn't have any more beds but we would get some and that there was a basic supply of food in the fridge. I didn't know how to apologize with my hands.

The woman was already in the room. She surveyed the scene before her and sighed as she turned and smiled on me again. "Ritz."

"Ritz?"

"Ritz." This time the smile had widened to reveal her teeth as perfect as white pearls. I guessed that, after such a tiring journey, our simple home felt like a five-star hotel.

"I am Mary Jo. Me Mary Jo." I pointed to myself several times and then I pointed to her, with the question in my eyes.

"Me Mary Jo"—she pointed to me in a beam of intelligence and then to herself—"Me Semira."

"Semira?"

She nodded and bowed and closed the door.

The family slept for the rest of the day and then on through the night. In the morning I found a cup of hot tea on my kitchen table. As I breathed in the aroma of cloves and cinnamon, I heard a rustling by the door and turned to see two small heads of curly black hair watching me intently with their four eyes. "Say thank you, Semira," I said as they scampered away.

There were many reasons why I needed and wanted to talk to Semira immediately and so I arranged for an Eritrean translator to come the next day. When he arrived, I explained to Semira that each person was responsible for her living area and that everyone in the house must be welcomed as a neighbour regardless of the person's gender, race, religion, nationality or political opinion.

"She says that is very good," relayed the translator. "It is good to be a big family."

"Does she have any money to buy food?"

"She says she had money but there is nothing left. Only a few American dollars."

"We will try to see she gets welfare as soon as possible."

"I explained to her what welfare means and she says she is sorry to be a problem."

"She's not a problem. She is a human being."

"She says thank you. Some places you are not a human being."

"Does she have a husband?" I wanted to take the question back for I had only then noticed the gold wedding band on her finger.

"She says she does but he disappeared in Eritrea."

It was then I learned that Eritrea was the small northern province of Ethiopia that had been fighting for its independence from Ethiopia for almost thirty years. Situated on the coastal area of the Red Sea, Eritrea was Ethiopia's only access to the sea. During the years of struggle, Semira and many other young Eritreans had fled their country and had eventually made their way to Saudi Arabia. It was there that Semira met and married an Eritrean man called Jamal. About two years before she arrived in Canada, Jamal had left Saudi Arabia to visit Eritrea and had never returned.

"She says she doesn't know if he is dead or alive," explained the translator, "but she has told the children he is visiting his parents in Eritrea."

"Could Semira tell me the names of her children?"

"The oldest boy is Turki and the next boy is Nesredin and then there are three girls: Jemilla, Juwaher and Muzit."

"Could you write the names and ages down? They all look the same to me."

When the list was complete I asked the translator if there was anything else Semira needed right away. The two of them consulted and then the translator replied: "She has asked me to find a friend of her husband's who may be here in Toronto. His name is Abdullah."

When the translator left, Semira and I had another cup of tea together. She held up five fingers and I tried to say the names of each of the five children. When my mouth wouldn't work, she would clap her hands as if to encourage me and then held up her five fingers again.

She stuck out her thumb on the next hand, "Semira," and then her index finger and said, "Jamal."

"Jamal." She pointed to her wedding band.

That day I taped the list of the children's names to the mirror in the washroom. I added "Jamal, husband," to the list and started to go through the names like beads on a rosary as I brushed my teeth every morning.

I dropped the toothbrush the morning before the children were to register at Keele Street Public School across the road. In a moment of panic I had seen the name of the oldest boy as if for the first time. Turki. Turkey. "Oh my God."

I raced to the phone to dial Semira's friend Abdullah who had become a regular visitor to Romero House and a great help to the family.

"Abdullah, you must come over. Emergency."

Through Abdullah I tried to explain to Semira that Turki was a wonderful name, a great name, in other cultures, but in our culture it was the name of someone stupid. I gobbled, cranked my neck up and down and flapped my arms frantically. "Children will laugh. Ha-ha-ha."

Semira assessed the situation for less than a minute. "She says no problem. Semira will give him a new name to celebrate the first day of school. Now he will be called Amir, the prince."

For Amir, the first day in a Canadian school was the beginning of his rise in the ranks of royalty.

However, school would not be easy for the new young prince. He had learned Tigrinya (the language of Eritrea) at home and Arabic in the streets. He had gone to a private school where his first two years of education had been in German and this had meant learning a third alphabet. English would prove to be more difficult for him than for his younger brother and sister who had also started going to Keele Street

Public School. However, Amir excelled at sports and soon became the prince of the pick-up baseball teams in the park.

English was not the only source of his frustration. One afternoon I heard a loud whack, whack coming from the backyard. It was Amir beating down all the newly planted tomato plants with a stick.

"What's the matter, Amir? Are you okay?"

"Big boy said my father dead. My father not dead," he shouted as he felled another plant. "My father go see mother and father in Eritrea. Not dead." Whack. Amir was old enough to realize that it had been a very long visit.

"Here. Let me show you something, Amir. This is a good plant. No hit. This is a weed, bad plant. Go whack."

Amir whacked away. "Sheet. Sheet." He had already learned one important word on the playground.

The teacher in Amir's school later told me that one of the boys on the playground had heard Amir was a refugee from Africa. "Where's your father, stupid?" the boy had yelled. "He's dead. They kill fathers over there. They starve people like you over there."

I picked up Amir from school one afternoon to take him to a dental appointment. It was obvious that there were many things on his mind as we drove along together.

"What means 'sheet'?" he asked.

"Ka-ka."

"Oh." He was silent for a while. "Women no drive in Saudi Arabia."

"Well, they do here," I replied.

"I know," he said thoughtfully. "Can mother Semira drive here?"

"Sure."

"Oh." He said nothing more until we reached the dentist's office. "I want be dentist. Money for car for mother."

The fragrance of Semira's freshly baked bread began to fill the house and almost every day I would find, on our kitchen table, a large flat round bread called *kitcha*, an Eritrean specialty. The eyes of the two youngest girls would watch from the doorway until I ate at least one piece of the sweet, cardamom-flavoured bread.

Watching me had become one of their favourite pastimes when the three older children were away at school. They would look through my back as I sat writing at the kitchen table in the evenings.

"I know you're there, Juwaher. I hear you, Muzit. You can come in. Welcome." Giggle and squeal and they were gone.

Then came the morning when I awoke before the alarm sounded. The two small girls were sitting on the floor by my bed—watching as their strange new neighbour began to awake.

"Good morning, Mary Jo, *habibte.*" They flew away like sparrows only to reappear at the beginning of each day. "*Habibte. Habibte.*"

I asked Abdullah, who was now called Uncle Abdullah by everyone in the house, what *habibte* meant.

"It means, my love or darling or my sweet."

Semira would later remember that first summer in Canada, the summer of 1991, as "the golden summer." She worried about her husband when she was alone but she was sure her children were safe and she could see that they were flourishing.

When some friends invited me to see a Shakespearean play in High Park, I took the children along even though I knew they wouldn't understand a word of it.

"I love it," said Amir as we walked home along Bloor Street. "What is name?"

"It's called a play. Theatre. The play's name is *Love's Labour's Lost.* It was written by a man by the name of William Shakespeare."

"I love Sheik Peer!"

In the weeks after the three older children had started school, all five children would jump on their beds in the early morning and sing "O Canada." Soon they were singing "One little, two little, three little Indians . . ." and then "Old MacDonald." They had "arrived"—or so they thought. Staying in Canada would prove to be much more difficult than learning the national anthem and some old campfire songs.

SIR GEORGE

He seemed rather tall, even patrician, when he first arrived with his arms flung over the shoulders of his two friends. His sharp features were almost tragically set off by his half-shaved head and the shock of long black hair that covered what looked to be a good eye. A large black eye patch covered much of the other side of his face. "His name is George," said one of his friends.

"Sir George to you," he said as tossed back his hair and winked his good eye. "So what kind of service does this establishment have to offer?"

Sir George had obviously fallen on hard times. His two friends had found him in a coma in a run-down basement apartment and had taken him to the house of Mama Nancee who had then called me to see if there was room at Romero House. Nancy Pocock is someone you can't say no to. Her husband had died of brain cancer and she had transformed her grief by opening her heart and home to refugees from Vietnam and Central America. They would arrive in town with nothing but her phone number and the name "Mama Nancee" on a crumpled piece of paper. Nancy told me that when George appeared on her doorstep all she could see was the face of her husband. "I don't have the strength any more to look after someone as ill as George. Could you?"

"Tell me more," I replied.

I learned from Mama Nancee what George's friends had related to her. George was a highly educated and successful naval engineer in Sri Lanka. He was not really involved in politics and was more interested in wine, women and song. Eventually he married Marina and more or less settled down to a comfortable life in a large house with servants.

They named their first daughter Maria Lourdes because they had visited Lourdes on their honeymoon to France.

His problems went back to the simple but indelible fact that as a Tamil teenager he had engaged in some rather foolish antics which resulted in his agreement to allow someone to tattoo a small tiger on the left cheek of his behind. His friends jokingly called him "Tiger." An innocent enough term of endearment here but it soon became a dangerous designation in Sri Lanka when the Tamil Tigers (LTTE) began their guerrilla campaign against the Sinhalese in the south of the country. Since 1983, the Tamil minority in the northern Jaffna Peninsula had been locked in an increasingly violent struggle against the Sinhalese majority. From this point on, all Tamils became suspect, not only those who were militant.

All it took was one night in a bar when a drunken friend yelled across to George, "Hey, Tiger!" Someone must have reported the incident since the police soon arrived and took George away for questioning. They discovered, in the course of stripping him, the tattoo of the tiger. He was beaten severely. An iron bar was pushed through one of his eyes and into his head. Only a hefty bribe paid by his family secured his release. He knew it was simply a question of time before he would be picked up again.

Fearful for his life, he found a job as an engineer on an ocean liner and travelled around the world, from Sri Lanka to India to South Africa to Argentina to Brazil to Mexico, then to the United States and to Montreal. There he left the ship and went on to Toronto to claim refugee status. Once accepted, he began working as a translator in hearings for refugees from Sri Lanka. His English was impeccable. Oxford. The refugee lawyers liked him as he was charming and witty and would joke with the refugees, putting them at ease.

About two months after taking on this job, he found himself increasingly dizzy. His speech became slurred and he became confused in the midst of translations. Such symptoms were not totally unusual for him as he was a rather severe diabetic. Because of this condition, with which he was familiar, he put off going to a doctor. When he collapsed in the midst of translating at a refugee hearing, he was taken by ambulance to Sunnybrook Hospital, where he was diagnosed as having a cancerous brain tumour. It was not clear whether there was any relationship between the tumour and the iron bar that had been driven through his eye into his head. The surgeons operated immediately, apparently without much success.

Because of hospital cutbacks, George was soon released after his operation and sent to a shelter for homeless men, to recover. There he was surrounded by drug addicts and alcoholics. His belongings were locked up and he was forced to go out onto the streets during the day. One night he was beaten by the man sleeping next to him. Desperate, he collected his papers and used what little money he had left to get a basement room in a boarding house. He had just enough strength to make one last phone call, giving his address. Alone, he lapsed into a coma until his friends found him.

When Nancy called, I knew that we had a room in our house that had only recently become vacant. It was the room next to mine. When she reminded me that her husband had died of brain cancer, I replied, "Well, my father has just died of a brain tumour. Maybe he has been reincarnated." It was decided.

Most of the refugees in our houses live under the threat of death in their homeland until they are accepted into Canada. But this was the first time we had someone who was dying in our midst. I knew it would involve a lot of care and I sensed we could not do it unless everyone in the house was involved.

We called a meeting and Winkie, the nurse on our board, attended. She explained to everyone what might be involved in accepting George—how he would slowly or quickly deteriorate, how he would soon be unable to move from his bed, how he would need help with all the basic things in life, like eating and going to the bathroom. I asked people to think about whether we could make such a commitment.

"I say yes," said Semira. "He have no family. He have no home. We each do a little. In our country, we help sick person at home. Hospital not home." Everyone else nodded and preparations began in earnest.

We set up a schedule so each of the adults in the house would take a turn at cooking for George once a week. We offered to find some money to reimburse them for the cost of the food. They would have none of it. They insisted on sharing what little they had with someone who was dying. Some of our friends in the neighbourhood also volunteered to cook one of the meals. A timetable was set for bathing and cleaning. Winkie borrowed some supplies from her hospital and was able to bring over a walker and a sheepskin for the mattress to prevent bedsores.

He needed all of this and more. Indeed, he insisted on more. The more physically helpless George became, the more demanding he became. Somehow, the other women in the house seemed to understand. "Must talk strong because no strong now." They patiently prepared his meals and often sat to talk with him as he was eating.

Part of George's routine was a bath three times a week. The chairman of our board, a busy principal of a high school, had volunteered to take on this part of the care. It was a lot more than he had bargained for. George had certain expectations regarding a real bath. It included three changes of water, numerous bath towels and three different massages on the back—each with a different ointment. Lorne soon learned that a "real bath" could take as long as two hours.

"Please don't tell anyone you are doing this," I said to Lorne. "If you do, word will get out that we are quite the bathhouse and we will have people lined up for blocks for your services."

After Lorne departed one evening, George summoned me to his room. "That Lorne is a good guy," he said. "He may be a good principal, but he certainly doesn't know much about giving a bath. Today he even let one of the towels fall on the floor."

One day I overheard George shouting at Semira who had brought him supper, "Your English leaves a little to be desired, my dear." I was furious. I walked in and lambasted him: "This is not Sri Lanka and these women are not your servants. Stop snapping your fingers and start saying please and thank you. They know what it is to have servants of their own. There are no more servants here. Just neighbours."

"He sick Mary Jo. It's okay," said Semira.

"Yes, I'm sick Mary Jo, and don't you forget it."

How could I? My part of this bargain-basement care was to help George during the night. He had a little bell by his bed and he would ring two or three times a night when he had to go to the bathroom. He liked ringing the bell, my bells.

At first it was easy. I would walk beside him until he reached the bathroom. From there on he was assisted by the handrails we had installed by the toilet. Soon I had to hold him by the arm and then I had to pull his arm over my shoulder and pull him along the hallway. He felt heavier and heavier.

Sometimes we would chat when he was finally back in his bed. His mind would wander.

"I'm a son of a bitch, you know."

"I know."

"Do you think I'll go to hell?"

"Probably not. You'd expect more service than they usually offer there."

"I have a bottle of holy water from Lourdes in my suitcase. Could you sprinkle it on me? It can't do any harm. I'd love to see my daughters before I die. By the way, Jo, you've got a great future as a night nurse."

I phoned Nancy who was already working to try to arrange for George's wife and daughters to come from Sri Lanka to be with him as he was dying. We discovered, to our horror, that he had neglected to fill out any sponsorship forms for them. Now it was too late. He couldn't write any more. He couldn't read. It was now impossible to say that he knew what he was doing or, as they say in legalese, that "he was in full possession of his faculties."

Finally one night I couldn't lift George out of bed any more. A tear formed in the corner of his good eye. "I'm wet." That's all he had to say as he lay there quietly.

I could hear the sound of Omar upstairs, on the next floor, chanting his prayers. He had recently arrived from Somalia with his wife, Fadumo, and was a devout Muslim. Two or three times a night he would rise to pray for, as he said, "When all the world is silent, that is when Allah hears our prayers more easily." It made me feel like a bit of a spiritual slouch.

I was aware that how I dressed and acted was mostly *haram*, or "unclean," to Omar. He would not shake my hand when I reached out because it was *haram* to touch a woman's hand. I did not cover my head and arms. *Haram*. And that night when George wet his bed I was dressed only in my pajamas.

Nonetheless, I decided to go upstairs to knock at Omar's door. "Please help me. Help George. Bathroom."

"Yes," he replied instantly. He came down in his sarong and together we hauled George to the bathroom. Every night thereafter, whenever George would ring his bell, Omar would come down to help us. He explained to me that it was more important to care for the sick and the dying than to worry about *haram*.

Then came the night when the bell did not ring. I woke up almost out of habit and went to get Omar. Neither he nor I could lift George, nor could we wake him. In the early hours of the morning we called an ambulance. As the paramedics brought him downstairs on a stretcher, everyone in the house was gathered by the door in their nightclothes. Some of the women started to cry. Later that day they went to clean his room and packed his suitcase for the hospital.

Nancy went to various government offices in Ottawa, trying to get a visitor's visa for George's wife and two little girls. She pestered and cajoled and eventually obtained the visas.

The day after his wife and daughters arrived from Sri Lanka, they went to see him in the palliative care unit. Marina was shocked when she saw his condition. She stared at George in disbelief. "You never told me you were sick."

This was not how she remembered him. "He used to love to dance and sing. He was the life of the party," she told me. The little girls stared mutely at the man they could barely remember, whom they only knew from the letters he had written home.

George had never admitted he was sick. "I have an excellent job," he had written. "I have lots of friends and my services are much in demand. Soon I will send for you."

George lived only two weeks. He was buried in a cemetery to the north of Toronto in a section reserved for indigents. All of George's neighbours from Romero House accompanied him there. As we were driving home from the cemetery, Semira asked me, "What means 'sunbeech'?"

"Sunbeech?"

"Yes, he keep saying 'I'm sunbeech.'"

I let the word turn over in my mind. "It means he was a good man but he didn't know it."

MRS. WOW

Omar and I had come to respect each other during and after our night-time trips with Sir George to the bathroom. I had yet to really meet his wife, whom I first got to know as Mrs. Wow.

When they arrived at our front door, Omar introduced himself and his wife, Fadumo.

"You are welcome here," I said. Omar would not shake my hand.

"Wow," replied Fadumo and kissed me on both cheeks.

I showed them upstairs to the open area third-floor room just above me. Omar could obviously understand most of what I was saying, so I showed him the various appliances and explained how the fire alarm worked.

"Wow."

They stood there in the middle of the room. Lost? Waiting for me to go? I went downstairs again.

I did not see them the rest of the day, but in the middle of the night I was awakened by the solemn and rather sad sound of someone chanting above me. The words were not audible but they had that quality of longing that I had only heard in the songs of the medieval monasteries.

The next morning I met Omar on the stairs and I said in passing, "I heard you chanting last night. It was lovely."

"I hope I didn't keep you awake," he responded politely. "I am a sheik and it is my duty to pray many times a day. In the middle of the night when all the noise of the world is finished, then the sky is free and God hears our prayers."

"Oh no, don't worry about me being awake. I might pray too in my own way." Then, as an afterthought, I asked, "But I thought you were a captain in the Somali army?"

"I had to join the army. No choice. But I am a sheik first." He started to go down to the front door, tall and lean. Then I realized that he was wearing only a light navy suit.

"Omar, it's cold outside. Winter. You can't go out with only that on."

"But I have to go. I must go to the mosque." He had already found out where the Jemi Mosque was, just a few streets over on Boustead Avenue.

That morning I called some tall, thin men friends and explained the situation to them. By the evening there was a coat, several sweaters and a pair of boots lying beside the door to the third floor. Earlier in the day, we had found a coat for Fadumo from what we called "the Romero Boutique" storeroom of donated clothes.

"Wow," she said when she tried on the coat.

That night the prayer rose once again from our third floor to heaven. In the grey beginning of a January day I rose to get a cup of coffee. As I looked out the windows of our back kitchen, I saw Omar in the driveway by the garage. He seemed to be dancing, one step forward, one back, two to the side. He was waving his arms slowly up and down. An angel of the morning.

In a few minutes, he said hello as he passed by the kitchen.

"I saw you dancing, Omar." I was teasing.

"Dancing? But we are only allowed to dance at weddings."

"Out in the back there. Just now."

"Oh, I just practise walking. I don't know how to walk on snow. We don't have snow in our country."

"Wow," I said. He grinned and let out a hearty laugh.

"Fadumo, she say that because that is only English word she know. When we wait in Buffalo at the shelter, she watch English TV all the time. All the, how you say, advertisements say always 'wow.' Wow hamburger. Wow car. Wow coke. Everything wow in America."

"I see." I made a silent resolution never to say "wow" again.

Fadumo seemed to be one of the happiest people I had ever met. She was more substantial than Omar and somewhat shorter. Each day she would appear in her long dress and veil of exquisite colours. I soon discovered that she did not wear her veil in their room and would rush to put one on only if a man appeared with me.

One evening, as we sat watching TV in the community room, there was a scene with a mother and a little baby.

"Do you have children, Fadumo?"

"Wow."

I made a rocking motion with my arms, pointed to the TV and then to Fadumo. She opened her hand and spread her five fingers wide.

From time to time, Fadumo would bring me down some of her meat pastries, called sambusas. She smiled, I smiled. She said, "Wow."

One evening, Omar joined us for tea.

"You have a lovely wife, Omar," I said. "She's one of the happiest people I know."

"Oh, but she suffer a lot. There was war. I was away. Five men from other tribe come to our house and set on fire. They take Fadumo outside and rape her—many times. Then they put piece of plant, plant that burns, up inside her. Burn her inside. I came home and find her like dead. I send children to my brother's village."

"The five children?"

"Yes. Only way out through Kenya, through jungle to Kenya. Too many big animals for children. I take Fadumo with me two months in jungle. Many times she almost die. I use many things in jungle to help her. We get to Nairobi and then take plane to Jamaica."

"Jamaica?"

"Yes, in New York City. When airplane arrive, Fadumo almost dead. Ambulance come and we go to hospital. But she still not well. All the time blood. No sex. Sex hurt. My friends say leave her because she rape. But I am faithful. It not her fault."

"We must make an appointment with a doctor, Omar."

What was there to say? The three of us sat in silence and sipped our tea. There was nothing more to say.

HER NAME IS HAPPINESS

François and Julie were the first of several French-speaking Africans who would stay at Romero House. Their French was elegant and we, who had supposedly learned the second official language of our country, struggled to make ourselves understood in "Franglais."

This husband and wife, fleeing from political persecution, had arrived from Zaire through the United States. We had been told by our friends at Casa El Norte in Fort Erie that their one-year-old daughter had chicken pox. So they stayed in a kind of self-imposed quarantine on their floor. Julie, we learned, had been a nurse and she was quite anxious not to pass on the disease to the other children in the house.

It was January when they arrived and we began with the essential task of finding the right clothes to keep them warm. Julie became concerned when François would shiver, as that was always a sign of a dreaded disease such a malaria. Our nurse, Winkie, explained that we shivered because of the cold, not because of a disease, and that shivering was one of the ways the body tried to keep warm. The two nurses exchanged many helpful bits of information.

Soon, we heard sounds of the little girl running around on the floor above us and the family came out of their seclusion. François was polite, unfailingly and almost painfully polite. He wanted to know what he could do to help around the house. His wife was an imposing presence in the room, in any room. She would move around the kitchen with her little girl riding on her back, secured by a wrap of brightly coloured cloth. At times, I interpreted her set face as either sad or angry.

One day a missionary from Africa was visiting us and, noticing the brightly coloured material about Julie's waist and her facial features, guessed where she was from.

"*Mbote, Mama.*"

Julie turned around and her face broke open with what seemed to be the widest smile on the earth. From that point on, I would begin every conversation with Julie with "*Mbote, Mama.*" And Julie would respond, "*Mbote, ma soeur.*"

During the spring break we received some free tickets to the Metro Toronto Zoo and we took a vanload of families for the afternoon. We began with the African pavilion and proceeded to the display of fish. However, Julie asked me to take her daughter and said she preferred to sit in one corner of the pavilion containing a majestic tree and beautiful foliage.

"It is like my home," she said wistfully.

When we returned to pick up Julie after two hours she seemed completely rejuvenated. Her eyes were like soft flowers, her skin was alive and her smile was fresh and bright.

There were so many matters to take care of in the first few weeks of their arrival that I had fallen into referring to the little girl as "bébé." One day I realized that I did not know her name.

"What is the baby's name?" I asked Julie.

"Félicité."

"I think that means happiness in English."

"I was praying for happiness then. I felt we needed a miracle to bring us happiness once again."

"A miracle?"

"Yes, François was in prison then. He had been taken to Mobutu's prison soon after I had learned I was pregnant, the day after the march for democracy in the capital. François had been put in prison before because he had been one of the leaders in the small Christian communities but this time we knew it was very serious. In this prison, people were executed every day. Each morning there would be lists put up on the walls outside the prison of those who were to be executed that day.

This meant the family could go and pick up the bodies in the evening.

"Every morning I would walk to the prison and look at the lists to see if I could find François' name. I was looking for his name but I didn't want to see it. I prayed every day that God would protect him, save him, and that we could be happy with our child. Our little girl was born while François was still in prison. Someone told me that they were beating him and torturing him, trying to find out the names of people in the pro-democracy movement. There was nothing I could do. I kept on praying and I named our baby Félicité when she was born. François was not there when she was born."

In a few swift strokes, Julie painted the picture of Zaire as it was in the grip of the dictator Mobutu Sésé Séko. Formerly known as the Belgian Congo, it was a vast country in Central Africa, rich in natural resources with all the possibilities of providing a good life for its people. However, Mobutu had seized power in 1965 and, using the army as his means of control, had waged a campaign of terror and brutality against any person or group who challenged his authority. The Catholic Church, in particular, was regarded with great suspicion by the government. A bishop of Kinshasa, a man very much like Archbishop Oscar Romero of El Salvador, had been assassinated because of his defence of human rights, and many priests and lay leaders of the parish communities had been arrested or assassinated. Each parish was composed of several small communities of prayer and service that provided support and encouragement for the people in their everyday life and in their hope for a more just and peaceful existence.

François, Julie explained, was a deeply religious man who did not want to get involved in politics. He simply wanted a society in which there could be more love and peace.

"He was saved, you know," she said, looking at me steadily. "There was a morning when I went to the wall and saw Francois' name on the list of those to be executed that day. I went home and prayed that God would be with him. I tried to look after Félicité that day and prayed that François would continue to protect her from heaven, because that is where I knew he was going.

"After supper I prepared to go to the prison to pick up his body. Then the door opened and François slipped into the house. I thought I was dreaming or that Jesus was appearing as François. Then he said in his own voice, 'I have been saved.'"

"François told me that he had a little copy of the Gospels with him and he would meditate every day. The evening he heard he was to be executed, he placed his life and our lives in the hands of God. On the evening watch there was a new guard. As he walked down the corridors of those waiting in cells to be executed, he recognized François as someone he had been with in the parish elementary school years ago. They had played together. The guard opened the door of the cell and told him to run. And François ran and hid until he could come to us later in the evening. We went to stay with some relatives until we could sell our house and buy the tickets and visas to the United States."

It was at that moment that François, carrying Félicité, came into the room where we were talking. I looked at the man who had come back from the dead. "You were saved, François."

"Yes, I was saved. Now I am living my life in gratitude to God."

ANA DE JESUS

Somehow I was not surprised when the young woman from Guatemala told me her name: "Ana de Jesus, like in the Bible." She had been holding a tattered brown Bible, *La Biblia*, in her hands since she had first arrived at Romero House. She held on to it for months and read it constantly in the evenings—especially, or so it seemed, in the evenings as I was watching the news on TV.

Ana and her small son José became my closest neighbours as we shared the kitchen, bathroom and small living room on the second floor. At first, I was a little disconcerted with the small signs of piety that kept appearing about me. On the door of Ana's bedroom she had pasted a sign: *Cristo es Vida*. Little prayer cards in Spanish and Portuguese were taped to the mirror in the bathroom and above the kitchen sink. But there were no crucifixes or rosaries. Ana had become an Evangelical Christian during her five years in the United States and she did not believe in such graven images. Neither did her seven-year-old son. One day he sat looking for a long time at an icon that I had hung in the living room. He turned and looked solemnly at me: "No one has seen God's face. Don't you know that?"

Every evening Ana and José went to pray at their little church on Dupont Street while I attended to more ordinary matters. She would put on a plain navy suit and a clean white blouse and José would be dressed in his solemn black suit, a white shirt, navy tie and brightly polished black-laced shoes. Yet nothing seemed to tone down the flashes of Ana's sunshine smile and the brightness of her laughter. She was short and ample, with a billow of beautiful curly black hair about her head.

"I like your smile," I said to her one morning as we were eating breakfast on the porch.

"Oh, I've lots to be happy for," she said. "It is a beautiful day. I have José and I have found Jesus."

She had found Jesus, she told me, after she arrived in California from Mexico. She had fled from Guatemala after her husband had disappeared, knowing that she was pregnant.

"He was a good man. He was in the army and they wanted him to do dirty things and he didn't want to. He told me about the dirty things some of those guys did. And he said they would try to get him. So he told me to get to the border and he would meet me there. But he never came and later his cousin called me in California and told me those guys killed him.

"So I had this baby all alone. I didn't know nobody. I sat holding him and I was so afraid. I didn't know what to do with a baby. I never had a mother. I didn't know nothing. 'What am I going to do with you?' I said to José. That's when I started to go to church. I needed somebody.

"I had a lot of bad things people did to me. When I went to church I started to forgive them. And I felt better. I started to live again."

"Was that when you learned English?" I asked.

"Yes, and I got work there. They showed me how to clean and I volunteered in an old folks' place. You know I really like to be with old people and to help them. But after four years they came and said I had to go. I donno why. The Americans think there's no problem in Guatemala. I donno why."

Ana got up to get another cup of coffee. We had almost begun to speak about her future in Canada, but I knew she didn't want to talk about it.

After her refugee claim had been refused by the Immigration and Refugee Board (IRB), she had packed her bags and taken the bus to Niagara Falls, assuming that she would have to go back to the United States and then somewhere else. But the immigration officer at the border told her that she couldn't cross to the United States without an appointment with the American Immigration and Naturalization Service. He also advised her to appeal the decision because he couldn't imagine anyone from Guatemala being returned there and referred her to some refugee advocates who had then sent her on to Romero House in Toronto to help her in the appeal process.

She returned with her coffee and José in tow. As she sat tying his sneakers and getting his lunch ready for school, Ana resumed our conversation. "You know, I really want to get a job. I don't like to be on welfare. I know this Portuguese guy who's got a cleaning company and he say I can work for him if I get a work permit. It's at night but I could be back in time to get José ready for school and take him there. Isn't that great!"

Ana smiled and then hugged José, covering his face with her mantle of shimmering hair.

While we contacted various lawyers for advice about an appeal to the Federal Court, Ana did what she could. She began to work for minimum wage ($6.85) on night shift with a cleaning company which had a contract with the Royal Alex Theatre. "That's where they have *Crazy For You*," she said proudly.

"But what's your work like there?" I asked.

"It's okay. I clean the gum off from under the seats and I do the stairs and the washrooms. The boss is okay. He doesn't go after the women." A smile. A giggle.

Every evening Ana would leave for work around eleven o'clock, returning about half past seven in the morning. José would get up on his own and sit by the front door, waiting for her.

However, after she had been with us three months, she began to pack her bags. I was extremely distressed when I saw her preparing to leave. She had offered no explanation. Had we offended her? Were we too Catholic for her? Finally, I spoke up. "It doesn't make sense, Ana. You should stay until you get your immigration status cleared. We would be very sad to see you go."

Ana put down her suitcase and sat on her bed. "I donno why I was packing. I never lived anywhere more than three months. I just thought it's three months and it's time to move on." She sighed. "Nobody ever asked me to stay before."

Ana stayed.

On her days off, Ana would clean the kitchen and the bathroom and the living room we shared. I was embarrassed by this, never having had a cleaning lady before. I begged her not to do it.

"I like to work," she responded. "Then I don't have to think. And I like to look at your pictures too."

"Oh? Which ones?"

"The ones that don't look like a photo. I like paintings like that. They make you think."

"You mean the abstract paintings. But I thought you didn't want to think?"

"Oh. You know what I mean. I don't want to think about immigration and about things like that. You know I like that old-fashioned music too—like you play sometimes. It's like what Pavarotti sings. I hear it sometimes. It makes my heart think too."

"It's called classical music. But you can listen to it at any time you want. I just don't want you cleaning my place on your day off."

"Well, it's my place too, you know." A smile. A giggle.

José was very proud of his mother's talent for cleaning. "My mom spends a lot of time cleaning this place up and then you just mess it up again. Don't you know how to clean?"

Because Ana was such a good cleaner, I had assumed that she knew how to do everything around the house. One day as I was cooking rice, I discovered how little anyone had taught her, how little family life she had had.

"How do you do that? When I cook rice it gets all like glue or burns." Ana giggled.

"Well, first you wash it in cold water until the water isn't cloudy any more." I continued with some more tips I had learned from my mother and from some of the other refugee women.

"Oh, I see," Ana beamed. "I'm going to try it out on José tonight. He never liked rice because it tasted so hard and burned."

"I thought every Central American knew how to cook rice and beans."

"Well, you see, I never had a mother. She was an alcoholic and she went with men. She sent me to my grandmother but she never talked to me. My grandfather used to come after me. There was another cousin there and she was jealous of me. I think because of my hair. My grandmother used to beat me and she would lock me in a room for many days. You know I was so lonely I used to go to a mirror and look at myself and talk to myself. I was so lonely."

Ana's lips began to quiver and a large tear rolled down the side of her nose. She wiped it quickly and took a large pot out of the cupboard and began to fill it with rice. "It's okay. It was a long time ago." She put the pot under the tap, covered it and placed it on the stove. It just didn't seem the time to remind her about the salt and the butter and measuring cup.

As the weeks passed, I could tell Ana was getting tired. After she had worked the night through, prepared José's breakfast and lunch and walked him to the school, she was able to manage only about five hours of sleep before he was home again. I started taking him to school just to give her a few more minutes of sleep. José and I had some wonderful conversations while we were on our way to the school on the corner of Keele and Bloor.

"You know what I wish most in the world?" he asked. "What do you wish most in the world?" "I wish that there is kindness in the world."

"Can people like us go anywhere in the world?" "Well, where would you like to go?" "To the land where Jesus was born."

"I'm a big boy, you know." "Yes. You're getting bigger." "See," he said, pulling up one leg of his jeans, "the hair on my legs is growing."

"My daddy's dead you know." "I know." "I'd like to get a new daddy. But I want one who speaks French because that's the official language."

José almost got a new dad. One of the Portuguese men in Ana's church, a Canadian citizen, started pursuing her seriously. One month after meeting her he had given her a watch, a ring and had proposed. For one brief moment it seemed as if all her immigration problems could be solved with a simple "I do."

"I don't want to do it," Ana said one morning when she came back from work. "Marriage is because you love someone and want to be forever. But I don't love him and he just wants my skin. He don't love me inside." And that was the end of it.

Ana's only remaining option was to hope that her appeal to the Federal Court would succeed. I stopped talking to her about the various procedures because any conversation about immigration invariably seemed to make her feel vulnerable and powerless. I did have to talk with her about the cost of retaining a lawyer to work on the "stay of deportation" procedure. I had done a quick calculation of her income and expenses and thought that she might be able to pay the lawyer fifty dollars a month. However, Ana told me she never had any money left at the end of the month and I believed her. I could see how frugal she was.

"Not even twenty dollars?" I asked.

"No. You see . . ." she hesitated, "I have another child."

"Another child? Who? Where?"

"His name is Otavio and he live in Mexico. I can show you his picture. They write me a letter every few months about him."

"Who's they?"

"World Vision. Otavio is my adopted son. I send him thirty dollars a month." She brought the tattered picture of her adopted son out of her wallet. "Isn't he cute?"

"But, Ana, you hardly have enough money to look after José. Why are you doing this?"

"Well, Jesus says that we have to look after those who don't have as much as we do."

"Yes, he did say that. But not everyone takes him this seriously." I walked away with a fresh sense of what Jesus meant when he talked about the widow who gave everything from the little she had. Blessed was she . . . is she.

Ana only initiated a conversation about immigration once and that was while I was trying to make a contribution to the cleaning by wiping out the crisper containers in the fridge. Her eyes looked at me over the open door of the fridge, her nose barely touching its rim, her hair slightly astride the jars of mustard and relish below. "If they send me back . . ." She started to sob and disappeared behind the door.

I stood up and looked over the door. She was kneeling with her forehead touching the floor, her hair spread out like a mop on its surface. "I only have a past. I'm only living in the past. I don't have any future. I never have any tomorrow."

"You've got today," I said putting out my hand, trying to find her face.

"No. I just got a big headache."

For the very rich, the future can be managed. The middle class plan for the future. But for the very poor, the future is what happens to you.

MAMA MIRIAM

Everybody called her Mama Miriam. Her name was the only thing we knew about her for certain.

Some of the Eritreans said she was single, others said she had a husband and children in Saudi Arabia but that she had left them or they had left her, and some thought all her family had been killed and she just didn't want to talk about it.

Whatever the case, she dressed in the traditional long white cotton dress worn by Eritrean and Ethiopian women, her jet black hair covered loosely with a thin white veil billowing about her face that seemed lined with the suffering of centuries. She lived at the Jesuit house for refugees, which was just down the street, and when she came to visit she would sail into our house, usually bearing wonderful goodies for the children. "Mama Miriam coming. Mama Miriam here." Her specialties were shish kebab and sambusa.

We knew she had already been refused by the Immigration and Refugee Board and was awaiting a deportation order, but months went by and nothing arrived in the mail from Immigration. At first she had seemed rather resigned to being returned to her country and then she gradually became more and more depressed. She would sit in a corner of the living room, sobbing and wailing. Soon she was unable to sleep.

"I have dreams, bad dreams, of the hearing. Two white women judges are two big white cats try to scratch my eyes. They no want me here. They no want my black eyes no look at them."

She covered her eyes with her hands and rocked back and forth on the sofa. "Want to leave. No want stay in Canada."

From that point on we began to talk about how and where she would go when she left. Since she had entered Canada via the United States, at the Buffalo–Fort Erie border crossing, I knew she would be "removed" to the United States at Niagara Falls. However, once she had decided to go, she did not want to linger around the United States, caught up in some futile asylum claim that would surely be refused.

Her decision, as she announced it to Sister Mary Power and me, was to fly directly back to Addis Ababa, the capital of Ethiopia. This was a signal to us that she really did not think she was at risk if she was returning to the country which had brutally dominated Eritrea for thirty years.

Mama Miriam told us that she had saved the money to pay for her plane ticket to Addis. All we needed to do was to get permission from Immigration to have her directly "removed" to Addis rather than to Niagara Falls, U.S.A. This was much easier said than done. We had to get a letter from the airline and from the British Embassy in Ottawa saying that she would not be allowed to leave the airport during the stopdown in London, England.

There was one further problem, a "big problem," which is how Mama Miriam put it to Mary and me one afternoon over tea. I knew she had been sizing us up for a long time. She would ask us many questions about what we thought about this or that other refugee. We told her it was none of her business, that she needed to respect the privacy of others. She wanted to know what privacy meant. "Like secret," I replied.

"This very private," she whispered and put her cup of tea down. "I have gold in New York. This gold for my old age. Like you say retire, insurance for life. In my culture women have many gold things to wear. This how they save money. My gold in New York with Somali man."

"A Somali man?"

"Yes. When I come New York, I no place to go. Walk in streets. This Somali man say come to his house. No choice. But him good man, very good man. Very good wife and children. Make me like daughter. He show me how go to Buffalo. He say no take gold to Canada. They take gold at border. So I leave gold with Somali man. He keep for me. Now I need gold. But me no can go to America. No visa. He no can come to Canada."

Mary and I looked at each other and we knew we were each thinking the same thing: the gold was long gone, long spent. I told Mama Miriam that this was fool's gold.

"No, he very, very good man." She was adamant.

Then Mary offered to fly to New York and get the gold. I was astounded at the offer but Mary was older and wiser than I. She knew that this gold was all Mama Miriam had for her old age.

"How much gold is there, Mama Miriam?" Mary asked.

"Black box. Not big. Earrings, rings, necklaces."

As Mary began to plan the trip with another sister, they became aware that they might face problems at the airport. No one knew exactly how the metal detectors at the airport worked, but we had a vision of the two older sisters walking through the checkpoint wearing pounds of gold jewellery and setting off alarm bells everywhere.

The alternative scheme was for Mary and her friend to drive down to New York City and to pick up the box over the weekend. At Romero House, the trip became known as "The Voyage of the Gold Dust Twins." We had a sad feeling that the twins would come back with nothing to show for all their effort. But Mama Miriam kept saying, "He very, very good man."

As Mary recalls the trip, she had directions to an address in Harlem but was prepared to find out that it was non-existent. Driving through Manhattan, she wondered whether this was much of an improvement on Mogadishu, the capital of Somalia, which was now in shambles. She was beginning to think that she might get out of Harlem with a black box intact but not with her car.

The address did exist. The two elderly sisters walked up a precarious flight of stairs to the second floor of a decaying apartment block and knocked on the door. "Mama Miriam sent me. Mama Miriam sent me."

The door was unlatched halfway and two bright eyes peered through the opening. "You Toronto?"

"Yes, Mama Miriam sent me for the gold."

"Welcome. Welcome. We keep for her two years now."

They walked into the very clean but sparse apartment where a lovely elderly woman, who introduced herself as Adar, offered them some tea. While they were sipping, the woman made a brief phone call. Within minutes, an elegant and kindly gentleman appeared.

"How is Miriam? She was very alone in New York. She was like our daughter."

"She sent me for the gold," said Mary, not wanting to get side-tracked.

"Yes, of course," said Yusuf. "I put it in the wall here." He carefully eased a cabinet away from the wall and pulled out a black box.

Mary still half-expected the box to be empty. But, no, there was the jewellery lying before her. Yusuf carefully laid the items out on the table while Mary went through them, ticking off the list that Mama Miriam had compiled for her in Toronto: one set of large gold earrings, two sets of small gold earrings, five rings, six bracelets, three anklets, one large, three-stranded necklace. It was all there. Mama Miriam's past and her future.

They carefully placed the gold pieces back in the box and had another cup of tea. Mary's interest now turned to Yusuf and his wife. Did they have children? How did they make a living?

"Oh, I drive a taxi. Very interesting work. Many poor people not happy. Many rich people not happy here. But we are happy. God is good."

"Did you ever think of selling the gold?" Mary blurted out the question which had been on her mind—and mine.

"Sell it? Why?"

"For yourself, for your family?"

"But it's Miriam's. She asked us to keep it for her."

And that was the end of the gold rush. Mary and her friend drove back through upstate New York and crossed the border.

"Anything to declare, ma'am?" asked the immigration officer at the wicket.

"I was there less than forty-eight hours, officer," said Mary demurely.

The officer waved them on. Two nice old ladies.

They went immediately over to Mama Miriam's on their return.

"You see," said Mama Miriam. "He very, very good man and you very, very good woman."

On the evening of her removal, we drove Mama Miriam out to the airport. Several of her friends came over to the house to say goodbye. Many of them sobbed as they kissed her on both cheeks. By now they were all starting to wonder whether the same fate awaited them.

At the airport we went directly to Immigration where a very business-like young woman explained to us that we would have to wait until everyone else had boarded the plane, then an officer would meet Miriam with her passport at the door of the plane and accompany her to her seat.

"We will give you your passport when you are seated," she said.

"Don't worry. I no want to stay here."

After the other passengers had left the waiting area, Miriam stood up and proceeded slowly down the entranceway. She was wearing her white cotton dress, a lot of lovely gold jewellery and looked as regal as the Queen of Sheba. She walked away from us and never looked back.

FUNNY GUY

Fred loved Farah. He was four years old and from Rwanda and she was twenty-one, recently arrived from Somalia. No one quite knows how it started, but Farah smiled at this impish little boy and seemed to take him completely seriously. They talked a lot in some language all their own.

"You funny guy, Fred," she would say.

"Ya, me funny guy. Me boyfriend."

"Who boyfriend Fred?" Farah would ask.

"You, Farah. Me love you."

In fact, we all loved Fred. He had charmed us all with his husky voice and audacious manner. Liking him was a little more difficult at times. For example, as I sat typing some supposedly important fax in the office, Fred would sneak in and sit silently under the desk. The minute I went down to the basement work area to get a cup of coffee, Fred would reach his hand up to the computer keyboard and plunk away. I would return to find a scramble of symbols and letters across the screen. This and other actions had earned Fred the names "small bandit" and "fearless Fred" around the office.

"Fred, please don't do that," I would scream as I looked at another scrambled computer screen.

"Ya, me funny guy," he would smile.

He also enjoyed jumping on the coffee table in the front room. One day it broke and Natan, our maintenance man, came over to repair it. Fred was ready to make his move again. Natan caught the glimpse in his eye. "Fred, you jump this and I put you in prison."

Fred looked at him solemnly and said, "I will do it." He positioned himself, ready to jump. We knew all our threats had failed to impress funny guy. Finally I pulled out the worst threat I could possibly think of: "You know what I do with guys like you, Fred? I hold them by the feet and I flush them down the toilet."

His eyes got very big. He never jumped on the table after that.

"Just wait," Brian, one of the volunteers, said. "Some day he'll be in a therapy group and you'll be blamed for all his troubles." Brian himself had been in the bathroom one day when Fred whizzed by and turned off the lights.

Fearless Fred struck again the next day as I was banging away on the computer. He pulled the plug. I looked under the table and said, "You know what I do with guys like you?"

"You funny girl."

Mon Général

It was a gentle winter night. The snowflakes fell slowly around the streetlamps on Wanda Road. I was late for supper after a long afternoon of teaching at the university. As I walked around the corner and onto our little street I saw someone going through our garbage. It was to be picked up the next morning and I had put it out well ahead of time.

A few steps further and I saw that the rummager was a handsome young man with a rather chubby little boy by his side. They were inspecting the broken pieces of wood and the fragments of fixtures in our garbage. I knew there would be nothing of use in our garbage or it would have been kept inside our garage to be rehabilitated by one of the refugees.

The man looked rather startled as I approached and put his hands in his pockets.

"There's nothing there," I said. "We have some good things in the garage. You can come back and take what you need."

The man looked down at the ground, then reached to take the boy by the hand.

"No, really. You can come and take what you need." I pointed to the driveway and the garage at the end of it.

The man turned and started to walk down the street with the boy. I started walking after them. "People gave us these things. You are welcome to them."

The man turned around and flung his arms helplessly by his side. "No English. No English."

"What do you speak? What speak?"

"Romania."

"Just a minute. Just a minute. Wait. Stay. Here." I pointed to the ground and ran inside to phone an Italian woman who had volunteered to help out with Romanian translations. I explained to Lauretta that I had been trying to tell the man about the furniture in the garage. Then I called him and his son to come inside.

The man took the phone and as he listened his eyes widened. When I came back on the line, Lauretta was howling with laughter. "He thought you were a prostitute trying to get him to come in."

"Well, tell him it's safe to come in. Ask him to tell me a little about his living situation."

After the two talked, Lauretta told me what she had learned. The man's name was Dan and the boy's name was Nicoli. He called his wife "Mon Général."

"Mon Général?" I asked.

"Yes," replied Lauretta. "I asked too, but he said you'll understand why when you meet his wife."

Dan had just arrived from Romania via Holland where he and his family had lived on the streets for a few days. When his interview with Immigration at Pearson International Airport was over, he had asked the officer where he could find a place to sleep.

"That's your problem," the officer replied.

Dan took his wife and son to the sidewalk outside the terminal. For half an hour they wandered around asking one person and another, "Speak Romania?"

Finally they knocked on the window of a taxi and showed a five-dollar American bill. "Hotel?"

The taxi driver left them at a motel a few minutes from the airport. For the next three days they stayed in the motel and used up their remaining American money. They could not see any stores, any place to buy food. They lived on chips from the machine in the office of the motel and water from the sink in their room. Then Dan remembered that someone he had worked with had a cousin in Toronto, so he looked in the phone book for that same last name and started calling all the numbers of people with that name. There were eleven people to call and he struck it lucky on call number seven. The cousin told them they could stay on his living-room floor for a few days. Then he got them a bachelor apartment over at Crossways, the large apartment complex near the Dundas West subway station.

Dan was apologetic, so the translator said, when he explained that they had no furniture, no sheets or blankets, nothing to eat with at the apartment. That was why he had been going through the garbage in the neighbourhood.

The next day we emptied out the garage and managed to provide Dan and his family with some of the necessities. Dan walked down the street with a bed on his back while we loaded up the old station wagon with the mix-and-matchless kitchen utensils from the Romero Boutique.

Dan would drop over frequently after that first encounter. He was quiet, self-effacing almost to a fault. It was clear who gave directions in the family.

When I first met Sophia, some days after I had met Dan and his ten-year-old son, Nicoli, I was taken aback. I had never seen anyone wear so much makeup. Her long hair was dyed jet black. Her face was coated with layers of dark beige foundation topped with bright circles of rouge, a heavy trellis of mascara, and a metallic overlay of eye shadow. Her lips were like big red flags as she sailed into the house. If I had seen her on the street, I would have assumed *she* was the prostitute.

One evening, when Lauretta dropped over to visit the family, she took the opportunity to give me her view of them: he's a little boring but she's really quite interesting. I took a chance and said to Lauretta that she maybe, possibly, could suggest to Sophia that she might be too interesting with all that makeup.

Lauretta sighed. "She needs that makeup. Her skin is grey. She's very sick."

It turned out that "Mon Général" had been working as a radiology technician in a Romanian hospital where faulty equipment had exposed her to excessive radiation. There were other problems at the hospital, as well. She discovered that some of the doctors were working with high-ranking army officers to harvest the bodies of dissidents for organs, which would be sold on the lucrative black market in Europe. Anti-government demonstrators who had arrived at the hospital still alive, were taken away dead and without some of their body parts. The officers tried to silence Sophia by accusing her of spying against the country. Deciding that this was a battle she could not win, she and her husband made plans to leave the country.

Mon Général relished the daily skirmishes with Canadian immigration officials and mapped out the city of Toronto like a battlefield. She became a self-appointed apprentice in a small real estate firm with a flamboyant certificate to prove it. She had fallen down a flight of stairs while going to the office but, no matter, it was the best thing that could have happened. When she went to the "head doctor" for an examination, he told her that she had a most unusual head, for she could see colours when she smelled things. He told her to go to a perfume company where she would probably be paid thousands of dollars as a research assistant. At least, this is what Mon Général had told me.

One day, as she wafted into the house, I noticed that she had put her hair up in a floppy bun on the top of her head. I complimented her sincerely. She started to do a modelling routine in front of Lauretta and me as she talked excitedly in Romanian, punctuating her remarks with a massaging motion on the top of her head.

For almost ten minutes Lauretta was doubled over with laughter. When she told me what had happened to Mon Général's hair, I couldn't contain my own laughter.

Sophia knew very little English, but she never let that get in the way. She shopped with aplomb and would often say to the cashier, "Keep change," as she sauntered off. That day she had gone to get some shampoo at the drugstore in Crossways shopping mall. She liked shampoo in tubes as it was easier to carry if you were travelling. That was what she got, or so she thought.

Up in their apartment, Mon Général went into the shower and began massaging the shampoo into her brittle, dyed hair. Within three minutes, great clumps of hair started coming out as she massaged the top of her head. She shrieked and Dan ran in to find his wife with a tonsured head and long stringy black forelocks. She immediately washed out the rest of the "shampoo."

Using their new English/Romanian dictionary, Dan and Sophia slowly translated the instructions for the shampoo. They discovered that the Neet "shampoo" was a depilatory which women in North America used to remove unwanted hair.

Undaunted, Mon Général boasted that she now knew some big English words like "deeply-tory."

Mr. Immigration

Soon, I noticed that Semira and Sophia always watched TV together on Wednesday nights. Sophia would brush her long now-blonde hair back over her greying face as she leaned to show Semira how to knit a sweater. While Semira would click away on the needles, Sophia would hold Semira's youngest daughter. They were watching "Melrose Place."

I wanted to ask: why are you watching that junk? Then I wondered if it was an assignment from their English class. Other refugees had been told that watching the soaps was a good way to learn English. People spoke slowly, only one person spoke at a time and the vocabulary was very simple.

Finally, I was too curious and blurted out: "Why do you watch 'Melrose Place'?"

Sophia smiled whimsically. "Because just once a week we want to remember what love is like. Now we have no time for romance. The only man in my life is Mr. Immigration. I wait his phone calls every day. I wait his letters every day. But he no have time for me."

Mr. X

"He's not who he says he is." This was the judgement of Ana de Jesus on the newest refugee in the house. "He say he's from El Salvador but he's not. I met lots of Salvadoreans when I was in the States. Sounds to me like he's from Colombia or somewhere."

Semira agreed. When the young man with the designer haircut and white silk suit went up the stairs, Semira pointed to him and shook her head. "No good."

Again and again, I would learn that refugees themselves are the best judges of each other. No refugee who has personally suffered wants to see someone take advantage of the system.

I decided to talk to the mystery man, using the little Spanish I had. "I must ask you to tell me the truth. *La verdad*. We do not work for the immigration system. We are not the police. We work as volunteers. We have very little space and very little money. We would like to use our time and energy for people who are genuine refugees, who need the protection of Canada."

Mr. X did not answer. The next morning he was gone. A few years later, I met him on Yonge Street in Toronto, looking as prosperous as ever, and asked what he was doing. "Thanks be to God, I was accepted by the Immigration and Refugee Board and I'm going to be landed."

He turned on his heel and sauntered away. "*Viva* Canada."

Who knows what line of work he was in. He seemed to have impressed the authorities, but he hadn't passed the most difficult test—the scrutiny of other refugees.

P.E. LEE

We were driving around the neighbourhood on an early Saturday morning, checking out the yard sales, when Nicoli, Sophia's ten-year-old son, noticed a man in a khaki uniform walking down the street.

"Stop the car. It's a Canadian soldier."

And so it was, or possibly a young reservist on his way to a week-end of training manoeuvres.

Nicoli climbed out of the car and ran up to the young soldier. "Please, sir, can I have your autograph?" He ran back to the car to get a piece of paper and a pen.

"Oh, good grief!" said the blushing soldier, quickly signing the piece of paper and walking away. He seemed so young and looked as if he had barely started to shave. Obviously, he was embarrassed by the adulation of this child from Eastern Europe.

Nicoli read the piece of paper signed "P.E. Lee," folded it carefully into his pocket and leaned back with a sigh of great satisfaction.

"I have the autograph of a Canadian soldier."

Nicoli pasted the autograph on the wall at the head of his bed, right next to the icon of Jesus.

ABBÉ JO AND THE LADY

After a year at Romero House, I began to discover that I had at least two new names.

Semira's youngest daughter called me Abbé Jo. As she got a little older, she seemed to know that I left every morning at about eight o'clock to go to the office in one of the other houses. She would rush to the foot of the stairs as I came down from the second floor. Her arm held high, she would point her forefinger at me and exclaim, "Abbé Jo! Abbé Jo!"

I started to wonder if my angel of the annunciation was a little olive-skinned Eritrean girl. I wondered if some day she would open her mouth and give me a message. And what would she announce?

But it was the second interpretation of my name that was even more astounding.

We could never quite figure out why so many refugees kept coming to our door. Our task had been defined as the simple process of helping to settle refugees in this country. We had never advertised Romero House as an advocacy group and we certainly never had any funds allocated for that purpose. Yet, we were often asked if we could speak to the prime minister, to the Queen, to someone from the Royal Family about a particularly distressing situation. One woman came in and threw herself at my feet, begging for help.

It always seemed so difficult to communicate the fact that we could not help someone unless we were able to present a convincing, well-documented case to whomever the decision maker was. Nevertheless, we would hear remarks such as "You can do it if you want to," or "Don't you like me?"

Then one of the volunteers noticed that a letter was addressed to Lady Mary Jo. We had also been getting calls for "the lady." The penny dropped.

I consulted with one of my friends from Eritrea and she confirmed what I had feared to be the case. Because my last name sounded like "lady" they had concluded that I was a member of the Royal Family.

Anyone who had lived in Saudi Arabia, and many Eritrean refugees had, knew that a member of the Royal Family could make all things possible simply by a snap of the fingers.

From time to time, I considered changing my name.

III

VOICES, ECHOES

No More Little Girl Semira

The woman who had smiled upon me six months earlier began to smile in English. "My name is Semira. I come Eritrea. I like Canada. I like tea. I like bread. I like God."

Semira had found an ESL class which provided a few hours of day care for her two youngest daughters and she had registered as soon as possible. After her five children had been put to bed, she pulled out her notebook and with great delight began to trace the letters of her new alphabet. "I like *a*. Good *a*. I like *b*. Good *b*." Indeed, it seemed that there was hardly anything or anyone that Semira didn't like. Her generous spirit moved through the walls between people and flew over artificial boundaries.

Although she had little time to study the language, her English improved rapidly. Semira wanted to communicate, to connect. Intelligence, courage and ingenuity helped her to use the simple tools she had been given in school with great effectiveness. I looked forward to the evenings when she would come into our kitchen and we would talk over tea. It was good to begin to hear her voice, unfiltered by the presence of a translator. As her facility with the language grew, so did my ability to fill in the blanks between the words.

"Good talk. Woman and woman," she said sadly one night. "I have no family here. No mother speak. No sister speak. Very difficult."

"Do you miss your family? Cry in heart because there is no family?"

"Yes. You have family. I see crayon your family in room."

"You saw the photo of my family in my room? The photo when I was a little girl like Jemilla and Juwaher and Muzit?"

"Yes. Very beautiful."

"Do you have photos of you when you were a little girl?"

"No. My mother and father put, how you say, many photo down in garden. Like dead."

It took a few more questions before I understood what had happened to Semira's childhood photos. When she was fourteen, her parents had taken all the photographs of Semira, placed them in a plastic bag and buried them under the house. Many years later, her mother had tried to retrieve the photos but the moisture in the ground had seeped through the plastic and destroyed all the photos.

"So no more little girl Semira. Like dead. But no dead now."

"Why did you leave your home, Semira?"

"Ethiopia come for children."

In the late seventies, the Ethiopian army had fanned out through Eritrea, searching for any and every teenager, boys and girls alike, in a program of enforced conscription into the army. Conscription was designed to demoralize the separatist movement by forcing Eritrean teenagers to fight against their own people. Those who did not join the Ethiopian army were killed or imprisoned.

The young people knew that eventually the moment of decision would come. Either they had to hide in the mountains of Eritrea, hoping to make contact with the separatist guerrillas or they had to flee from their country. In either case, they had to leave their families.

Semira was just fourteen when the Ethiopian soldiers came to her village, a prosperous farming area just outside of Asmara, the capital of Eritrea. She hid in a shed at the back of her family's property until they left. Her parents, who had just buried the pictures of Semira under the house, told the soldiers that all their children were under ten. The evidence of Semira's existence had been hidden but her parents knew she was no longer safe at home. In a few days, they drove her to another village where they paid a guide to include her in a group of teenagers who would be taken out of Eritrea and through the desert to the Sudan. That was the last time she saw her parents.

The teenagers hid until dark and then began walking north, as much as possible by night, through some secret desert routes. By day, Ethiopian helicopters scanned the desert and strafed any visible escapees. It took Semira more than thirty nights to reach the Sudanese border. She prayed constantly and tried to help the others but several of them died from exhaustion and the heat and had to be buried in the sand. Eventually, worn out and thirsty, they reached the border and she found her way to the home of some distant relatives who had fled to the Sudan earlier. The cousins had barely enough food for themselves and so Semira went to work immediately as a house cleaner. The Sudan was a beautiful country with great agricultural potential but it was obvious to Semira that something was wrong politically and the people remained very poor. The influx of refugees from Eritrea was not something eastern Sudan could support for long. Semira saved carefully until she had enough money to pay for passage on a small boat to Saudi Arabia. Her visa was issued for her to make a *hadj*, a pilgrimage to Mecca.

The Saudi culture was a shock to Semira. In Eritrea, the boys and girls had played together and mixed freely. The girls were able to wear blouses and even long shorts in the heat. Semira's family was Muslim but they had never had any strict prohibitions around women. Now Semira was forced to wear a long black dress and veil every time she left the house where she was working. While she was single she could leave her face exposed, but after she was married only her eyes could show. She had to adapt if she was to stay.

However, Semira was never under any illusion about the rules for women. They had little to do with religion. Once, as a servant to royalty, she had accompanied one of the prince's daughters on a trip to

London, England. As soon as the plane left the ground, the princess threw off the black covering and revealed her new miniskirt and tank top underneath. In London, the princess and her friends went to discos and did everything they had been forbidden to do. When they arrived back at the Riyadh airport, a taxi came to the plane and in it was a long black covering for the princess and each of her friends.

Semira met her future husband as the result of the elaborate protocol through which marriages were arranged in the Eritrean community living in Saudi. One of Jamal's aunts had seen Semira at a gathering of women and was quite taken with her beauty and her character. The aunt arranged for Jamal to have a brief look at Semira through the window so he could see her without the veil—too many marriages collapsed when the husband had finally seen the face of his new bride. Jamal and Semira met a few times in strictly supervised circumstances, with Semira fully veiled. They talked about their families in Eritrea, about what was important to them, about the family they would like to have. Jamal proposed and Semira accepted.

At twenty-two, she would be marrying into one of the best-known families in Eritrea. Jamal's father and his uncles owned most of the warehouses in Eritrea and exercised a virtual monopoly over trading in the country. Outside the capital city of Asmara, the family's warehouses covered several acres. They had all been confiscated by the Ethiopians and were being used as barracks for the army.

Jamal had also left Eritrea as a teenager but had proceeded from the Sudan to Italy and then to East Germany where he studied for several years and became very active in organizing the Eritrean students. He became quite comfortable with European ways, cultivating a taste for beer and dancing. Eventually, he went to Saudi Arabia to work for a European import company and was quickly promoted to a managerial position. It was now time to settle down and raise a family.

They had their five children in quick succession, and soon moved to a large apartment to make room for the family and for the numerous relatives who would arrive as refugees from Eritrea. Jamal would often drive around in the evenings, dropping off food and clothing for the Eritreans who had recently arrived in Riyadh.

Semira knew that Jamal went out to Eritrean gatherings in the evening and that he invited men in for political meetings. But that was all she knew. Most men did not tell their wives about their political activities because they were afraid the women would reveal some information when they gossiped together. Women spent a great deal of time exchanging the small bits of information that added a little interest to their lives. Jamal, we later learned, was not worried about Semira gossiping. He wanted to protect her and the children.

In 1989, they learned that a section of Eritrea had been liberated from the Ethiopians by Eritrean fighters. Jamal told Semira that he wanted to go to Eritrea and assess the situation first-hand. He left by plane for Khartoum, in the Sudan, where he was to meet an escort which would take Eritreans into the northern part of their country. The guerrillas known as the Eritrean People's Liberation Front (EPLF) had issued an announcement to Eritreans living abroad that it was now safe to visit the liberated zone and that visitors would be escorted in convoys from Khartoum.

Jamal never returned. Semira called his employer, who then made extensive inquiries in the Sudan and at the airline office. The only information was that he had arrived in Khartoum but had disappeared from there.

Semira became alarmed. A woman without a husband or male relative was not allowed to stay in Saudi Arabia. For a few months, her brother helped her out and did the food shopping but he was soon to get married and she did not want to force him to continue to live with her. In desperation, she sold all her jewellery and their BMW car to purchase the tickets and visa to go to New York City. She knew she could not return to Eritrea because of what had happened to her husband and her plan was to head for Canada, the country which she had heard was very beautiful and helped those in trouble. A Saudi prince she had worked for helped her to get the visa and an agent offered to make all the arrangements for a small sum. In the end, she had paid almost fifty thousand American dollars to be able to escape. All she had left were her children and whatever fitted into an overnight bag.

"But it was so long and so far," she told me later. "I wondered who I would meet. It seemed as if I was going to the end of the earth."

For more than twenty-four hours Semira had travelled by plane to New York City. The only English words she knew were "Buffalo, Canada." Somehow she found her way through the airport and then by taxi to Port Authority where she caught a bus for Buffalo. A very kind lady, seeing her standing in the midst of the beggars and drug addicts at the bus terminal, had helped her find the right bus and had written out something on a piece of paper. When Semira arrived in Buffalo she showed the paper to the bus driver who put her in a taxi which took her to a motel. She showed the paper to the manager of the motel and he nodded his head when she said, "Canada." The next day a taxi arrived and he paid the driver to deposit the family at the Peace Bridge. As she walked across the bridge with her children, an officer saw her and took her over to the office. A translator was soon found and the officer said she could enter immediately because it would be too difficult to wait several days with five children. She was given a set of immigration forms and told a lawyer had been assigned to her case.

A woman who had hardly ever been permitted to leave the house during her nine years in Saudi Arabia had travelled halfway around the world with her five children and an overnight case.

"Everyone was so very kind. God look after my children," said Semira as she recalled her journey. And you were very brave, I thought.

In May 1991, shortly after the family arrived, there were extensive television reports on the fall of the Ethiopian dictator, Mengistu. All of Eritrea had been liberated and a provisional government had been set up, run by the EPLF. I thought this would be wonderful news for Semira and called her down to watch the coverage. She seemed rather serious—not the reaction I had expected. Local news broadcasts had carried reports of how thousands of Eritreans in Toronto had gathered to celebrate the end of Ethiopian rule.

"It will be better," said Semira carefully. "But you know, still many problems. New government want power. Freedom big problem." I didn't understand what she was saying. Hadn't the liberation movement been fighting for freedom? Only later would I realize the implications of this statement for the future of her family and the safety of her husband.

The ripple effects of Mengistu's fall would soon be felt at Romero House. We would begin to receive some refugees from the other side of the conflict, those who had worked for the Mengistu government. At the same time, Canada started to deport Eritreans back to their new country. The panel members at the Immigration and Refugee Board were already deciding that Eritrea was "safe" now that Mengistu was gone.

What I could not yet tell Semira was that her husband was alive. Abdullah, her husband's friend, had sworn me to secrecy in the summer of 1991. "Jamal's brother never gave up hope. He kept raising the money and paying people to find out where his brother was. They know where he is now. He is in a desert prison camp in the Sahel region of Eritrea. Don't say anything to Semira until we know for sure. We don't want her to hope until we are sure he is safe."

It was a secret I kept. Jamal still had to escape from prison, cross a desert and continents and brave the Canadian immigration system before he could rejoin his family.

I NEVER THOUGHT I WOULD BE A REFUGEE

After the phone call from one of the local parishes, I wondered whether our house would soon become a little Mogadishu, a place of beauty and harmony torn apart by seething tribal conflicts.

The caller had explained that her parish had raised money to sponsor a Somali family but, because they had heard nothing from Immigration for over two years, they had decided to use the money for some more urgent projects. The sum of money had been substantial two years ago, she said. It was enough to cover all living expenses for a family of five for a year.

"Unfortunately—or fortunately—there's only one member of the family left," she said with evident distress. The concerned parishioner said that they still had enough money to cover some of the doctor's living expenses, but they could no longer cover the rent.

"The doctor's?"

"Yes, she's a doctor."

"She?"

"Yes, that's all I know. Something happened to her husband and three sons. He was a mathematics professor at the university in Mogadishu."

Then I received the official request from the sponsorship committee—could Romero House provide the doctor with shelter? We discussed a few of the details regarding her arrival and the matter was settled.

Almost as an afterthought, I asked, "What tribe does she belong to?" I had been learning a little more about the complexities of the situations that were forcing refugees to flee from Somalia and elsewhere.

"I don't know." The parishioner paused. "I think it begins with an *H*. Does it really matter?"

"It shouldn't," I said, "but it might . . . let's see how it goes."

I had guessed that "the doctor" was from the Hawiye tribe and I knew that she would be coming to live in the same house as Omar and Fadumo, who were from the Darood tribe. And those two tribes were not, to put it mildly, on the best of terms.

With this in mind, I tried to prepare the way for the doctor. I told the other people in the house that our new neighbour was from Somalia, that she was alone because something had happened to the rest of her family and that she had been in a refugee camp in Kenya. I told them she was a sponsored refugee, which meant that she had been accepted by a Canadian immigration officer in Nairobi, and that a group in Canada had raised money for the family a long time ago but that, thinking the family would never arrive, had since used the money for something else.

But nothing could have prepared us for Asha. She strode through our front door, elegant, gorgeous, almost confident. Unlike all of the other Somali women I had met, she wore a chic business suit and her short, wavy hair was fully exposed. I could see Omar shrink at the sight of such brazen beauty while Fadumo looked on with quiet curiosity. Semira stepped forward and gave her new neighbour a kiss on each cheek and then a third one.

"*A-Salaam Alekum.*"

"*Ma'a Salaam.*"

The doctor turned to me and held out her hand. "Hello. My name is Asha and I am grateful for your hospitality." She spoke in almost perfect English with a slight Italian accent. "If you will excuse me, I must sit down. I am very tired. It was a long flight from Nairobi."

Semira looked at her with compassion, remembering, understanding. They began to speak in Arabic. Fadumo sat down with the two of them and soon they were having tea together. Omar watched and then went upstairs to pray.

Soon Asha went to her room to sleep. And Fadumo said, "Wow." Semira said, "She very sweet."

The three women soon began having tea in the evenings after the children had gone to bed and Omar had left to pray. Asha would wear jeans and a sweatshirt and Fadumo would take off her veil when only the women were there. When I could, I would join them and float with the waves of conversation in Somali, Arabic and English.

At first they talked mostly about their children—about Semira's ever-present five, about Fadumo's completely absent five and about the three of Asha's who had disappeared. I learned that Asha had been separated from her husband and three sons when they were trying to flee from Mogadishu to Nairobi in 1989. She and her husband had tried to leave the country by separate routes and had hoped to meet at a hotel in Nairobi. Her husband and sons never arrived.

"This very bad," said Semira sadly. She put her arm around Asha and rocked her gently. "My boys, your boys."

"Yes, this very bad." Fadumo looked at the floor and through it to the other side of the world.

Later, as I began to inquire about Asha's credentials to see what courses she could enrol in, I heard more about the twists and turns in the history of the Horn of Africa which had brought her to this point. Her own family had owned one of the most fashionable hotels along the beach near Mogadishu. During the Italian occupation it was patronized by Italians, after the Second World War it was frequented by the English and was popular again with Italians during the Italian trusteeship of 1948–58. After the 1969 coup, in which Major-General Mohammad Siyaad Barre seized power, the hotel became a favourite haunt of Soviet diplomats and development experts. The large, white building which looked out onto the glistening blue waters of the Indian Ocean had seen the powerful come and go.

Asha had gone to one of the finest high schools in Mogadishu, which was run by an order of Roman Catholic nuns from Italy. Because she had done exceptionally well, she was encouraged to go on to university. When she confided to one of her teachers that she had always dreamed of being a nurse, the teacher responded that Asha should also dream about becoming a doctor because Somalia had need of women doctors.

It was 1973 and the Soviet Union was offering generous scholarships for African students who wanted a post-secondary education. Asha left her home by the Indian Ocean and went to Moscow to study medicine. It meant learning another language and leaving the warmth of her country and her family for seven years.

"But it wasn't just the weather that was hard," she recalled. "The people were hard. I never really felt that they liked the Africans."

It was during those years in Moscow that Asha let go of her traditional dress, her veil and many of the restrictions she had grown up with. However, she was not sure she wanted to live like the women she had seen in the Soviet bloc countries. She didn't want to be so alone, so separated from her family.

Nevertheless, it was an exciting time for Asha. Every day she was learning something new in the school of medicine and she was convinced that it mattered, that it would make a difference in the lives of the women and children in her country.

She returned to Somalia hopeful and confident, planning to look for work in a clinic as soon as possible. However, her family had grown concerned that she was getting older and was, as yet, unmarried. They started a series of discreet introductions to several potential husbands. Although they knew by then that they could not force Asha to marry anyone, the family wanted to provide some guidance in such an important matter.

When Asha met the young professor of mathematics, she was more than interested. They shared the same intellectual interests and the same desire to improve the situation of the people in their country. And he was from the same tribe. He had been married before to a woman from the same small village, but they had divorced during the years of his graduate study in Italy. His first wife had returned to Somalia with their small daughter. In due season, he and Asha were married and had three boys in rapid succession.

"We had a wonderful life together," said Asha. "The trouble in the country didn't affect us too much. I never thought I would be a refugee."

Asha's mother-in-law helped with the three boys so that Asha could begin to work part-time in a clinic that was run by an Italian aid agency. She usually wore a veil in the clinic so that the women who came there would not be uncomfortable. Asha had hoped to spend most of her time doing family planning education, but she soon found that her time was being taken up with the medical care of women who had been raped. Although women and children had usually been off-limits in tribal warfare, they were now becoming casualties of the vicious struggle between the government forces of Siyaad Barre and various tribal factions.

In 1989, the army began its campaign to subdue high-profile members of the clans who opposed Siyaad Barre. Troops moved through Mogadishu, picking up influential or potentially dangerous members of the Hawiye tribe. Asha's husband called her to say that several members of the faculty had been dragged away and that he had escaped only by hiding in a storeroom. He asked her to stay at the clinic until he could get the children from his mother and make arrangements for all of them to leave the country.

One week later, a messenger came to the clinic with a package from her husband. It contained her passport, some money, an airline ticket and the address of the hotel in Nairobi where they were to meet.

Asha waited in Nairobi for her husband and sons. She went directly to the hotel where they had planned to meet; rarely venturing outside the building, she waited in her room. She waited for three months—until she had run out of money.

Asha walked out onto the streets of Nairobi as if from a tomb. She walked and walked, oblivious to cars, passersby, the distance or direction of street. She walked until she reached the outskirts of Nairobi where she found herself in the midst of a refugee camp.

"Who are you?" asked one of the children playing in the dust at the entrance to the camp.

"I'm a doctor," Asha answered. "Or I was. Or I think I am."

"That's good," said the little boy. "We need many doctors."

The smells in the clinic near the camp drew Asha once again to other human beings. She was welcomed. She was needed. She was soon dispensing medicine, delivering babies and bandaging the wounds of those who had been wounded in fights in the camps.

Workers with the United Nations High Commission for Refugees (UNHCR) would often visit the camp and the clinic. Asha enjoyed their company and some of them took an interest in her situation. A young Canadian woman recommended that Asha go to the Canadian High Commission in Nairobi to apply for refugee status so that a sponsorship could be arranged.

Asha's Canadian friend arranged to get her the application forms and the required medical examinations. All that remained was the interview with a Canadian immigration officer. Months passed. Asha's friends explained to her that the few immigration officers at the Canadian High Commission in Nairobi were responsible for all the refugee applications from east and central Africa. "You would have a better chance in eastern Europe, where there are more immigration officers, than in east Africa," quipped her friend.

Eventually Asha had her interview, but most of the time was taken up with questions regarding the qualifications and the whereabouts of Asha's husband. The frustrated officer wasn't sure whether Asha was applying as a single refugee or as one of a family of five.

"I don't know," said Asha sadly. "I don't know if I am alone or if I am still a wife and mother."

"I'm sorry," replied the officer. "It's been a hard day."

In 1990, the fighting between the Hawiye and the Darood tribes escalated. The Somali government of Siyaad Barre was overthrown in January 1991 and the country descended to yet another level of violence. That was when Omar, a captain with the government forces, and his wife were forced to leave. Six months later Asha arrived on a sponsorship request "for a family from Somalia" from a parish in Toronto.

As the weeks and months passed at Romero House, Omar began to pray more and even attended all-night teaching sessions in the local mosque. Fadumo started to smile and wink and then think out loud in English. Asha, on the other hand, became more and more withdrawn. She even stopped having tea with Semira, Fadumo and me in the evenings.

I would see this many times at Romero House—the refugee who struggles to survive, who has kept on moving in spite of everything and who finally makes it to a place of safety. It is then, and only then, that the grief surfaces and threatens to engulf everything.

There is nothing that can be done. The sorrow must be granted a space within the soul.

Asha slowly emerged from her isolation. Omar and Fadumo welcomed her back with great gentleness. They knew where she had been.

"I am sorry about all the fighting," Omar said to her one evening. "It is not good for any of us. Your children gone. Our children gone. The people at the top play their little games and we get thrown away."

"Yes," replied Asha. "We have all been thrown to the other side of the world . . . and I am sorry for what has happened to your family, Omar."

I was a witness to this small peace. If they can do it, I thought, then maybe we all can do it.

Asha began reading some of the books which were lying around the house in an effort to stop herself from slipping back into a depression. She picked up *Man's Search for Meaning* by Victor Frankl and found herself profoundly moved by his description of what had kept him going during his time in the concentration camps of Nazi-dominated Europe.

"I learned a lot from him," Asha told me. "I am beginning to believe that there must be some meaning and purpose in all of this. Someday I may understand why all of this has happened. I don't know now. But I believe there is some reason for it."

Asha received a letter from her friend with the UNHCR. "You will be astounded by the information I have to share with you: there is a young girl, thirteen years old, and she is the daughter of your husband's first marriage." Asha was beside herself. She was simultaneously thrilled to hear news from her family and then terribly concerned.

"You have no idea what it is like for a thirteen-year-old girl, alone, in one of those camps," she said to me. "She could be raped. I have to do something. In my culture, I'm responsible for her as if she were my own daughter."

There was a determination in Asha's eyes that I had never seen before. I resolved to do what I could although I was unsure what that might mean.

The next day an elderly woman called to say that she had seen a television program about the terrible situation in Somalia and she wanted to do something about it. Could we use two thousand dollars? I assured her that we could and that it would be used to bring a thirteen-year-old girl out of a refugee camp in Nairobi.

For two years the money sat in the bank while we wrote back and forth to Nairobi trying to make it possible for Asha to adopt her husband's daughter—in the Canadian way. Throughout that whole period of time, Asha never gave up. She could not afford to give up.

Finally, we received word that her stepdaughter was arriving on a flight from Nairobi. I drove Asha out to Pearson International Airport. She was quiet, very quiet.

We waited by the gate as the passengers came through the metal doors in the international arrivals section.

Asha started forward when she saw the girl in the veil with a small suitcase. And then Asha stopped, only for a moment. The frail little girl with the sunken eyes was holding her stomach with one hand, holding herself where she was very big and very pregnant.

✳ WE SANG DISSIDENT MUSIC

"So how did you two meet?" It was a quiet moment of celebration at a little Mexican restaurant on Bloor Street and I was finally able to ask a question that had seemed relatively unimportant until now. But now that Hanna and Yuri had been accepted by Canada, other dimensions of their lives, which had been submerged by the refugee process, began to surface. We sipped some Corona beer and they warmed to the question.

"Well, we were, like you say, Romeo and Juliet," said Hanna. Her dark encircled eyes seemed to flash with memories. Yuri leaned back to listen. He was used to his wife doing the talking. Her English was much better as she had been working as a housekeeping supervisor at a large Toronto hotel and his work as an expert jeweller had made fewer linguistic demands. Besides, she was the feisty one. She should be, Yuri had told me earlier, she's a Kurdish princess.

"Romeo and Juliet? But you didn't kill yourselves!" I teased.

"No, but our families did not agree. My father was like a chief, a noble, to the Kurdish people in Iraq. My family had to leave Iraq because of all the persecution for our people. We went to Georgia, which was then in Soviet Union. But my father always wanted me to marry a man from an important Kurdish family.

"And Yuri was not Kurdish. He was Russian. His family had gone to Georgia at the time of Stalin's famine so they could eat. You see, Romeo and Juliet."

"But how did you meet?"

"We were both in a band. How you say, under-the-ground band. I was the singer. Very good, very sexy singer and Yuri played the guitar." They looked at each other and laughed. "I almost forgot. We have been so worried for so many years."

"A band? How interesting. What kind of music did you sing?"

"Well, dissident music of course!" Hanna raised her glass of beer and clinked it with Yuri's.

"Dissident music? What does that mean?"

"The Beatles," Yuri replied.

"The Beatles?"

"Oh yes, everyone we knew at the university was singing Beatles songs when we were young. The government hated this music but we loved it. 'Yellow Submarine.' 'Hey, Jude.' You know." Hanna poked me.

"Well yes, I do, but I guess I didn't realize the extent of their political influence."

"I like 'The White Album' the best," said Yuri. "But we never sing for years and years."

"No." Hanna saddened. "After Soviet Union broke, life became very hard for us. My sister was raped and killed because she was Kurdish. It was not safe for us in Georgia any more. And Yuri had a big problem because he knew about dirty business with national art treasures. People stealing jewels from the country. Georgia is very beautiful country but we couldn't stay there any more.

"But you know," she looked at me pensively, "it was that time we began to believe in God. Yuri's grandmother died and we went to clean her little farm. We found an old black piece of wood and Yuri say it may be a holy picture. Icon. We took it home.

"You know in a few months we began to see picture of Mary and Jesus. The black went away. We take this icon everywhere. Before that I was nothing. We had no religion in my family and Yuri didn't know too much about religion. We couldn't know in Soviet Union. But all these troubles . . . we needed God."

After that night in the Mexican restaurant, Hanna and Yuri prepared a party for all their friends and supporters in the little Russian cultural centre not too far from our place. The walls of the rather small basement room were covered with lavish scenes of Russia as it once was. Hanna and her friends had prepared tables full of various Eastern dishes. And there was plenty of vodka and red wine.

I went to the party with some of the volunteers who had met Hanna and Yuri during their visits to our office and had heard me recount the conversation in the Mexican restaurant. Many of the other guests were older Eastern European women and some of the staff workers at the Russian church. There was also a very beat-looking Russian musician playing the guitar in the corner. His shaggy hair and beard grew down into his black suit, black shirt and big black boots.

After Hanna gave a short speech of thanks to all who had supported her, she invited us to enjoy the music and food. "Sing some dissident music!" I blurted out.

She laughed and grabbed the microphone while the black-robed musician propped himself up on a chair. The words came slowly at first and Hanna had to cough several times. She started to sing "Yellow Submarine" and then launched into "Hey, Jude."

And everyone else in the room seemed to know the tune. Whenever Hanna faltered for words, they would fill in, if not with words, then with gusto. Soon the whole room was joined arm in arm around the U-shaped table and swaying to the beat.

Then there was another song. "Especially tonight," said Hanna as she coughed again. "You know I haven't sung for twenty years." Somehow the years seemed to fall away as she stood there and sang the song that had been the beat of freedom when they had lived under a soulless regime—"Like a Bridge Over Troubled Waters."

This is what we sang in the basement of the Russian cultural centre in Toronto.

I AM AN UPSIDE-DOWN MAN

It was on Hallowe'en that I first learned that Cheeva had been subjected to torture in a prison in Sri Lanka. He had seen a paper skeleton at Zellers and brought it home and hung it upside down from a rope attached to the light in the front hallway. On the skeleton he had pinned a button from Amnesty International which I had left lying around the house. The button said: Stop Torture.

After I saw this desperate statement, I invited Cheeva to go for a walk with me. The children on the street were hauling home their bags of booty, the rewards of looking scarier than thou.

He began to tell me his story: "After I got out of prison, I went into hiding at a friend's house. I wanted to stay in Sri Lanka any way I could. I couldn't imagine being away from my family and I had such a good job. But then my friend said I was putting his family in danger. I had to go.

"You see, maybe I was lucky. I worked for a large spice company and I had a very good job. I had gone to many places in Europe and the Far East on company business. It was easy for me to get a visa by saying it was another business trip. But certainly not from the Canadian High Commission in Colombo. They just don't give visas. But I could get one to the States.

"I had to go. And my wife and children had to go into hiding in a village where she had some relatives. My children, they are not schooling." He began to sob.

He looked at the local goblins trotting down the street. "These children don't know what monsters are, they don't know what human beings can do to each other."

"Were there monsters in the prison, Cheeva?"

"Yes, yes. They were like animals. You can't imagine. I am so ashamed. They hung me up. They . . ."

"You don't have to go on."

"I am an upside-down man. . . . The worst thing is I don't know why they arrested me. I knew that my brother had disappeared a month before. There were only two of us. He was working in the hotel business. He was my best friend. The police kept saying he was a member of the JVP [an ultra-leftist terrorist group in the south of Sri Lanka]. But he wasn't, he was just like me. We were trying to make a good living. He wanted to get married. We didn't want to become involved in politics.

"They kept asking me and asking me. For sixteen days they kept asking me. They would have killed me, I know. But my father was waiting."

"Your father was waiting?"

"He had already lost one son. I was all he had left. We all lived together in his big house. When I was taken by the police he went around to every prison until he found out where I was. He went inside and asked to see me. He kept going to the desk. And he waited outside for sixteen days. He slept there at the doorstep at night. Finally, a friend of his in the police heard about my situation. He came to see me and told me he had arranged for me to go but that I had to leave Sri Lanka.

"But I didn't want to go. It was my whole life, you know. My kids. My wife. I knew I could not take them with me or they would be suspicious and would not give me a visa. I was somebody there, you know. I was Sinhalese, not Tamil. I had a car. I was the best salesman in the company. And I was very sportive. I played cricket for the best team in Sri Lanka. Everyone knew me. My picture was in the paper—that's why my friend didn't think I could hide forever in the country.

"When I arrived in New York I couldn't sleep and I couldn't stay awake. I just stayed in a friend's apartment for a month. I didn't know what to do. I was very depressed. Then my friend helped me get a bus ticket to Buffalo. I had no money left. I wasn't able to take my savings with me or they would have been suspicious. They could have been watching the bank. I couldn't sell my house. It's just boarded up now. The servants have gone.

"I have always been working, you know. When I was in Buffalo I stayed in a shelter. I volunteered a lot, doing the dishes. I even got a certificate of merit for all the work I did. Then I had my appointment with Canada Immigration at the bridge. They asked me why I left my country. Do you know what I said? I said I didn't know. I just started to cry. I have never cried. It's not right for men to do that."

I remembered Sir George's efforts to maintain his dignity, and how he was finally forced to cry in humiliation.

"Cheeva, there's a place here in Toronto called the Canadian Centre for Victims of Torture. There are other people who have been tortured. The people at the centre can help you. You will never be the same. But you can learn a little about how to live with what happened during those sixteen days."

"You don't know what it was like."

"No, I don't."

At the Centre for Victims of Torture, the doctor wrote a medical opinion which was to be presented at Cheeva's hearing:

> Hearings can be very traumatic for those suffering from post-traumatic stress disorder. They can resemble the previous experiences of interrogation. Any adjudication process can bring back memories associated with a kangaroo court, with a time when the refugee was at the total mercy of his

questioners. Victims of torture have sometimes survived only by repressing memories of what happened. They may be unable to remember details of what happened under torture. The effects of torture seem to be most devastating on those who had no political conviction or motivation.

Three days before the hearing, Cheeva went to the local clinic because of severe congestion. The day before the hearing he was taken to the hospital because of an asthma attack. His doctor phoned and said he did not think he was in any condition to go to a hearing. I begged Cheeva to postpone the hearing. I was sure he would be unable to give any credible testimony at the hearing.

"I will go even if they have to take me in a coffin. I have to get this done as quickly as possible so I can sponsor my wife and children."

He cried in quiet little howls on the subway the morning we left for the hearing. The other passengers looked away in discomfort.

"Why's he crying, Mommy?" asked a little girl with big blue eyes. "Are you okay?"

It was such a gentle question. "I'll be fine," he sniffed and smiled back. "Do you know I have a little girl just like you?"

Cheeva was lucky with the panel members at his hearing. They had read the medical report, they said, as the hearing commenced. There would be no necessity for him to go into detail about what happened at the prison. They started with what they thought would be an easy question: "Can you explain to us why or how you were released from prison?"

"It was my father . . . he waited for me." Cheeva covered his face with his hands so we could not see his tears. But we could hear them.

With great sensitivity, the judges switched to another set of questions to allow him to establish his identity: "I understand you were a well-known cricket player. Can you tell us what position you played. What were some of your best games. Can you tell us a little about your company. Tell us how you earned the best salesman of the year award."

Their questions restored his sense of worth. His lawyer
press clippings, convincing documents and a letter from the p̶
dent of the spice company. Cheeva pulled out two medals from his
pocket.

Then one of the panel members asked again: "Can you tell us why
or how you were released from prison?"

And Cheeva answered. He told them what he had told me. He was
accepted. The next day he applied for landed immigrant status so he
could sponsor his wife and children. This was in 1992. There was no
"head tax"* then. All he had to raise was the money for their airfare.
While he waited for their arrival, he looked for a job and volunteered
at the Kidney Foundation.

Almost miraculously, his landed papers came in five months. It is
the fastest process of landing that we had ever seen and we have not
seen anything like it since. We expected that he would be elated when
his wife and three children arrived. He was, sometimes. But at other
times he was withdrawn and sad. It was something I couldn't understand but I didn't want to ask about.

Then one day he said to me, "I thought when they came that it
would all be the same as before, but it isn't."

I was learning, slowly, that there are things that can create a great
divide within human beings between before and after, and that surviv-
ing involves two choices: the choice not to die and the choice to live.
And the two choices are not the same.

✳I WILL NEVER BE SAFE

Suleyman had never asked me for anything. He had come over to the
Romero office several times but always with another Kurd. Suleyman
came as the translator, as the leader of his Kurdish community and
that meant he was the unofficial, unpaid, but full-time social worker.

---

* The "head tax" was imposed on all immigrants and refugees in
February 1995.

"He needs some assistance," Suleyman said with great courtesy. "Twana's wife is trapped in a village in the Kurdish area of Iraq." The crisis was always understated just as Suleyman was understated. He did not want pity—neither for himself nor for his companions—and he had long ago abandoned any hope of mercy.

His presence was striking and you would look at him twice on the street. Large bushy eyebrows shadowed his ruggedly handsome face. It was a sad face but occasionally there was a wide and generous smile and the hint of some mountain sunshine from long ago in his eyes. He seemed strong and physically fit—except for the limp, except for the black fingernails and the patches of orange skin at his fingertips.

Suleyman did not speak about his black fingernails. They simply rested on the briefcase on his lap. They were there. Nothing special. Nothing to be discussed. I guessed but never asked.

The Kurdish centre was a few blocks from us on Dundas West in the Junction area of Toronto. It was small compared to the centres of most ethnic groups in the city. The front room had a few old tables and straight-backed chairs where a small group of men sat drinking sweet tea. The room behind was covered with rugs and served as the place of prayer. It was here that Suleyman could be found almost any day—listening to the people who dropped in, helping to translate documents, organizing the latest demonstration outside the Turkish Embassy. He was one of the most educated members of the Kurdish community and the task of acting as the interlocutor with various agencies had fallen to him.

Every now and then I would drive over to the centre with clothes and food which had been donated for refugees. I could never leave without a cup of spiced tea. "Sorry we don't have crumpets," quipped Suleyman.

"Where did you learn your English, Suleyman? It's very good."

"Well, I obtained a degree in mechanical engineering in Turkey so I didn't study languages. I only learned to speak English here."

"Did you work as an engineer?"

"Oh yes," he sighed. "I had a very good job with the national railways until I was put in jail."

I waited. It was his line to cross.

"I became active in the union movement in 1979 and I started to speak up about the rights of the Kurdish people. They put me in jail for a year and tried to find out information about the Kurdish organizations. Really, there wasn't much to tell them. They used electricity. That wasn't the worst thing. The worst was hearing the screams of other people in the corridors. Then they let me out."

"Was that when you left Turkey?"

"No. I wanted to stay there. It's my country, you know. It's a beautiful country. I wanted to go back to work. I wanted to get married and have a family, but then I was drafted into the army."

"The Turkish army?"

"Yes. I even became a lieutenant because of my education and because I did so well in the training school. I was the best in my class. But they would never give me any position of real responsibility because I was a Kurd. They used me, that's all. They sent me on assignments to areas that nobody else would go because it was so cold. They even sent me to the Kurdish areas in the east. I could never have fought against my own people. Maybe they knew that.

"Anyway, it didn't last forever. After two years I went back to my job, but soon I was arrested again because of Kurdish uprisings in the east. They used more electricity. That was when they beat my feet. I knew then I could never be safe in Turkey. It didn't matter what I did or didn't do, I would be arrested just for being a Kurd. I was in there for about sixteen months. When I got out I used the railpass to go through Europe and to get as far away from Turkey as I could.

"I went to Ireland because I thought it was about as far away as you could get. It was a great place. The people were so friendly and the music was so happy. But—can you imagine—they couldn't find one Kurdish translator in the whole of Ireland! This meant I couldn't have my interview for refugee status. So I came to Canada. It was my last hope."

"When did you come to Canada?"

"Oh, about four years ago, in 1991, but I'm still waiting for my landed immigrant papers. They're pretty tough on the Kurds. They think we are all terrorists waiting to blow something up. I just want to go to university so I can work as an engineer. I've been accepted at the University of Toronto and McGill but they say I have to be landed first. So I just try to spend my time helping people in the community."

"Is there anything I can do to help?" I asked.

"Well yes, of course, if you could help Twana get his wife out of that village in Iraq."

A few months later, Suleyman was sitting in our kitchen when I went there to make supper for the volunteers. He sat at the table, rubbing his hands on his knees. "Are you busy tomorrow?" he asked.

"Yes, I am. Tomorrow's the day I have to teach at the university."

"You have to?" He seemed worried or puzzled, I could not tell which.

"Why? What's on tomorrow, Suleyman?"

"Well," he hesitated, "I got a letter from Immigration that I must go for my security interview tomorrow. It's required for the landed immigrant status." He hid his hands in the armpits of his jacket.

He had never asked for anything for himself and he would not do so now. "I'll go with you," I said.

"But you have to teach. Your students. University is very important for them."

"And for you, too. I'll make arrangements for them if I'm late. How long will it take?"

"Well, they said to be there at nine in the morning. Maybe two hours."

"No problem. I'll still make it for my afternoon class." It all seemed a matter of course to me. First the security interview and then on to the halls of learning.

I met Suleyman at the Dundas West subway stop early the next morning. He was wearing an immaculate white shirt and his one good, very bright red sweater. He stood solid in the middle of the aisle with his arms crossed and fingers out of sight. "You know," he smiled only slightly, "no one ever cancelled an appointment for me before."

Around us were people in business suits on their way to work, teenagers in their uniforms heading, I guessed, to Michael Power High School at the end of the line. Some of them had painted their fingernails black.

We got off at the Kipling station and walked through the parking lot and over the road to the tall white building with slats of windows. The only visible sign on the ground level was that of an arrow pointing to the coffee shop. On the door were the small black letters that indicated this was Canadian Immigration Centre Etobicoke.

It was like most other immigration centres in the area: the Canadian flag, the Canadian coat of arms, rows of seats and then two or three wickets with someone behind them. It wasn't too crowded at the time so we went directly to the wicket with Suleyman's call-in notice. The woman took the notice, glanced at it and then asked us to have a seat.

We waited for about half an hour. I was mentally running through the outline of the class for the day. I was still treating this all as a mere formality.

"Mr. Suleyman Goven. Please come to the wicket."

We walked in the direction of the wicket but were intercepted by a young woman in a tailored suit. "No. Come this way," she said. She took out a plastic card and opened a door which had neither a handle nor a window. Down a long corridor and then to the right, another door. This one opened with a handle. Inside was a large oval table with several chairs around it, a boardroom type of table. On the wall a Canadian flag and the Canadian coat of arms.

A slight young man with straight blond hair and wire-rimmed glasses was already sitting at the table with a file folder. The young woman sat down beside him and instructed us to sit on the opposite side of the table.

The two of them took out two small cases and opened them quickly. Badges. "We are agents with the Canadian Security and Intelligence Services." They gave their names.

"We are here to conduct a security interview. Our recommendations will directly affect whether or not you receive landed immigrant status in this country. Is this clear? You have someone with you. Is she a lawyer? Is she here with your permission, Mr. Goven?"

"Yes. She is a friend."

"Are you sure you want her here? We will be asking some very personal questions which may be embarrassing to you."

"I have nothing to hide."

The woman began to question. She was polite, deferential. Slowly she went through Suleyman's papers from his refugee claim, checking the details of his family history, birthdays, the whereabouts of relatives, etc. Then she began to walk through the information form he had filled out at the time of his refugee hearing. It was clear that the form had been highlighted in pink in some places, yellow in others.

"You were in prison twice. What happened?"

"It wasn't that long. I got out alive."

"Why did they put you in prison?" she inquired politely.

"As far as I can tell, because I was a Kurd."

"Were you a member of a terrorist group?"

"No." She checked a box on the page in front of her.

"Were you ever a member of the PKK?" She seemed to have done her job. The PKK is a Kurdish resistance movement which had recently been involved in the bombings of some Turkish offices in Europe. The party had been banned in Europe but not in Canada.

"No," answered Suleyman.

"Are you sure?" she looked up at him, waiting.

The slight man never looked at Suleyman. He was doodling on a piece of paper.

"Yes. I sympathize with the effort to get justice for the Kurds but I do not support any violent tactics."

"But you have been involved in demonstrations outside the Turkish Embassy in Ottawa," she noted as she opened another file.

"Yes," replied Suleyman. "I helped organize them. We wanted to protest what was happening to our families in Turkey. The villages burned. All the innocent people they have killed. They will not even let us speak our own language. We have a right to protest."

"Of course you do," she smiled sweetly. It was now eleven o'clock. "I have no further questions. Do you?"

The bone-edged man pulled a bundle of folders from the seat beside him. "A few."

"Now, Mr. Goven, you realize that if we find you credible and if you cooperate with us, we will recommend you for landed status?"

"Yes. I would like to be landed. I hope to get my engineering degree in Canada so I can work. I have been accepted to go to McGill but I must be landed."

"We'll see about that."

The security officer took off his glasses and squinted. His mouth was tight and he talked with an audible French accent. "You are an engineer, Mr. Goven. Now that would qualify you to build bombs, wouldn't it?"

"I never learned how to build bombs."

"But you were in the Turkish army. Didn't they teach you that? Didn't they teach you how to use weapons?"

"I learned how to use a gun, but they never gave me any sophisticated weapons because I was a Kurd."

"Why did you go to Ireland? Did you make contact with the terrorists there? What did they teach you?"

Suleyman recounted his stay in Ireland just as he had told me months before.

"Did you make contact with the IRA? Did they teach you terrorists activities?" His mouth got tighter, his voice more monotonous.

"I only met a few people in Ireland. It was hard for me to speak. I couldn't find an interpreter. Listen, if I wanted to fight, I would have stayed in Kurdistan or I would have stayed in Europe. I just wanted some peace. I wanted some peace of mind."

"Do you belong to the PKK?"

"No."

The CSIS agent put his glasses back on. "But you said you sympathized with them. Doesn't that mean you are a member?"

"No. I sympathize with their goals but not their means." Suleyman placed his hands on the table. "How would you feel? How would you feel if your home had been destroyed? If your family had been killed? If your people were suffering?"

"You're here to answer questions, not to ask them." The slight, precise man opened another folder with photographs in them.

"Do you recognize this woman?"

"Yes, she's a journalist from Kurdistan who came to visit Canada with a delegation to explain the situation of our people to politicians here."

"And you were the one who took her around the city and to Ottawa?"

"No."

"This woman is a member of the PKK."

"She may be. But even if she is, what is the problem? The PKK is not a forbidden group in Canada. The government here recognizes that it is trying to save the people of Kurdistan from genocide. The world needs to hear about this."

"There was a demonstration at the Turkish Embassy in Ottawa and someone threw a stone. Did you know that?"

"I heard about it but I wasn't there. I was doing a radio interview."

"Do you sympathize with such violence?"

"I don't support violent action. My father was killed by Kurdish extremists."

Suleyman paused and looked down.

"But you sympathize with the PKK." He stated this as a fact and wrote something down.

Suleyman took his hands off the table. He clutched his hands tightly together until they appeared almost white.

"Why were you made the leader of the Kurdish community here? Why would they trust someone who had been an officer in the Turkish army?"

"Well, I am one of the most educated persons in our community. As my English improved I was able to help people. And I guess they like me. They are grateful."

"We have transcripts of phone conversations from your office."

"I have nothing to hide."

"Can you give us the names of PKK members who are in the Kurdish community here? Remember that we will base our recommendation for landing on your replies."

So there it was. You inform for us and we will give you landed status.

"I can't give you information I don't have. But I would like to be landed. I have been waiting for years trying to do something with my life. I used to be able to build things. Now I am just picking up pieces."

Suleyman began to rub his knees with his hands.

The guardian of the files continued to question. At one o'clock we were allowed a ten-minute break to go to the washroom. The questioning continued until three-thirty. It had become an interrogation session. I had been told I could not intervene in any way during the "interview." My mind started to wander, seeking relief from the agony of it all. On the wall there was a picture of the Queen, a plaque from Jean Augustine (the MP for the area) commending the centre for its service to Canada. I looked at the Canadian flag and tried to remember the words of the anthem. "Our home and native land." And where was I? Where were we in this room which had become a prison cell?

My fist slammed down on the table. "Just a minute. Are you trying to say that the PKK is an illegal organization in this country? It is not. Even if Suleyman were a member, there is nothing illegal about that. You have no right to interrogate him in this way."

"Well yes, you are quite right," nodded the man. His lips became a thin line. "You understand we have to protect the security of our country. We're just doing our job. We can't have people going around bombing innocent people."

"None of us want that. It's my country too."

I was seething by now. "Let me make it simple for you." I turned to Suleyman and asked, "Do you know of anything or anyone that would harm innocent people, children, in this country?"

n't have this information. If I did, I would do everything possi-
to prevent violence. I have seen too much violence. I have seen too
many innocent—" Suleyman stopped.

The young woman intervened. "That will be it for today. We will be
sending in our recommendation to Immigration."

The two agents picked up their files and walked out. It was now
after four o'clock. The interrogation session had lasted almost seven
hours and I had missed my class at Regis College with students who
were asking sincere questions about the meaning and purpose of life.

I put my hand on Suleyman's shoulder. "I'm okay," he said as he got
up and walked out. Neither pity nor mercy nor justice. He expected
none. We went down the long corridor where an immigration officer
opened the door with a plastic card.

I suggested to Suleyman that we get a coffee at the little shop. As we
went outside the doors of the centre and along the walkway, Suleyman
turned and put his face against the wall of the building. He pounded
his fists once against the wall and then he slumped down on his knees
with a strangled scream. "I will never be safe."

Suleyman is still waiting for his landed immigrant papers.

✳ WE JUST WANT COOL

They had finally received their photo album which they had left with
some friends back home. "Come and see how we are before," said
Svetlana. It was an important invitation. Very few refugees had
pictures of what they used to be like. Some, like Semira, had none.

Svetlana and Natan had arrived at Romero House several months
earlier and Natan soon proved himself to be a mechanical genius. He
had completely overhauled the old 1980 Volvo belonging to the house
so that it looked almost new.

What did they used to be like? She was the only daughter of a
Byelorussian intellectual and his wife. Her father had lived in the
forest for three years during the time of the Nazi invasion. There are

pictures of the beautiful young woman with long blonde hair who graduated from university with an accounting degree. There are pictures of the staff of the university bookstore where she had become the manager.

Photos reveal a tall, dark and very handsome young army officer playing cards in a lonely light tower on the far Pacific coast. In his next transformation he is standing in paint-splattered old clothes outside a Russian Orthodox church he was helping to renovate. There are pictures of his parents, Samuel and Sarah, and their five children. "Natan's father was a very frightened man," explained Svetlana. "He had seen his own father shot during a pogrom and he never thought the Jews would be safe."

In the wedding pictures, they seem like a carefree young couple. "This is our first apartment. It was in Minsk," points Svetlana. "We worked so hard on it. It was really beautiful. Natan redid all the walls and I made the curtains. We wanted it to be ready for the baby."

She shows me the picture of small Sasha. Bright fine features. Blue eyes in a porcelain dish of a face.

And then there are no pictures for the next year.

When the Chernobyl reactor blew on April 26, 1986, Natan was working unawares on the outside of one of his restoration projects in Minsk. Initially, no one knew what had happened. According to information from that period, the government did not know what to do with a disaster of such magnitude and, not wanting to cancel the May Day parade, decided not to tell its citizens right away, even though scientists warned that a radioactive cloud had drifted up from Kiev and was blowing north and eastwards.

Instead, the Soviet government decided to "seed" the cloud, to drop water bombs on it, so it would rain to the earth before it reached Moscow. It was to fall instead on Byelorussia and other "lesser" countries in the Soviet Union.

As the citizens of Minsk gathered along the roads of the city to watch the May Day parade, they noticed that the weather became inexplicably hot. A few days later they were told about the disaster, warned to stay inside and instructed to spray their houses with water.

That summer the grass in Minsk grew ten feet tall, there were no insects left and the birds that did survive had no feathers. Svetlana and Natan vomited throughout most of the summer. Sasha found it difficult to digest his food and had to sleep at a forty-five-degree angle. A bluish haze began to form around his eyes.

Svetlana's long blonde hair fell out. They had been expecting their second child but the doctor told her she had to go to the hospital and have an abortion and to wait for ten years before thinking of having another child. It was unofficial but operative policy: no child would be delivered in Minsk hospitals for the next two years. They were both warned not to have more than one X-ray a year.

Government policy prevented them from moving out of the radiation zone. Natan thought that perhaps they could go to America as there was still an open-door policy for Jews from the Soviet Union. However, Natan's father panicked. He seemed sure he would be killed if his son did not stay to protect him. Natan and Svetlana decided they could not abandon the older man. Samuel died two years later from radiation sickness. By that time, the doors to the U.S.A. had closed and they decided to go instead to Israel where they hoped that clean air and uncontaminated food would help them to recover. But they had not counted on the effects of the sun in Israel. In the great summer heat, their skin began to turn bright pink, to burn, and they found it difficult to breathe. They did not know what was happening to them.

Then one day Svetlana saw an advertisement in the Russian-language paper inviting people who had suffered from the Chernobyl radiation to come to a medical clinic. She went. One of the doctors at the clinic told her that the family was suffering from "heat sensitivity reaction," a medical condition that often affects radiation victims. He explained that Israel's climate would accelerate the effects of radiation and would prove dangerous, if not fatal, for the family. They should leave soon.

They thought of a cool country such as Canada.

"We just want cool," said Svetlana. "That's all. Just cool."

During the hot summer days when they first arrived at Romero House, Svetlana and her son would both turn bright pink and Natan could barely breathe as he went up to their two rooms on the third floor. We decided we had to invest in an air conditioner and the family stayed inside on the days when the weather was particularly unbearable. "Hot day like jail," said Svetlana. "No go out. Chernobyl prison."

As the fall chill set in, the family seemed to come alive. Svetlana had enrolled in computer classes and was doing very well and Sasha, who was looking much less blue, had taken up classical violin classes. Every evening we would hear him squeaking away on an old violin someone had donated to Romero House. Then one night it sounded like music, real music magically coming from the third floor and from another century.

And on another night, Natan danced for the first time since "before Chernobyl." It was the evening of his birthday party and some of his friends had gathered for a celebration in our little dining room on the back porch. There were mushrooms and eggs and potatoes which Svetlana had spent most of the day decorating in the most inventive way. A cassette of Russian rock music was playing in the background. After the meal, Natan got up from his chair and began slowly dancing around the table.

"First time he dance after Chernobyl. It's cool. No?"

However, I knew the heat would come again, and I was perplexed with the problem of their obtaining some kind of status in Canada. I knew that technically they did not fit the definition of a refugee, as someone who faced persecution because of nationality, religion, social group, gender or political opinion. Yet, I knew that their lives were in jeopardy. In one sense, they were environmental refugees, but there is still no category in the world to account for such vast problems.

My first suggestion was that they get an expert medical assessment and I contacted Dr. Rosalie Bertell, a recognized expert in low-level radiation and someone who had visited the Chernobyl area and written on the ongoing medical side-effects of the disaster. She reviewed all the medical documents they had brought with them from Russia and Israel and ordered a series of specialized tests.

I held my breath as we awaited the results. She had told me that if the radiation had penetrated the bone, there was a very strong possibility that they would get cancer. This would have made them "medically inadmissible" by the standards of Immigration Canada.

However, her reports said that the radiation damage had not yet reached the bone and that, in a cool climate such as Canada's, they had an excellent chance of leading healthy lives with no unusual medical supports. "By the way," said Dr. Bertell when she called me, "you might want to ask Svetlana why her radiation count is higher than that of her husband and child."

Svetlana responded to my question in a matter-of-fact way, as if, well, that was life in the Soviet Union. Her family had moved to the eastern part of the country after the Second World War to try to make a new beginning. While Svetlana was still a young child, there was a nuclear spill or a nuclear test in the area and she, along with many other children, became quite ill. No one knew the reason for the sudden "flu" symptoms at the time but the family decided to move back to their homeland, Byelorussia, in the hope that the clean air of the Black Sea would help their child.

"We didn't know this problem in old time. Gorbachev said it," said Svetlana. "Me have two Chernobyl."

From all of my inquiries to various immigration lawyers, I had concluded that the most appropriate route for this family to take was that of an application to become landed immigrants on humanitarian grounds. It was another rather obscure procedure and category but it implied that the family would meet all the requirements of regular immigrants, i.e., command of English, employment opportunities, contribution to the country. Evidence of their particular medical problem was to be included.

It all seemed very straightforward at the time: Natan had three job offers from firms specializing in the restoration of historic buildings and it was clear that Svetlana would soon be working as well. Of course, they thought their son, the budding musician and one of the most avid fishermen at Grenadier Pond, was their greatest contribution. All that remained was to obtain a work permit for Natan.

Thus they began their paper chase which would last for over two years. It would turn into a paperweight.

DO THEY THINK WE CAME FOR THE MONEY?

After their arrival, I started to notice that I would tilt my head from side to side whenever I was pleased. And it was a pleasure to have the three young people from Sri Lanka. "We are happy to have you here," I had said when I first met them on the porch of Romero House. "But we are just in the middle of renovations in our new house. Everything is a mess."

"Yes," said one of the young men on the doorstep, "and we are very, very happy to be here. We are used to camping out so we can help in any situation." The three of them smiled and tilted their heads slightly from side to side.

The slight young man with a well-trimmed beard and deep brown eyes stepped forward and shook my hand. "My name is Nihal and this is my sister Samantha and this is her fiancé, the man I will be proud to call my brother-in-law. We will be most grateful for whatever arrangement you can offer us." The note of propriety echoed the tradition of British schooling in Sri Lanka. Polished, like Sir George.

I showed them the basement where there were two bedrooms which had only recently been renovated. There was an awkward moment when I suggested that they could use the two bedrooms in whatever way they wanted.

Nihal smiled and said in a discreet tone, "You see, I am the older brother and the chaperone. I will share the room with my sister and Mark can sleep in the other room—at least until they are married.

They had planned on a wedding in Sri Lanka but we had to leave."

True to their word, the three new residents started scrubbing down the walls, cleaning the floors and removing old and mildewed carpets. We put an all-points bulletin out for furniture and soon some friends started dropping off beds and a few dishes. Nihal and Mark pulled and pushed and lifted the furniture down into the basement. But only after they had made sure there was at least some furniture in the rooms in the rest of the house.

"We have to make sure there is something for everyone who comes," said Samantha. She was lovely. A pool of clear-water peace in the midst of the chaos of the house.

By the evening, they were exhausted from the day's efforts. Nihal and Mark would put on their brightly printed sarongs and Samantha would cook supper. It was mostly rice and curry. Samantha invited me for a bowl of rice. "It is very nice and good for you." I asked them whether rice was their national dish.

"We eat it with everything," replied Samantha. And then I understood.

"Do you have any money for food, any money at all?"

"No," Nihal replied. "We could not take the money with us or they would have suspected something. We paid for our tickets and brought a little but we have run out now. We were in Montreal for about a month before we came here. We didn't think we had a chance there because we don't speak French."

I was appalled. "You should have told me," I said. "We will phone to make arrangements for you to be on welfare."

Nihal responded, "This is a terrible thing for us. We know what welfare means. You see, we were doing well in Sri Lanka. I had an executive job, a beautiful house and a car. Samantha was working in the accounting department of a major airline where Mark was a manager. He had a car, too. That was our problem. We were young and it looked as if we had a lot of money. But welfare means you aren't working, you are poor. This is very hard for us. We are proud."

"But you have to eat more than rice," I said. This argument didn't seem to carry much weight and so I tried again. "Nihal, you have to keep strong so we can get your wife and daughter here, and the two of you won't get married if you collapse before the wedding."

"Yes," Samantha replied.

We went to Welfare. It was humiliating.

Shortly after Nihal arrived he explained to me, carefully, how he would bring his wife and child in two or three weeks. "They have been in hiding but her auntie who loves her has said she will pay their airfare. Now that I am here I can sponsor them."

I could hardly bear to tell him the reality he would have to face. "Nihal, you haven't been accepted as a convention refugee yet. Because you came in on a visitor's visa and made your claim inside the country, you may not have a hearing for about another year or year and a half. And then you must become a landed immigrant—possibly another year or two—before you can sponsor your wife and child."

"But I didn't know that," he exclaimed. "I never would have left them if I had known. They are in danger, hiding. I couldn't bring them with me because they won't let families leave the country. I must go back and protect them."

Samantha put her arm around him. "Nihal, you will be killed if you go back."

From that time on Nihal had headaches. He found it hard to sleep at night and Samantha began searching for stores which had special herbal teas which would help him sleep.

We started preparing the personal information forms which were necessary to their application for refugee status. I listened to their story as they unfolded it for me and tried to note the essential points for the lawyer who would be representing them. Most of these points would be presented at their hearing but the details, the bones and nerve of who they were, that I was privileged to hear, would remain unspoken.

Nihal and Samantha were the children of an upper-class Sinhalese family who lived in the stunningly beautiful area of Kandy in Sri Lanka. Both parents were practising Buddhists, but they had come to appreciate the Christian religion due to their time in Catholic private schools. Their father, Chandana, had made a great deal of money in the private sector and was happily married to his childhood sweetheart, Kumari. He rented an apartment in Colombo so he could stay there while on business. The apartment also provided a place for Samantha who had just gone to Colombo to work as an accountant with the airline company. It was there that Samantha met Mark, a dashing young executive who had worked his way up through the business and had recently been promoted to a position as manager. Mark had many connections in the travel business and had a multiple-entry visa which allowed him to visit Australia, Europe, the Middle East and Far East countries on business. While he was in Singapore, he bought the golden threaded material which was intended to be given to Samantha when they got married.

However, Mark had a secret that would be known only to the person who could check all of his identity documents. His mother was a Tamil and his family had decided to keep this fact hidden as long as Mark was living in Colombo. In the summer of 1989, "Bloody July," many of the Sinhalese in the city had gone on a rampage, killing any Tamil they could find. Thus far Mark had managed to escape detection. He always claimed he was a Burgher, a minority group in the country, and he spoke English as his first language, not Sinhalese or Tamil.

In 1992, the government asked that each resident in the city be registered at a local police station. Fearing detection, Mark asked Nihal if he could stay with him. Nihal and his wife agreed and welcomed Mark warmly into their spacious house. The two young couples tried to live a normal life in spite of the political difficulties in the country. They went sightseeing, spent evenings dancing at the local clubs and attended all the social events sponsored by their companies.

Then came the knock at the door. It was late in the evening, and when Nihal went to see who was there, the door was pushed in as he unlocked it. Immediately, there were ten armed and masked men inside his house, members of the JVP, an ultra-leftist Sinhalese terrorist group, and they issued Nihal an ultimatum: you must join our group and you must pay us a large sum of money. Nihal's wife and Samantha and Mark had then been rounded up in the front room as well. A man who appeared to be the leader questioned them all and issued the same ultimatum. The terrorists said they would return in a week.

Everyone in the house was in a state of shock. They knew very well that the JVP meant what they said and they were worried that these militant Sinhalese would discover Mark's Tamil background. These radicals, young people drawn from the universities and the lower classes, felt the policies of the Sinhalese-dominated government were too lenient on the Tamils and were engaging in a campaign of bombings, assassinations and kidnappings of moderate Sinhalese and Tamils. The JVP had been driven underground by a recent government campaign against it but there were rumours that it was regrouping and resurfacing—seeking new recruits and money for a new campaign of terrorism.

Nihal and his wife, Samantha and Mark were now on the JVP list. They knew they could not get off the list alive. The JVP was known for its persistent vindictiveness toward anyone who did not cooperate.

The young people talked for hours about the intruders. Nihal decided he would try to reason with them when they returned. He got a copy of all of their bank books so that the JVP could see that they could not come up with the astronomical sum that had been demanded.

Precisely one week later there was another knock on the door. Nihal had already sent his wife and child to stay with her aunt. He and Samantha and Mark stood ready to talk with the terrorists as they entered the house. Their reasoning was to no avail. The leader of the terrorists said they would return in one week and if their demands were not met, if the three did not join the cause, they would be killed.

Talking late into the night, the three young people agreed that they had no choice but to leave the country as quickly as possible. Mark sprang into action, contacting his friends in the airlines and the Canadian High Commission. Within a few days he had arranged visitors' visas and tickets for the three of them. It was impossible to include Nihal's wife and child because the immigration officials at the Canadian High Commission in Colombo would have suspected them of fleeing as refugees.

Samantha and Nihal moved numbly through the days—trying to sort out what they could take in their suitcases that would maintain the appearance of being tourists. They drove up to Kandy to tell Samantha's parents about the catastrophe that had befallen them. The wedding would have to be postponed, they explained. Perhaps they would soon be back. They could not say goodbye to their friends because of the risk of being exposed. They simply said that they were taking a two-week vacation with Nihal to see the sights in Canada.

Nihal went to see his wife and young daughter at the aunt's. "I will send for you in a few weeks," he said. "Until then, don't go outside the house." Returning to their home, Nihal put shutters on the windows and drove his car into the garage. He arranged for a friend to check the place while he was away. "It's just for a while," he told his friend.

A few friends from work came to wave the three off. It was difficult for Samantha and Mark and Nihal to appear excited about their vacation to Canada.

They made every effort to create a new home in the basement of our house, with wicker furniture from a garage sale and some Sri Lankan travel posters Mark had wangled at one of the local travel agencies. They purchased a little Canadian flag and a Sri Lankan flag and had them both in a jar of artificial flowers as the centrepiece of their rickety dining table.

Nihal withdrew more into himself. He tried to contact people who could invite his wife to Canada as a guest. Every letter of invitation was turned down by the Canadian High Commission in Colombo.

"Nihal, why doesn't she just go to the High Commission and tell them the danger she is in? They can interview her and grant her refugee status there," I suggested.

"If only that were possible, but everyone knows that the visa officers there will never declare anyone from Sri Lanka as a refugee. They say there is no trouble there." There was a note of bitterness in Nihal's voice. "Why would I come here if there is no trouble? Do they think we came for the money? I was making good money at home. If I wanted to make money, I'd go to someplace in the Pacific Rim. I came here because there was trouble in Sri Lanka, because I wanted to live."

Mark remained more cheerful and tried to make the best of his new situation. He could not work because the Canadian government at that time, in another shift in policy, had decided that refugee claimants should not work. He joined the local public library and began reading voraciously. He had always loved English at college and dreamed of becoming a writer before he had managed to succeed so well at business, but he couldn't take any university or college classes because he was not yet landed. However, he managed to get permission to audit some extension courses at St. Michael's College at the University of Toronto. He studied the American novel, the classics of the West and Shakespeare. Samantha spent her time taking computer courses which were offered by the Board of Education.

A few months after his arrival at our house, Mark showed me the rough draft of a short story he had written for the *Toronto Star* short story contest. I had a feeling it wouldn't win but it was a brave, a bold effort. He also composed a poem to his fiancée titled "Dream Goddess of Elaborate Power."

I am not sure when it happened for these three. I only know it happens to every refugee at some point. It is the realization that they will not, cannot, go back to their own country. It is the realization that everything they had and everything they were is gone forever and they must make a new beginning in Canada.

That was when Samantha and Mark started to talk about getting married here. They weren't even quite sure what that could mean. It was hard for them to imagine what it might be like to get married without any family or friends.

Except for Nihal, that is. Except for the friends they had made at the Romero community. We enthusiastically took up their first tentative remark that the summer might be a good time to get married. Mark took out the sari he had bought for Samantha in Singapore and had carried in his suitcase from Sri Lanka. He phoned my mother to ask if she would take the place of his mother and give Samantha the going-away sari during the wedding service.

MR. MULRONEY, MY FAMILY AND I SAY HI

The three Sri Lankans had become good friends with the young Russian couple who had moved into the house two months after they did. Lev and Olga were full of energy, and their daughter, Dana, was a little blonde-haired girl with the face of a doll. Lev was short and muscular with a shock of brown hair that was starting to thin. His wife seemed more pensive with long auburn hair and fine features. She had studied at a specialized institute for textile design in Leningrad. Their little girl seemed so innocent and unafraid. No matter who came to the front door, she would run up and greet them with a smile. "Hi."

Neither Lev nor Olga spoke English. However, as they learned the language, they spoke with such a heavy Sri Lankan accent that whenever I wanted to talk with them, I had to take along Nihal as an interpreter. Nihal and Lev were soon in great demand by some of our friends, for Lev, like Natan, was a mechanical genius. He could fix just about anything with nothing. He explained to me, through Nihal, that you have to learn how to fix things by yourself in Russia because there are no spare parts.

He was a man of many talents. He could lift a whole refrigerator on his back. He upgraded our community room TV considerably. I wondered why we were getting more channels all of a sudden but didn't know the reason until the neighbour appeared at the door with his bill. Someone from our house had tapped into his cable line. Lev and I had a long chat about how things are different in Canada.

Within two weeks of his arrival in Toronto, Lev had discovered an illegal wine outlet which sold jugs of wine for five dollars. I was astounded at the price and asked him where he had got it. He explained, through Nihal, that you drive up this street and then into this alley and knock on the back door.

"Well," I said, "I've been in Toronto for years and have never discovered the places you have."

I recommended the wine to some friends but most of them got sick on it and ended up pouring the coloured liquid down the sink.

Dana loved her new friends from Sri Lanka. Every morning she would run down the stairs to the basement and say, "Samantha. Samantha good." Dana was the first real ray of sunshine in Samantha's life. She taught Dana how to say "Samantha good. Mark naughty." When Mark would come into the TV room Dana would run to him and kiss him and say, "Mark naughty." For Nihal, it was like having a daughter again and Olga was very glad to have babysitters since she had started English classes.

Dana was a giving child. She gave joy and a smile and that was priceless. She also gave me green tomatoes. In the springtime we had started growing tomatoes from seeds in egg cartons and we had planted them carefully in the backyard. I gave Dana a tour of the plants and pointed to each one saying, "Tomato good." My strategy was to show her that pulling up the plants was naughty.

In September there was an early frost warning and I went outside with Olga and Mark to bring in the still-green tomatoes and place them on the windowsills. The entire house was bedecked with green tomatoes.

One evening, as I was getting into bed, I felt the mattress was a little bumpy. I turned on the light and found four green tomatoes in my bed. And the next morning I found more green tomatoes in my purse, beside my toothbrush in the bathroom and in the drawer with the forks and knives.

"She wants give you present," explained Olga. "Something good."

For the next month I discovered little green tomatoes in places I never knew existed.

"Dana good," I said.

The day after Lev and Olga arrived, I explained to them, through a translator, that they needed to get a lawyer to prepare for their refugee hearing. Olga said that they already had a card for a lawyer. I could not imagine how they had contacted a lawyer so quickly but that was their business and I left it to them.

Over the next few months, I got to know Lev and Olga better, and when their English had improved we used to talk in the summer evenings on the porch. They would smoke tax-free cigarettes they had bargained for and sip the bottled wine in the jug.

"It's hot here but more hot in Israel."

"In Israel?"

"Yes, we were there two years. Very difficult time."

Olga then began to trace back the journey which led them from Leningrad to Israel to Toronto. She was Jewish and things were difficult, although not impossible, for them in Leningrad. The economic situation was deteriorating and there seemed little future for a young couple. When the Jews started to get permission to emigrate to Israel, she saw this as an opportunity to escape from Russia. They had heard that they would be accepted in Israel and would receive some money to help them settle and that they could save and move from there to America or to Canada.

They might have stayed in Israel, she said, but there was a lot of hostility against anyone from Russia. The Arabs saw them as taking over their land and the Jews who were already there saw them as opportunists. Many Russian women were seen as potential prostitutes. Lev had received a call-up for military service and he simply wasn't interested, saw no value in going to fight the Arabs on the West Bank.

In the Russian-language newspaper they noticed an advertisement from an immigration consulting firm which stated that, for a certain fee, a large fee, the company would arrange airline tickets, visas to Canada and guarantee that the customers would be accepted as refugees in Canada. Lev and Olga worked for two years, saved several thousand dollars, paid the consultant and thought that their long journey to find a new life was over. The consultant had told them to contact a specific lawyer when they arrived in Toronto.

I was appalled by this story. It was clearly a scam. I also knew that Lev and Olga would never be accepted as refugees in Canada. Indeed, they were not refugees. If they had applied as immigrants through the usual channels they would probably have been accepted on the merits of their skills.

The only ones clearly benefiting from this scheme were some immigration consultants and lawyers. The family had lost its savings. Israel had lost its investment in them and Canada had lost as well. Determined to put an end to this senseless suffering, I arranged to see a high-ranking official at the Israeli Consulate on Bloor Street, and I suggested to him that he could stop this scam by arranging to have a notice put in the Russian-language papers in Israel, explaining that these schemes were doomed to failure. He didn't seem very surprised or very interested but he asked me to find out which newspapers the ads had appeared in and to let him know. I explained to him that I couldn't read Russian and couldn't easily access the papers from Israel. There seemed little more that I could do or that he wanted to do.

As time went on, Lev and Olga began to realize that the promises made by the immigration consultant in Israel were false. Little by little, they tried to come to grips with the fact that they would eventually be returned to Israel or to Russia. They knew if they withdrew their refugee case and returned to Israel or Russia voluntarily, they had the possibility of returning again as immigrants.

Lev began to buy more jugs of wine. Olga started to wear more make-up. It soon became apparent that she had struck up a relationship with a guy she had met at the English class. Dana wandered around the house calling for Samantha, who had recently moved out with Mark after their wedding.

The agony might have been prolonged had not Lev's father died in Leningrad. After he talked to his mother, Lev was determined to go home and to take his daughter with him.

It was a rather bedraggled group that we took to Pearson International Airport. Samantha was crying. Mark and Nihal were struggling to help Lev repack his bags as they were several kilos overweight. As we pushed through the crowds and past the bar in the terminal, we saw the prime minister on the large TV screeen.

"Mr. Mulroney," yelled Lev. "My family and I say hi."

"Hi," said Dana as she waved at the television screen. "Bye-bye."

YES, SHE'S THE FIRST

The visitor to our house was admiring the newborn baby that Beatrice held in her arms. Madonna and child. "Is this your first child?" the visitor asked innocently.

I knew that Beatrice would forever pause at this question. "Yes, she's the first."

The first to be born. The other child had been conceived in Rwanda just after Beatrice's marriage to Boniface at the beginning of 1994. She had felt well during the pregnancy and had continued to work in the hospital where she was the head nurse. Boniface had just left on an excursion to survey some land when the machetes began to hack away at her country.

Members of the Hutu militia came into the hospital and began killing anyone in sight. She saw the other women forced down on the floor. She was pushed down herself. At first, when she came to, she wondered whether or not it had been a bad dream. She then realized she was lying in a pool of bodies and blood. Beatrice dragged herself into the jungle nearby. It was then that she discovered that she was hemorrhaging profusely and that she had been raped.

She had a miscarriage alone in the jungle. The child was buried among the trees. Beatrice never told me whether there was a name. She waited there in the jungle for a month, not hungry but eating what she could, until she heard a van with a microphone drive by announcing that it was safe to come out.

She wandered back to the hospital in a daze and eventually found her husband in the home of some relatives who had survived. She told him what had happened. Boniface refused to give in to the paralysing grief which had gripped his country after the massacre of so many thousands of people.

"We will begin again. We will have more children," he said. "We will bring life to this world together."

CAN'T I STAY, MR. WOLF?

It sounded like two older voices and then it melded into one. I had heard it first through the crack in the sliding doors which separated the little Romero office from the front room.

By day the front room becomes a place of welcome for those who drop in and by night it serves as the community room for the people in the house.

In that late afternoon I sat typing some correspondence when I recognized the sound of Steve talking in two voices, one very loud and one very meek. Steve had been named after Steve Biko, the South African human rights advocate who had been murdered. He had said very little when he first arrived.

At night, the other people in the house heard the eight-year-old boy crying but he rarely said anything by day. His mother explained that he still had nightmares about what had happened in Burundi, the African republic next to Rwanda. Little by little, Steve began to loosen up. At the Romero celebration he soon proved himself to be the best dancer in the whole group, adults and children included. As soon as the music was turned on he started to move, perfectly attuned, amazingly free and inventive.

As I listened more closely to Steve's two voices in the front room, I realized that he was engaged in some very serious drama. Peeking through the crack in the sliding doors, I saw him with a sock puppet in each hand, one grey and one brown. They bobbed and weaved about each other. Then Steve held the brown one up high:

"What are you doing on my skating rink, little sheep? This is my skating rink." The voice was deep and menacing.

"But I like this rink. I want to skate here. There's room enough for both of us." A squeak.

"No, there's not. This is my rink. I do what I want here."

"Can't I stay, Mr. Wolf? Please?"

"No, if you stay, I kill you."

I Want to Pick Up the Dead Animals

Young Elias kept pointing to the animals that lay crushed by the side of the road. Most of them were porcupines, too slow to avoid the oncoming cars on the highway to the north. He was speaking in Somali to his father who was sitting next to me in the front of our van.

"He says he wants to get a car when he grows up," said his father, a former English teacher. "He wants to drive along the highway and pick up the dead animals and make sure they have a burial.

"Why would he want to do that?" I asked.

"I think it's because he was in Koran school in Mogadishu when it was bombed. Some of his little friends were killed. It stays on his mind."

Its Name Is Snow

As it falls, the children gather shyly by the windowpane to watch its strangeness through this slight shield against wonder. Soon they will open the door and venture onto the porch to touch it ever so tentatively. And then they will stand there, just stand there, for a very long time.

"Its name is snow," I whisper, as if to introduce a wonderful old friend.

"Oooh." Soon the children will reach out to touch the snowflakes with their hands.

And once again I see my winter world as if on the first day of creation. Very good. Something grand and given.

It is one brief moment every year and then the children move out to the streets playing shinny and designing their first snowman. It is a white world, this winter world. This, too, they will discover.

IV

MIRRORS

SEMIRA'S MIRROR

As she smiled upon me, Semira's face became a mirror in which I began to see myself and my world in a new way.

After the golden summer of 1991, we received notification from a lawyer, whom I will call Mr. Smith, that Semira's hearing was to be in the early fall. He had been assigned to her case by legal aid, he said, and wanted to meet with her for a few minutes before the hearing. A few weeks later he phoned and asked Semira to meet him in his office the next day. He suggested that she write up her story on a piece of paper and have it translated. "It will just take a few minutes," he said.

At that point in my life, I too thought it would take only a few minutes. Semira's story had seemed simple and straightforward and I could not imagine any reason why she would be refused. I phoned Abdullah to come over in the evening and translate what Semira would write out.

As I was drafting an article in the kitchen after supper, Abdullah and Semira came in and asked me to write out Semira's story in good English. She had written it out briefly in her own language and Abdullah translated it orally.

Until that evening, I had remained largely ignorant of the details of the Eritrean political situation. Like many immigration officers and refugee judges, I now knew that the Eritreans had fought for their independence from Ethiopia for thirty years and that in May 1991 the Eritrean People's Liberation Front had defeated the Ethiopian dictator Mengistu. Abdullah began to read out her words to me.

"I left Eritrea as a teenager to avoid military conscription by the Ethiopians. I went to Saudi Arabia to work, and there I met and married Jamal who was active in the Eritrean Liberation Front (ELF). When the EPLF told the Eritreans that they could go to visit the liberated zones, he decided to go with a group leaving from the Sudan. He never returned. A woman without a husband cannot stay in Saudi Arabia."

I wrote it as I heard it. "It sounds clear to me," I said. "But there's a mistake in the acronym of your husband's party. It's EPLF not ELF."

"No. It's not the same," Semira insisted through Abdullah. "Explain to her."

Abdullah proceeded to outline the factions of the various Eritrean groups on a piece of paper. He explained that the ELF and the EPLF had been involved in a bitter struggle in the past over the future direction of their country. Lives had been lost and destroyed in the process. Jamal's family was an extremely high-profile supporter of a faction of the ELF called the Eritrean Liberation Front–Revolutionary Council (ELF–RC). It espoused a multi-party social-democratic state as opposed to the single-party Marxist-oriented model favoured by the EPLF. The EPLF had defeated the ELF–RC in 1981 and then had gone on to defeat the Ethiopians. "This party will never share power with another party," explained Abdullah.

"My husband is ELF," Semira insisted again. "I know this. It's a very different party."

Now I understood why Semira had been so subdued when the reports of the fall of Mengistu were being relayed on the nightly television news. While other Eritreans had gone out to wild and joyous celebrations in different community centres in the city, she had remained quietly at home with her children.

After our discussion, I asked Abdullah to take what I had written and to type it out on his computer at the college so it would be presentable for the meeting with the lawyer. "No *P*," I reminded him teasingly.

"You don't have to tell me that," he replied as he left. "Any Eritrean knows this." I asked Abdullah if he would take Semira to the lawyer's office the next morning. It never crossed my mind that it might be important to monitor the lawyer's way of proceeding.

"How did it go?" I asked when they returned.

"Good. Just five minutes. We gave him the story," said Abdullah.

Semira's story arrived in the mail a few weeks later as part of her personal information form which would serve as the key point of evidence at her refugee hearing. The form contained the substance of her refugee claim—why she feared persecution in her own country. Since both Abdullah and I were away at the time, Semira simply placed the envelope from the lawyer in a drawer.

Two weeks before the hearing, Mr. Smith called the house and said he wanted to see Semira twenty minutes before the hearing. "Is that the only preparation she is going to get?"

The more defensive Mr. Smith became, the more concerned I became. I explained to Semira and Abdullah that they had a right to expect a little more from their lawyer. Together we decided to ask for a postponement of the hearing and to get a new lawyer.

Through a series of inquiries to refugee advocates, we found a new lawyer. Belva Spiel, a committed and competent lawyer, would represent Semira and her family for the next two years with all the resources her feisty spirit and careful intelligence could summon up.

Semira brought the envelope with her personal information form to the first meeting with Belva. As Abdullah was translating Semira's story, I saw a strange look come over Belva's face. "Could you repeat the name of the group your husband is associated with?" she asked.

"ELF of course," said Abdullah.

"But that's not what's written on this form," said Belva. She laid the paper out on her desk and showed it to the three of us. My mind swerved and stopped on one single letter. The letter *P*. Jamal was listed as poilitically affiliated with the EPLF. Underneath the story was Semira's signature attesting to the truthfulness of everything in the document.

"Semira, did you sign this? How could you sign it? When did you sign it?"

"She signed it in the lawyer's office," said Abdullah. "When we gave him her story."

"But the story hadn't been typed onto the form. It was blank. How could a lawyer ask anyone to sign a blank form?" I looked at Belva and she looked at me.

"I signed it because I thought he was my lawyer and he was right," said Semira.

A few days later, when I took a young Eritrean girl to her lawyer, I learned that Semira's experience with her lawyer was not unusual. Hiwet was just sixteen, so I knew I would have to act as her legal guardian. She described her journey from Eritrea to the lawyer with the English she had learned from a teacher during one of her many stopovers.

After listening for half an hour, the lawyer placed a blank personal information form in front of her and said, "Just sign here."

Once again my mind swerved and screeched to a halt. "You can't ask her to sign an empty form. You should type it up first and then send it to us in the mail. She'll take a look at it and I'll make sure it gets interpreted to her. Then, and only then, will she sign it."

He looked at me with a certain exasperation. "Trust me, sweetie. I do it all the time. This will make things go faster."

"Sweetie" didn't trust him and he finally agreed to send the completed form in the mail.

I was disturbed by what I had heard and seen and I began to discuss the situation with other refugee advocates and some lawyers who worked long and hard with refugees. Almost no one else was shocked. Everyone seemed to know that there were lawyers who were cashing in on the suffering of refugees. I learned that Mr. Smith did a lot of the legal aid work for refugees from Africa. He had been working in personal injury law until the auto insurance was changed and then he switched to refugee law.

Mr. Smith had done hundreds of Eritrean cases and most of them had succeeded—before May 1991. Until the fall of Mengistu, any Eritrean was almost automatically granted refugee status. The Eritreans were, in effect, cash cows. During the summer of 1991, word spread about the first Eritrean rejections. Members of the Immigration and Refugee Board were concluding that with the Eritrean victory and declaration of independence, it was no longer necessary for Eritreans to fear returning to their own country. The question of the P was becoming more and more crucial to Semira's case.

I would have preferred to forget about Mr. Smith except for the fact he sent Semira a copy of the bill he was forwarding to legal aid. He was billing for almost a thousand dollars.

I determined to make a formal complaint against Mr. Smith to the law society and to complain to the director of legal aid regarding his billing of this case. I met with several officials from the law society and legal aid who seemed unsure how to proceed. They said that this kind of practice fell between the cracks because legal aid could not remove a lawyer for conduct and the law society could not pursue questions of legal aid billing.

"What about all the refugees who are falling between the cracks?" I asked. I still thought it would be possible to ensure that other refugees didn't suffer from such negligence. I told Abdullah that he would have to write up a statement for the law society. He told me he was afraid but he would do it.

"Why are you afraid?"

"Because Smith comes from a very large and very powerful tribe."

"Pardon? What tribe?"

"Smith tribe. I looked in the phone book and I could see all the names. He comes from a large and powerful tribe."

There were days when I began to think that Abdullah was right. My letter to the law society was passed on to Mr. Smith for his comments. He immediately wrote me and threatened to launch a lawsuit against me. He wrote bishops, church organizations I worked for and several employers about my destructive actions. Most ignored him, a few did not.

However, more shocking was the document that he submitted to the law society in his defence. He included a copy of what he said had been Semira's typed statement which had been given to him and faithfully retyped. Throughout the statement, Semira's political affiliation and her husband's was that of the EPLF. I could not understand this error and I asked Abdullah if he still had a copy of what he had given Mr. Smith. Yes, he said, he had a disk of letters he had written on his computer at George Brown College.

Abdullah's statement had no *P*. What had happened? I blew up sections of Abdullah's and Smith's statements and saw that one of the statements had been altered. It seemed to me that the matter could easily be resolved by a forensic test. The law society said it did not do such things but that perhaps the RCMP could do it.

I met with a sergeant from the Immigration investigation unit and we talked for several hours in the presence of my lawyer. He wanted to know if I knew anything about refugee frauds.

"No, I don't, but I'm more concerned about legal fraud."

The day after the interview the sergeant called my lawyer to say that his superior had rejected the request for a forensic test because "the RCMP is concerned with refugee fraud, not legal fraud."

Mr. Smith is still practising refugee law. He and other lawyers like him have a distinct advantage over clients who feel they have been wronged. Even if a refugee lodges an official complaint, he or she will probably be deported before any investigation is complete.

However, Semira's difficulties have made a difference at the Immigration and Refugee Board. During a meeting with Gordon Fairweather, the chairperson of the IRB, I spoke to him about our discovery of the practice of signing blank personal information forms and filling in stories without a refugee's final consent. A gracious and honest man, Mr. Fairweather immediately instructed that panel members check whether a refugee had seen and understood the personal information form.

I think of Semira and Abdullah every time I hear the opening questions at a refugee hearing: have you read this personal information form? Have you understood it? Is this your signature?

I talked to Semira and Abdullah about lawyers from very large tribes. "I still don't understand it," I confessed.

"I do," said Semira through Abdullah. "He does it for the money. You do it for the love of God."

"For the love of God?"

"Yes. In our religion it is important that you do some things for God alone. You do good but in secret so that only God sees."

When she said this I knew it wasn't true. I had looked in the mirror of her face often enough to realize that I probably had many other motivations for what I had done. Liberal guilt? A personal need? Yet when Semira said this I knew I wanted it to be true. She went on to explain to me that you can only trust people who help you for no reason, for nothing in return. When you pay someone to help you, as she had paid people to help her escape, you do not know whether they help you because you are in need, or because someone is paying them.

And, I thought, this is how God loves us: for nothing in return.

I had a premonition that this was something I would need to remember.

Abdullah called and said, "I have news about Jamal. We need to talk this evening."

It was the first time we had talked without Semira. Abdullah had been so faithful to her, missing his classes at the community college in order to act as her translator, driving the kids to their medical appointments. They called him "Ami Abdullah" or Uncle Abdullah.

He arrived after Semira and the children had gone to bed and it was obvious that he was intensely excited.

"I wanted to let you know that we got him out."

"Who's 'we,' Abdullah?" I asked.

"His brother in Sweden and the members of his ELF group from Riyadh. Jamal and his brother were very close. They studied together in Germany for years and lived together. After Jamal went to Saudi Arabia, his brother was accepted as a refugee in Sweden. He phoned all the members of Jamal's group and asked them to contribute to a support fund. We had to get a lot of money so we could bribe some people in Eritrea to find out what had happened to Jamal."

I wondered how Abdullah could afford it on his small student budget. As if anticipating my question, he continued: "We all agreed to send in ten per cent of our income every month to Sweden and the brother would make arrangements. I couldn't give very much but I gave what I could."

"All Semira knows is that her husband disappeared from Khartoum," I commented. "Have you found out what happened?"

"Well, actually we have," said Abdullah, lowering his voice. "We know now that he was kidnapped by members of the EPLF in Khartoum and driven to one of the prison camps in the Sahel, the desert region in the northern part of Eritrea."

"That's wonderful news," I exclaimed. "Is there anything we can do to help?"

"No. Just pray. God knows what they have done with him."

I prayed. Weeks passed. The leaves began to fall. And then another call from Abdullah asking to come over later at night. I had no idea what to expect. The best? The worst? An answer? More questions?

"What's happened?" I blurted out even before offering him a cup of tea.

"His brother was able to contact some desert nomads who live in the area. They have found out the camp where they are keeping Jamal and they have seen him. He is alive. They think they may be able to bribe one of the guards to turn the other way so they can bring him out."

"We must tell Semira."

"No. Not until he is safe. It would be cruel to raise her hopes. She wouldn't even believe me if I told her now."

During the following days, I was so aware of Semira and the children as they went about the ordinary business of living. She was still wearing her wedding ring. When she had been asked to fill out her marital status on the immigration form she indicated that she was "married," her husband "whereabouts unknown." She continued to tell the children that he was visiting his family in Eritrea. They were too young to make the connection between his departure for Eritrea and their departure from Saudi Arabia.

The next time I saw Abdullah was during his noon-hour break from the college. He had taken a taxi over to the house and had raced up the front steps. Bursting through the front door he gasped, "He's on his way here."

After he caught his breath, Abdullah told me that the nomads had indeed bribed one of the guards to look the other way while they placed Jamal on one of the camels. They had travelled all night and the next day to reach the Sudan where he was then turned over to some members of his group in eastern Sudan who made arrangements for him to return to Saudi Arabia. He was there now and had contacted his friends and employer. As Semira had written to tell them her address in Canada, Jamal was now making arrangements to leave for the United States on a false passport. He would be arriving soon in Buffalo.

Abdullah collapsed on the sofa after he had delivered his marvellous news. "Now we can tell Semira," he said proudly.

When she arrived home after her morning English class, I asked her to come up to the kitchen to have tea with Abdullah and me. I had never had to deliver such news and had no idea how to proceed.

I started to run water into the kettle and then wheeled around and said, "Semira, your husband is alive. He's in Saudi Arabia and will be here soon."

She looked at me blankly, almost like the day she first arrived at the house.

"It's true. It's true," I said. "Abdullah knows."

Abdullah recounted the whole story of the efforts of Jamal's brother and the group. She sat very still and said, "I will believe it when he phones me." Her eyes were solemn and searching.

Two weeks later there was a phone call in the early evening for Semira. I ran to get her. She lifted the receiver and began to speak very slowly in Tigrinya and then a little more quickly. She put down the phone carefully and then said quietly, "It's true. I will go to tell the children."

Later that evening she came up to the kitchen, her eyes glistening. "October here is many colours. This October golden October." And she smiled.

Jamal had to wait at La Casa, the refugee shelter in Buffalo, for a few weeks until the dates of his immigration interview at the bridge. Semira and the children could not go down to see him as they were not yet landed immigrants with permission to leave the country. However, they talked to him twice on the phone. Amir ran into the TV room after the first call and said solemnly, "I talk my dad. See, he not dead."

Some of the members of our board who had come to know Semira decided to drive down to Buffalo to visit Jamal. It was the first Sunday of Advent when we set out, laden with bread and winter clothes from Semira and pictures of the children.

As we were driving along the QEW towards Fort Erie, Lorne said, "Well, this guy better be good." He said what we were all thinking. Semira and the children deserved the best. We had never really seen his picture since Semira had to leave behind all their photo albums in Saudi Arabia. To have brought them would have cast suspicion on her "tourist" visa.

When we walked up the stairs of the old St. Matthew's parochial school which was now La Casa or Casa San Matteo, a slightly balding and solidly built man of average height came towards us. "Hello, I'm Jamal. Thank you very much." He was polite, stiff.

Lorne gave him the bread and clothes from Semira. "Thank you very much," he said again. Then Winkie gave him the photographs of the children. He sat down slowly at the table in the old classroom and looked at them one by one. Tears started to roll down his cheeks. He looked at the pictures again, slowly revisiting each, and he did not try to brush away the tears.

After several minutes, he glanced up at us and said, "I'm sorry. It's been a long time. This one," he pointed to the picture of Muzit, "I don't even know her. She was so little when I left."

By this time we were all crying. He had our affection and friendship from that day on.

A week later I drove Semira and the children down to the Elizabeth Street bus terminal to meet Jamal who was coming in on the early-afternoon bus from Fort Erie. They were all dressed up, the boys in ties and white shirts and the girls in pretty dresses that Winkie had provided. Not a word was said during the ride to the terminal. I drove around the block discreetly after I left them on the platform where the bus had already arrived. When I circled by the platform again they were standing there with Jamal and his bag. On the ride home nobody said a word.

They spent the evening as a family and the next night we had a wonderful party to welcome him. My sister had given us a frozen lamb earlier in the season and we were able to serve the guests who kept streaming through the front door. Word had spread quickly about the party and people arrived with food and cassettes of Eritrean music. Soon everyone was swirling in a large exuberant circle in the living room—men, women and all the children moving in a circular slow-step rhythm that was from another time and place.

I had a minute with Semira while we did some of the dishes in the sink. "Jamal looks a little tired," I commented.

"He no sleep. All night he cry and take children on the bed and kiss them and cry."

"But he is safe now," I breathed.

"Yes, thanks God."

How wrong I was. I could not have foreseen that most of the next four years of my life, most of my time and energy, would be taken up in the struggle to ensure this family's safety.

THE LAWYER ASLEEP ON THE JOB

It was Palm Sunday, the beginning of Holy Week, a few months after Jamal's arrival and I was planting tomato seeds in the egg cartons on the kitchen table when Zeinib, another Eritrean woman, came in with a woman she introduced as Medhanit. There were no pleasantries, none of the polite questions which were customary in any Eritrean encounter. Zeinib was focused and clear. It could not wait until Monday.

"Medhanit received a letter saying she will be deported in two weeks."

It was a meeting that would mark a turning point in my life and in the life of Romero House. Until that day we had seen our work as the process of resettling refugees, of helping them integrate into the life of the country. Most refugees were being accepted and those who weren't would not, as far as we could see, be at risk if they were returned to their own countries.

"We don't understand why she would be deported," said Zeinib. "Her family is very well known in Eritrea. Her sister-in-law is the foreign minister of the main opposition group to the government. Medhanit and her children would be used as hostages if she were returned. They would never let her leave the airport."

Medhanit had brought the documents from her application and the negative judgement of the Immigration and Refugee Board she had received a few months earlier. She told me, through Zeinib, that she had asked her lawyer to appeal so she thought everything would be fine. And then the letter arrived on Friday, saying she was to be deported in two weeks. I assumed this meant that her appeal had been refused by the Federal Court.

It was a situation I had never really faced before. I could not imagine what could be done in two weeks. As far as I could see, all of Medhanit's options had been exhausted. She looked beaten and there was fear in her eyes. As I read her personal information form and then the IRB judgement I was even more sure that there was little that could be done. The panel members had dismissed her claim, suggesting that she was a simple woman who had come to Canada from Saudi Arabia to improve her economic situation. "She seemed confused and uninformed about the political situation in Eritrea," they wrote. "And, furthermore, there is no risk for Eritreans now that they have won the war against the Ethiopian dictator Mengistu."

"I don't think there is anything we can do," I said rather sadly. "But perhaps we could help you make the arrangements to go so that it won't be too upsetting for the children."

Zeinib stiffened and locked her eyes on mine. "This is different from Mama Miriam. I'm telling you that this woman and her children will be put in prison. They will be tortured."

I had been summoned. My thoughts scurried about in my mind, like a mouse trying to find a way through the maze of immigration regulations. It was a maze I had barely entered before.

"I think they make tapes of the hearings," I said tentatively. "Try going down to the hearings office at 70 University and ask for the tapes of your hearing and then bring them to me. Perhaps there will be something on them that we can use." To this day I do not know why that thought came to my mind.

By Wednesday, Medhanit returned with her cousin Tecle who had come with her to act as a translator. They gave me the brown manila envelope containing the tapes. It was not until the evening of Holy Thursday that I had the time to listen to them. I turned on the cassette machine in the living room and settled in for a long night. I heard the panel members begin with the usual formalities, the questions and Medhanit's faint answers repeated through the translator in English. I was getting drowsy. Then I was jolted back into consciousness by what sounded like a tractor, a motor ticking on and off. I went into the kitchen to see if something was wrong with the fridge. No, the sound was coming from the cassette player. No, it wasn't the machine, it was something on the tape. I replayed the section twice. The refugee hearing officer was questioning Medhanit. She was floundering. The judges called for a brief recess.

Then I realized that the sound was that of someone snoring.

A slow fury gathered within me. I phoned Tecle. "Call Medhanit right away and ask her if her lawyer fell asleep during her hearing and call me back immediately."

Tecle had been accepted as a refugee several years before and was now a citizen, working as a manager of food services in a large Toronto hospital. He knew the correct way of proceeding in Canada. He was trying to control his voice when he phoned back. "She said the lawyer was sleeping. One of the judges told him to wake up. She didn't think there was anything she could do."

"Where did she get this lawyer?"

"She said they gave him to her at the border. She only spoke with him about twenty minutes while he was preparing the refugee application. Then she saw him in the corridor just before the hearing. He was about an hour late."

It was a vigil of sorts as I listened to the rest of the tapes before I finally went to bed. In the morning I tried to prepare the reflection I was to give on one of the stations of the cross in the annual Good Friday walk through downtown Toronto.

In the end, I had only one thing to say at the service in the Church of the Holy Trinity in the Eaton Centre. "If you want to know what crucifixion might mean today, then listen to these tapes. Listen as a woman sits alone in a hearing room before two judges as her lawyer, her defender, is snoring away. Listen as she fumbles for the words to explain why she is afraid. Listen as she listens to the deafness around her. Listen as she grows silent."

It was eloquent but it would do nothing to help Medhanit, or so I thought. After the service a young man with his four children came up to the front of the church. His name was Steve Foster, a lawyer I had met briefly once before, who was working with the Jesuit Refugee Service as a volunteer. "I'd like to try to help her," he said simply. We arranged to meet the next day at his house.

Steve put almost all of his work at the Etobicoke Community Legal Aid Services on hold while he struggled to find a way to stop the deportation. Tecle took a week off work to help us talk with Medhanit. It soon became clear to us that Medhanit was a very intelligent woman with immense inner reserves. Why had she come across as so simple, almost illiterate?

"Let's check the translation at the hearing," suggested Steve, and we assigned Tecle the task of transcribing the tapes.

"This is impossible," lamented Steve to me privately. "We just don't have enough time."

Tecle rejoined us the next day in a state of great excitement. "The translator was terrible. He obviously didn't know the acronyms for the different political factions in Eritrea. He translated Medhanit's political party wrong so it made it sound as if she belonged to the government, not the opposition. His English is terrible."

"So it made Medhanit sound ignorant," commented Steve.

"Yes, and he made it sound as if she came from a simple peasant family," added Tecle, "not from the family of one of the largest landowners in the area."

"That's grounds for an appeal to the Federal Court. But the lawyer already tried that—or did he? Let's check the records there."

What Steve found out was that the lawyer had sent in a standard form notice requesting an appeal but that he had never "perfected" it, i.e., sent in the accompanying documentation and detailed reasoning.

"It happens a lot," I explained to Steve, "and then the lawyer bills legal aid for the costs of a full appeal. He makes money and the taxpayer loses, but most of all the refugee loses."

Steve now had a strategy. He would file a request to the Federal Court in Ottawa, asking for a stay of deportation so that Medhanit could make an appeal to the court. What he didn't have was sufficient time. "Normally this kind of thing would take two months' work."

Still he forged ahead with Tecle and me acting as willing, although not too competent, backups. We wrote the panel members, asking them for an affidavit regarding the sleeping lawyer. However, they replied that they couldn't remember. The refugee hearing officer remembered but was not willing to make a statement. After some hesitation, we contacted the translator. We felt guilty about asking him because we knew we were going to cite his incompetence in the documents to the Federal Court. He did remember. "The panel members see him sleeping and said recess. They turned off the tape then. One say to him, 'What's the matter with you. Wake up.'" The translator was willing to swear an affidavit to this effect. The one just man.

It seemed to me that the negligence of the lawyer would constitute grounds for an appeal because Medhanit had been deprived of the "natural justice" of being able to present her case well. However, we found out that such was not the case. In a previous ruling, the court had said that a sleeping lawyer did not constitute a lack of natural justice. By any other name it was not justice. We encouraged Medhanit to complain to the law society. She was already learning that she had "rights" and she was ready to fight—if not for her rights, then surely for her children.

Two weeks after Good Friday, Medhanit and I went with Steve to the Federal Court building. The request for a stay of deportation was to be conducted over an open phone line between the Toronto office and a judge in Ottawa. The case was to be heard at two-thirty. The court closed at four o'clock and Medhanit was to be deported Monday morning at nine. This was close to the wire.

We entered the small windowless room that would connect us with the federal judge in Ottawa. There was a microphone on the desk and a lawyer from the Justice Department, sorting through his papers. "Mr. Foster," he said curtly.

Steve motioned for me to go with him to the corridor. "We're in trouble. I locked horns with him on another case and I won."

Medhanit and I sat just behind the two lawyers and listened as the judge's voice filled the room. Steve began to present Medhanit's case methodically and politely. He apologized for not being completely prepared as he had only recently inherited the case. Then the lawyer from the Justice Department, representing the minister of employment and immigration, launched into his arguments as to why Medhanit should be deported. "She has been granted fair and due process under the law." The lawyer's voice dripped with sarcasm. "This is a frivolous use of the court."

Medhanit caught the tone of his voice and I could see tears falling from her eyes. It was the first time I had seen her cry.

"Thank you," said the voice over the speaker system. "I will be back in ten minutes with my judgement."

We sat in silence, waiting while Steve and the other lawyer ruffled through their papers.

And then the voice: "I have decided to stay the deportation and to allow time to prepare for leave to appeal at the Federal Court." The lawyer stomped out and I saw Medhanit smile for the first time.

Steve and I went back home with Medhanit, where Tecle was waiting with Medhanit's three children. She had barely seen them for two weeks and the two oldest held on to her legs as she scooped up the little boy and smothered him with kisses. We were introduced to Robel, a slight young boy with a sheepish grin, and Rahel, a beautiful girl with a wide halo of curly black hair.

"She wants to be a doctor when she grows up," beamed Tecle. "And this little one is Metawi. That means 'gathering storm,' because he was born just before the Gulf War, just before Medhanit's husband disappeared."

I realized that we had never really talked about Medhanit's husband over the last two weeks. It was just a fact listed in her personal information form: "Missing in the Gulf War."

"The Saudis ordered the foreign workers, many Eritreans, to drive the trucks to the Kuwait border in 1990–91. Many never returned," Tecle told us. "A woman without her husband was forbidden to stay in Saudi so Medhanit and many other women had to leave the country. They had no rights of citizenship there, and women like Medhanit could not return to Eritrea because they were associated with the opposition."

I had been involved in some serious protests against the Gulf War in January 1991, but I could not have predicted that I would become so involved with so many of its unrecorded victims over such a long period of time. The Gulf War, as with all wars, continued to claim its casualties long after it was officially over.

But Medhanit had won this battle and for a young lawyer it was his finest hour. It was also a turning point for "The Lady," for the word was out by the fastest grapevine in town that she knew how to stop a deportation.

A House for a Car

Hiwet, the young Eritrean girl, and I had sat at our kitchen table on the back porch the first afternoon she arrived at Romero House. We were having a cup of tea and I enjoyed listening to this teenager practise her English as much as she seemed delighted to describe her long journey to Canada.

Suddenly, she looked out the window that faced onto the backyard. "Who live out there?" she asked.

I looked out at the old familiar space. It was just a garden-variety yard, in need of a little time and attention.

"No one lives out there," I replied. "Well, maybe a few birds."

"No, person live there." She was adamant now. "Person there. House there."

"House?"

I looked out and for the first time I saw the garage for what it was. There was only one reply that I could make and my words fell like stones, one by one. "It's a house for a car."

"A house for a car?" She looked at me in disbelief.

Over the next few days I looked long and hard at the house for a car in our backyard. Given the housing shortage in the city at the time, it began to seem like a poor use of precious space. We talked about it at our team meeting in the morning and decided to get a building permit to insulate and drywall the garage so it could be used as a space for someone to sleep.

For the next few months I went around and around city hall trying to get a permit. Again and again I was told, "You can't do that."

"Why?"

"Because then everyone would do it."

"Would that be a bad thing?"

"The housing would get too dense. And besides, where would you put the cars?"

We had hit the proverbial brick wall. The matter might have ended there except for the fact that the house for a car loomed before us every time we had a cup of tea. The little structure refused to settle in our minds as just another garage.

One day it came to us. We would turn the house for a car into a house for God. Only this time we would not ask for a permit. I was sure there would be some regulations against building a house for God.

Some volunteers from nearby Bishop Marrocco-Thomas Merton High School insulated the garage and drywalled it as part of their community service project. It is now a very small room with a blue rug and sandy-coloured walls. It has become a little house where people of all faiths can find some space to be with themselves and with God.

THE MAIL MAKES THE MAN

It was imperceptible at first, the slight additions in our mailbox. A catalogue for office equipment one day, a flyer for cellular phones the next day and then a brochure for VCRs. It was nothing I had ordered and everything we couldn't afford at Romero House. Junk mail, I thought, and ditched it into the wastepaper basket without bothering to read it further.

The mail continued. Day by day, packets arrived from travel agencies, from government information offices, garden clubs, book and music companies. There was a gold-embossed envelope with a sidebar on the outside: "You have been selected for an all-expense-paid trip for two." Coupon books, postcards from companies, directories of services. "Thank you for inquiring." "In response to your request." Pitch and ditch.

Then came the morning when I had to make two trips from the mailbox to my desk. It took me twenty minutes to find the two or three letters which seemed to relate to Romero House business. The wastepaper basket fell over with its lopsided weight as I threw the last catalogue "For That Special Person" at it. I marched out to the mailbox and taped my protest against consumerism: NO JUNK MAIL PLEASE.

The volume of mail seemed to decrease dramatically in the following days. I was relishing my small victory in the cosmic war against junk when Gugan appeared at the door of the office. "Has my mail arrived?" he asked expectantly.

"No, I didn't see any for you, Gugan. Were you expecting a letter?"

He slumped in the chair by my desk. "It was just some catalogues I had sent for. I saw the advertisements in the paper and I, well, I thought it would be nice to get some mail even if I can't buy anything. I don't get much mail now. I used to get a lot of mail every day in my office."

Gugan had told me that he had been a senior vice-president of an insurance company in Sri Lanka. With a sigh of contrition I realized that I had thrown out some of the few remaining props for whatever was left of his identity.

"I'm sorry, Gugan. I didn't realize the catalogues were addressed to you. I should have looked more carefully."

"What you need is a good executive secretary, like the one I used to have." He smiled modestly.

"Well," I said, "why don't you take responsibility for distributing the mail to everyone in the houses and to the office? I'm sure it would be much more efficient."

"I would be delighted. It's what you call an entry-level position." He straightened up and walked out like someone you would call a "suit."

As soon as he left I ran to the front door, ripped the sign off the box, and scribbled a note to the mailman: "All mail gratefully accepted."

MY COLOUR

Almost everyone who comes to the Romero office is greeted by a young Somali woman who seems to be the receptionist. She sits in the large cushioned chair by the front door and she is usually talking and laughing on the phone. Visitors feel welcomed by her presence although she will never cut short a phone conversation or move to greet them.

Deequa lives on the same floor as the office because she finds it difficult to go up and down the stairs. The phone is her lifeline to the world.

When she arrived at our house, in her gorgeous long dress, we could see immediately that she had a limp and so we tried to make things as accessible as possible for her, arranging for Wheel-Trans to take her to English classes. Little by little we were able to communicate through more than smiles and chuckles.

One Saturday evening, Deequa finally confided in Winkie, our almost-resident nurse. "I need new leg," she said.

Slowly pulling up her dress, Deequa revealed the stick which was attached to the rough wooden stump just above where her knee had once been. Winkie examined the festering sores around the piece of old wood and then called in one of the Somali women to translate.

As the story slowly came out, Deequa told them of the day the house she had been living in had been bombed. Her leg had been torn to shreds and she was filled with pieces of the bomb. Winkie explained that we called this shrapnel. With great delicacy, Winkie examined the rest of Deequa's body and saw that there were pieces of shrapnel in her abdomen and chest and in her arms. She had been in continuous pain but all of that was veiled behind her smile.

Winkie referred Deequa to a doctor, and every few weeks one of the volunteers would drive her to get a few more pieces of shrapnel removed.

The process of getting a new leg was to prove more of a challenge. Deequa was taken to a hospital where she was carefully, meticulously measured for a better prosthesis by some very fine medical technicians. In the meantime, she was given a thin metal pole to which a large shoe was attached. This enabled Deequa to walk more easily, but it was a little disconcerting when people noticed the thin rod just above her shoe.

At last the much-awaited day came, and Peter, one of the volunteers, drove Deequa to the hospital to be fitted with her new leg. We had planned a big party and had posted announcements in all the houses for the "Take Back the Leg Party."

As they were driving home, Peter ventured to ask, "Well, how does it feel, Deequa?"

"Good," she replied, and then she lifted her dress modestly to mid-calf level.

"They didn't have my colour," she laughed.

Peter looked down and saw a very white leg. He was at a loss for words.

Later he said to me, "I wonder what Lucien Bouchard would have done if the doctors had told him they didn't have his colour!"

THE VEGETABLE PEOPLE

Some English words I found almost impossible to translate, even with the help of a translator. However, "potluck" is a word everyone understands.

The celebrations at Romero House are always, of necessity, potluck. However, it was also by choice, for it was a matter of pride for the residents of Romero House that they provide something, no matter how small, for every celebration. It was one sure way that they could contribute now that most of their usual ways of contributing had been cut off.

It never ceases to amaze me how delicious the dishes are and how attractively prepared. It is truly international cuisine at its finest and I have sometimes been tempted to invite some of the local restaurant critics. I am impressed because I know how little money these people have to spend on food and how they are usually forced to go to food banks at the end of the month. Nevertheless, we always manage to share in a magnificent banquet.

As I lived in the Romero community, I grew to appreciate the Eritrean and Ethiopian national dish called *enjarra*. This consisted of a large sour-dough pancake on top of which were placed various helpings of spiced meat in a sauce called *tsigny*, or lentils and vegetables. The Somalis made excellent sambusas and the Sri Lankans specialized in various curry dishes. I discovered that there are many varieties of curry, some of them composed of twenty or more spices. A true cook will always mix his or her own curry rather than buy it already prepared.

In any case, I found my tastes were expanded and refined through the cooking of my neighbours. And I lost a taste for some of the dishes I had grown up with—like turkey.

We have always had a big Christmas meal at Romero House—a meal which has now expanded to include over a hundred people. The turkeys are generously donated by friends and by St. Francis' Table, an alternate restaurant for the poor in Parkdale. At our first Christmas celebration, I noticed that most people took only a little piece of turkey meat and then proceeded politely on to other dishes.

After the celebration I asked Semira whether people ate turkey in her culture. "Yes," she answered.

By that time we knew each other well enough so that she could give me the full answer. "The Christmas turkey wonderful tradition. Christmas for friends and giving. But you know, Mary Jo, this food like hospital food. No taste. No spice. This for sick people."

As I laughed, I imagined all my meat-and-potato Irish ancestors turning over in their graves.

The next Christmas, I transported the five turkeys each to a different family to be cooked for the evening supper. We had an Eritrean turkey cut up and steeped in *tsigny*, Sri Lankan curried turkey, Russian turkey notched with garlic and stuffed with salty rice, Thai turkey with basil, lemon grass and coconut milk and one fat North American turkey with stuffing, gravy and cranberry sauce. This time my neighbours partook a little more of this strange turkey and seemed to enjoy it.

I thought I had provided for every possibility until Semira pointed out to me that I had forgotten the vegetable people.

"The vegetable people?"

"Yes. You know. No meat. They need Christmas too. The vegetable people."

VOTE YES

It was during the great Meech Lake debate. As we watched the nightly news together I tried to explain the situation in the country to my neighbours.

"What means 'separation'?"

"Like in a marriage. Some problems. Some say better to become two. Some say better to stay one."

My neighbours were very impressed that all this was even being discussed. Some were Eritreans who had been involved in a devastating war for their independence from Ethiopia for thirty years. Others were Sri Lankans who felt in their bones the savage civil war that had wracked their country. And Somalis. And Rwandans.

"At least you can talk about these things in Canada," observed Sirak, the former civil servant from Ethiopia. "Why do people have to go to war over such things? In the end, no matter how long you fight, you still have to come to a table to discuss. So why not stop the fighting when so many innocent people are killed? I think they fight because there are people who want only power. They don't care even about their own people."

A few days later, someone came to the door passing out "Vote Yes" buttons for the occupants to wear during the Meech debate. Perhaps she had come selling them, but when she found out no one could afford to buy them and why, she left a couple of buttons.

One of my neighbours came to my room with five buttons pinned to his shirt. "Maybe me wear like this for hearing." I suggested maybe one button might be a good idea but more than that might be too obvious.

He did wear the button to his hearing. It was discreetly placed on the lapel of his suit jacket. There was a flicker of a smile on the panel member's face as he announced the decision: "We have decided to vote yes. Ahem. We have determined that you are a refugee in the sense of the Geneva Convention."

SPECIAL PEOPLE

The trip to Ottawa has become an annual spring event. Some of the volunteers will take a vanload of Romero residents to the capital where they are billeted with various religious communities in the city.

The tour has been intensely prepared for and anticipated. The member of Parliament for the area, Jesse Flis, is usually able to obtain many seats in the Visitors' Gallery so that the refugees can watch a question period in the House of Commons.

One particular spring, the whole vanload was clutching their tickets as they waited to file into the gallery. One of the security guards asked them to wait. "We have some very special people here today and there may not be room for you."

Sasha, the aspiring young violinist who seemed unusually cheerful after a long skate down the Rideau Canal, stepped forward to the security guard and said, "But we are very special people too, sir."

Sasha's parents beamed and many of the other refugees nodded quietly.

Sasha gave the guard his ticket. "Well, I'll see what I can do," he replied. They were jammed into a back row but they were there.

"You see, he's Canadian," his mother said.

THE WORLD OF WORK

Zeinib had arrived with a flourish at Romero House not too long after Semira and Asha had arrived. She had three small children in tow and no husband in sight.

"He is an architect, you know. He is Somali but studied in Denmark and is very . . . Western . . . modern." Perhaps she was trying to tell me she was not like the others.

"Where is he now?" I asked.

"I really don't know." Her bravura seemed to fade to genuine sorrow. The story was by now all too familiar: men at war, women left with children.

Zeinib was elegant when she dressed up. Henna was her specialty and she had so perfected the dying of her hair that no one would guess she was rather grey at the roots.

Her children were a handful, visibly upset and disoriented by the loss of their father and their sudden move. "I don't have anyone to help me. I had my husband and servants or some of our relatives to help us."

Through Zeinib I became aware of how isolated child-rearing has become in our culture and what an adjustment it must be to be ripped away from a whole network of familial support.

"When I was growing up in the village it was very simple. The kids just played outside and could run everywhere. Nobody worried about them. But then the wars started in Eritrea and the famine came. Sometimes we would line up for hours for a little bit of food from an aid organization. By noon the line would break up and you would find dead people on the ground. They had just died from exhaustion standing there."

There was something of substance to Zeinib which began to show itself the longer she stayed. "I look at my kids when they are asleep and I think: now I have to be mother and aunt and uncle and grandmother and friend to them. I have to do this."

Little by little the children began to calm down and soon Zeinib was able to go to school. Her language skills enabled her to go to high school and she resolved to get the training that would enable her to support her children.

Finally the day of her graduation arrived and we all sat as proud members of her extended family as she waited to walk up to the podium to get her diploma.

The principal of Monsignor Fraser College had tried to personalize each presentation.

"Congratulations, Rosa, who has now found her place in the world of work.

"Congratulations to Osman who is now seeking his place in the world of work.

"Congratulations, Lee, who has two offers in the world of work.

"Congratulations, Zeinib, who will be going to George Brown College so she can find her place in the world of work."

I leaned over to Jack Costello, the Jesuit priest on our board of directors who had also been invited. "God help us. The world of work is starting to sound like heaven."

"It probably feels like it—in this recession time."

After we had all taken the required photographs I asked Zeinib what she was going to study at George Brown. "Well," she laughed, "travel and tourism. What else? I already have a lot of international experience!"

TRYING TO GET A LIFE

At first I knew Ghenet only through her two boys, Abel and Amanuel. Zeinib or Asha or Semira would look after them while their mother tried to finish her adult education classes. "Boys', Mama Ghenet, she work very hard at school," said Semira. "Very good woman." It was a sort of informal day care that the women in Brother John Masterson's house, the Jesuit Shelter for Refugees, had worked out with the women in our house. The two houses were only blocks apart and the arrangement was convenient for all concerned.

Ghenet was indeed a good woman and very intelligent. However, her training as a hairdresser was abruptly cut short when she received a "removal order" saying she had to leave the country in ten days. As far as we knew every legal route had already been tried by her lawyer. She had received even less notice than Medhanit and we knew that an appeal to the Federal Court was impossible.

By the time she received the removal order, Ghenet was living in her own apartment. When one of her neighbours phoned Brother John and said that Ghenet had been crying hysterically for days, John went over and tried to help her get packed. He also made sure that one of the neighbours would sleep with Ghenet until the departure date on Monday morning.

I was aware of the situation through John but had not been directly involved. However, on Sunday afternoon, after I had returned from a weekend trip, I turned on my answering machine to hear Ghenet's faint voice: "No want to live. Thank you. Goodbye. Me kill myself."

I called John who had just received the same message a few minutes earlier and together we drove to Ghenet's apartment.

"She has no sleep all week," said the neighbour lady as she opened the door. "She want kill herself."

Ghenet's hair straggled around her face, her eyes seemed fixed in their sockets, her skin grey-yellow. Her two little boys were huddled in a corner of the room—looking, just looking.

I moved immediately to phone the doctor on call at the local Four Villages Clinic on the corner of Keele and Bloor. The doctor advised us to take her immediately to emergency at a hospital and to make sure she got some medication. John and I drew her arms over our shoulders and pulled her down the corridor to the elevator and then to the car. We were carrying a human suitcase of sorrow.

The hours dragged by in the waiting room of the emergency ward in the nearby hospital. We told Ghenet not to worry, that the doctor would help her for sure, for sure.

Finally, she was called into a small room where three other people were waiting in chairs as the man in pale green medical fatigues talked and took notes. Two other patients were lying in beds close by.

Then it was Ghenet's turn. Finally, I hoped.

"So, lady, what's your problem?" he said for all the world to hear. "What's the matter with you? I'm talking to you."

"She doesn't speak English very well and she's exhausted," I replied, moving my chair to be closer to her.

"So where's she from?" he asked, pulling out a form.

"Eritrea. She's going to be deported tomorrow and she's very depressed. The doctor she knows at the clinic thought she might need some medication."

"Well, listen, honey, people get deported every day." He had wheeled his stool around so he was head to head with Ghenet. "Listen, stop feeling sorry for yourself. Get a life."

"That's what she's trying to do," I said.

"Listen, everything's fine over there. Just go back and start a new life."

"I think she needs some medication," I persisted. Then I lost it. "You know, you really are ignorant." The doctor ordered me out of the room.

John and I conversed briefly about the situation and he went in to try to retrieve Ghenet. They emerged in about half an hour with a prescription form. For the next few hours we drove around trying to find a pharmacy. The doctor had not told us where to find a pharmacy that was open on Sunday nights.

The neighbours kept watch over Ghenet in the night. By the time John arrived in the early morning to help take her to Niagara Falls, he could see that Ghenet was almost physically paralysed and decided to take her over to the house of some people he knew and asked them to look after her until a doctor could come to check on her. After about a week Ghenet seemed to be getting stronger and John felt sure that she would soon be able to make decisions about her future.

However, Ghenet had missed her appointment with "removals" and was now an illegal in the country. She was not really trying to hide. Within a few days, immigration officers went over to the school and picked up the two little boys in a security van. Then they went to the house where Ghenet was, shackled her and led her to the van, and from there to the detention centre and then quickly across the border. In official terms, she had not been removed but deported.

John was shattered by the turn of events but proceeded with steady resolve to correct the injustice that Ghenet had experienced. He found a religious community in Buffalo willing to shelter Ghenet while she was trying to get a life. He also found three church groups willing to sponsor Ghenet and the children back to Canada. I talked to my hairdresser, who was more than willing to hire Ghenet on her return. He wrote a letter to this effect, stressing how much he needed qualified and hard-working people such as Ghenet. The local member of Parliament wrote to the Canadian Consulate in Buffalo, urging that the sponsorship for this woman proceed. The chief executive officer of the hospital where Ghenet had been treated so callously wrote a letter expressing his profound regret for the way in which the medical staff in emergency had failed this woman at a critical time. The CEO had told us that the doctor had been fired shortly after our encounter with him because of his unprofessional manner with other patients.

John and I drove down to Buffalo on three occasions to wait with Ghenet as she was summoned to an immigration interview at the Canadian Consulate. The waiting room at the large bunker-like building on Marine Drive was usually filled with what looked like tourists from the Far East. Perhaps they were investor immigrants, I don't know. I do know that they were dressed in the latest and classiest clothes and that they were served promptly. They had appointments. They were called on time, ushered in and left with papers.

Ghenet waited—sometimes for hours. The first and second interviews ended in a matter of minutes. The officer told her there was some mistake in the file numbers and that the whole process would have to be started over again. The third interview took about an hour and Ghenet came out trying to put a brave face on things. No one had been allowed to accompany her—no friend, no interpreter.

"I tried to explain night at hospital and showed letter but the officer no read."

As we walked out of the building Ghenet told me that the officer had asked her what she could contribute to Canada.

"What did you reply?" I asked.

"I said . . . 'my children.'"

CELEBRITY INN

Someone was knocking frantically at the front door just before eight in the morning. As I opened the door, Semira's husband, Jamal, rushed in and tried to tell me something terrible had happened.

"My friend Zein phoned me and said that immigration officers came and were taking the family. Then the phone stopped. No sound."

Jamal couldn't understand what had happened as Zein had not received any removal order and was still in the process of appealing his case.

"I called over to another friend who lived in the same apartment block and he said no one was at home and the door was open."

I was guessing that enforcement had picked the family up—but I didn't understand why, and where could they be? We called enforcement in Niagara Falls but they said no one was in detention there.

"They have probably taken them to Celebrity Inn," replied the voice.

"Celebrity Inn?"

"Yes, it's the detention centre just near the airport." It sounded like a rather sad joke but I knew that he was telling the truth. I had never been to Celebrity Inn although I had spoken to a few Quakers and some lawyers who had been out there. The conditions, they had said, were appalling.

Jamal and I ran to the car and drove up Airport Road, north of highway 401. Just beyond the Red Lobster was the large sign for Celebrity Inn. We entered the front door and saw a bar to the left and a restaurant to the right. It had the same worn-out interior as most of the motels in the airport area. Nevertheless, this didn't seem like the place we were looking for. A rather cheery waitress told us that we could find the place we were looking for by going around to the back entrance.

Celebrity Inn took on a new face as we walked around to the motel. The windows have bars on them and there is a tall wire fence surrounding an enclosure at the back. A small glass door observed by a security guard at a glassed-in desk indicated that we had come to the right place.

We buzzed. We showed our ID and asked to see the Zein family. "No. Come back in the afternoon."

"When can he be released?"

"Tomorrow morning is the earliest time for his detention review. Come back then," said the voice through the intercom.

"What about his wife and little children?" asked Jamal. The place had already made him visibly nervous but he wanted to help his friend. "Today is the big feast of the year for Muslims. I know the children were all dressed in their new clothes to go to the mosque."

"Too bad. They're in here as long as he is in here."

"But what has he done wrong?"

"How should I know?"

We contacted Zein's lawyer, a young woman named Kristin Marshall, and she agreed to go to the detention review the next day. She urged us to come up with some bail money in case that was necessary.

The next morning we found our way to the detention review centre located behind the International Centre at the airport. The front of this enormous building usually hosts events such as the large Cottage Show in the spring, but behind is a labyrinth of immigration offices. Any time I had been out there, it had been a challenge to remain sane in a scene of total chaos.

Once I had gone out there trying to find the file of a particular refugee. "Could be anywhere right now," said the harried officer at the desk. "We found a couple of boxes of files in the washroom last week." Someone's chance to work. Someone's life. Someone's future.

After we were seated in the small room, Zein's wife and four little children were brought in by a security officer. After they were seated, he was brought in, shackled with handcuffs and leg irons.

The adjudicator dispensed with the matter rather quickly. It appeared the Zein family had been picked up because they were not at their old address. Some immigration officers thought the family had gone underground and so they traced him to his new address. Zein's lawyer brought a document to prove that he had indeed reported his new address, not only to her but to Immigration. The adjudicator ordered the family released immediately on the condition that we post a performance bond. "And get those kids out of here," he said sharply. "They shouldn't be in a place like this."

The family sat frozen in the back seat and the rear section of the old station wagon. When we finally reached their apartment block the oldest son turned to his father and asked, "Daddy, what did we do wrong?"

I turned to him and replied, "Nothing."

My next visit to Celebrity Inn took place on the evening of Good Friday. I had gone to church in the afternoon, but as I listened to the readings of the solemn service I began to think about the silent and hidden suffering I had seen at Celebrity Inn. That evening I drove to the northern part of the city near the airport.

I gave my passport to the man behind the thick window and spoke through the microphone. "I'm here because it's Good Friday. Is there anyone in here who is being held simply because they don't have an address to go to?"

"I donno."

"Could I speak to a supervisor, please?"

"I donno."

"Well, I'll stay here until I can speak with someone who knows."

He left the little room behind the glass window.

After fifteen minutes, a rather young man with a crew cut came to the window. I repeated my reasons for being there. "Well, I don't think there's anyone here like that. They're all criminals as far as I know. But come into my office and I'll go through the lists."

He walked ahead of me, down a dingy corridor and up a flight of metal steps. Everything in his office seemed metal, too: metal desk, metal filing cabinets, metal chair. He offered me a cup of coffee and plunked his feet on his desk while he started to read through the pages on his clipboard. I asked him what his name was. "It doesn't matter."

A security guard came into his office and opened the filing cabinet. "Hey, do you know of anyone here who is here because he doesn't have an address to go to?"

The guard paused, "No. I don't think so. There's that guy Mohammed who's been here a couple of months, but I don't know why. He doesn't speak English."

"Mohammed?"

"Yeah. Mohammed. The guy from Iran."

"Oh yeah. But he doesn't speak English."

I asked if I could see him. "Sure. But he doesn't speak English."

I was taken into a bare room with a table and two chairs. I was told this was the room where lawyers met with their clients.

Mohammed shuffled into the room and sat down in one of the chairs. His clothes bagged around his bones and his eyes were ringed with circles.

"How are you?" I asked.

He lifted his head slowly and looked me in the eyes, "I'm very depressed."

For the next ten minutes he spoke, and in English: "When I got deportation letter I was very afraid. I try to suicide. They took me to hospital and give me medicine. Then they take me here. I no hope any more."

I gave Mohammed my card and promised to speak to the supervisor. Then I went back to the supervisor's office. "He does speak English," I said. "I think he is very depressed and maybe a doctor should see him. Do you have any record of what hospital he was in?"

"He speaks? Well, what do you know. Let's take a look at his file." He flipped through the few pages and looked up. "Yeah, it says he was picked up from the psych unit in a hospital."

"Where will he be deported?" I asked.

"Iran."

"Well, that's enough to depress anyone."

"I guess so. That's kind of sad. I mean, no one knew he could speak."

"Have you worked here long?"

"Too long. I just do weekends. I go to university during the week and I'm almost finished. Then I'm out of here. Too much pressure to go out and pick people up. They say there's lots of criminals out there."

"If there are," I said, "why don't they pick them up instead of picking up innocent people by mistake, or women and children."

"Listen, it's easier to pick up the women and children. Easier than criminals. All they want is numbers. Makes me sick sometimes to see the kids in here with druggies. Sometimes it's for months. But I can't think about it."

"Who's they?"

"People up higher. They don't want any refugees in this country."

"Why?"

"I don't know. They've got a thing about it. They dig up any dirt they can find and feed it to the media. They ask us to feed them the dirt."

It was snowing as I drove down Airport Road. The flakes melted on the windshield and it seemed to me that the city itself was silently crying.

Mohammed never called me. Two weeks later I called Celebrity Inn to make an appointment to see him. The person who answered the phone put me on hold. "He's not here," the voice answered.

"Where is he?"

"I donno." Silence and the sound of ruffled papers. "Maybe Iran."

I asked to speak to the weekend supervisor with the crew cut. "He's not here."

"Where is he?"

"I donno."

On December 17, 1995, a Nigerian refugee claimant called Michael Akhimen died of diabetic shock while being detained at Celebrity Inn. The matter was eventually reported in the media. Somehow I was not surprised.

According to information gathered by Parkdale Community Legal Services, he was thirty-nine years old and had a master's degree in criminology from the University of Benin in Nigeria. Because he was involved in an attempt to overthrow the military dictatorship, he was arrested and tortured for eight months.

He was apprehended in Canada in October 1995 when he was trying to cross into the United States on a freight train. He was trying to reach the United States to make a refugee claim. When he was caught he decided to make a claim in Canada but he remained in detention because the officers did not think he would show up for the hearing.

In desperation, in November 1995, Akhimen tried to withdraw his refugee claim. He wrote this note to immigration officials: "I can no longer stay in detention when I have committed no crime and my family back home cannot be located. I would prefer to suffer in Nigeria for a reason than wasting away here far from my wife and kids. I will take my chances with the security forces. I want to be removed from Canada immediately, please."

In early December, he began to complain of health problems, including blurred vision, nausea and joint pains. On December 13, believing he was suffering from malaria, he offered to pay for blood-work and a proper check-up. He wrote a letter to the kitchen staff, offering to pay for bananas, juices and milk as he was unable to digest solid food.

On December 11, he was placed in solitary confinement because he had attempted to get some water from the kitchen. He was suffering from severe thirst, a symptom of diabetes. A fellow detainee said a guard tried to stop him and this was why he was put in solitary.

There was an inquest into his death in which Akhimen was repeatedly portrayed as a troublemaker. Many of the key witnesses who saw his illness had already been deported from the country at the time of the inquest.

However, the inquest heard evidence that immigration officials have no authority to place individuals in solitary confinement and that there are no rules governing solitary confinement. Detainees have no recourse to any outside body of complaint. The guards who kept close watch over him as he died presumed that he was faking it.

The jury at the inquest found that Michael Akhimen had died of natural causes while detained at Celebrity Inn.

My Tribe

"So what tribe are you from?" Amir, the oldest son of Semira and Jamal, had been studying about the various tribes and nations of the native peoples of North America. He was trying to locate me and my loyalties.

It was a question I had begun to ask myself as the months became years at Romero House. At times I felt like an empty field of snow with no footprints compared to the geographies of identity which, for better or worse, had shaped the lives of so many of my neighbours. I had begun to talk to my older relatives and to read a little more about the history of this country.

"Well, Amir, I come from a long line of Irish kings and queens."

"You do?"

"Not really. That's just blarney."

"What's that?"

"It's a special language in my tribe. Really, I came from a big tribe called the Irish Catholics. There was a famine, no food, in their country in the nineteenth century, a long time ago. There was no food because there were problems with the land and problems with politics. They would have died if they hadn't been able to leave."

"So your family was a refugee too?"

"I guess so, but they didn't call them refugees then. They called them immigrants. There was a young man from Ontario called Peter Robinson who went to try to help some of the people come here. He found them boats to sail in and food to eat on the boats and doctors to look after them. I think my great-great-grandfather came with Peter Robinson. They landed at Port Hope and they went to the area near Lindsay, and Peter Robinson gave them some good land and food to start. Very soon they were growing their own food and growing food for others and paying taxes. The people were so grateful that they called the area around there Peter's Borough or Peterborough. That was in 1824. Peter Robinson was from a different tribe. He was a Protestant and my family were Catholics. He was English and my ancestors were Irish. Yet, he was a good man and he knew how to help people become Canadians. He helped them stand on their own feet."

"I think that sounds great," said Amir.

"It was, for my family. But then there was another great hunger a few years later and there weren't many Peter Robinsons. The people from the Irish tribe went on boats and they had no food. And when they came here they were very sick. They didn't give them good land and food to help them make a home here. They had a hard time and they couldn't make a living. People didn't like them and they didn't feel welcome. People said they had too many kids, that they had an accent, that they were lazy and that they wouldn't be loyal to the country."

"That's very sad," said Amir. "How long ago was that?"

"Not that long ago."

V

FILES, NUMBERS

The S Files

Semira's smile was folding away into a file. Her laugh was disappearing like a fax into a machine. The process of her refugee determination hearing had begun and she had become another number in the immigration system. She had an Immigration and Refugee Board number, a client ID number and a CIC file number.

The first session of Semira's hearing, in the fall of 1991, had been consumed by the effort to introduce a new personal information form. Both Abdullah and I had to testify about the statement Semira had originally prepared and about how insistent she had been that her husband belonged to the ELF and not to the EPLF. The distinction had now become critical as the refugee board was issuing decisions which reflected the widespread conviction that, after the fall of Mengistu, any Eritrean could safely return to a now independent country.

The refugee hearing officer (RHO), the person assigned to help the panel obtain all the necessary information, was a man who was obviously at least an acquaintance of the lawyer from the very large Smith tribe. Although he was supposed to be neutral in the proceedings, he assumed an adversarial role. When Semira tried to explain that she had signed a blank form, the RHO openly mocked her and asked why anyone should take her word against the word of a reputable lawyer. At one point he even laughed at her. "I note for the record that the RHO is laughing at my client," said Belva. During this portion of the hearing he left the room several times to consult with Mr. Smith who was attending a hearing in an adjacent room. Outwardly Semira remained dignified, although inwardly she was terrified. As she told me later, "In our country, something like court is for people who do something very bad. I try to think of my children."

Nevertheless, at the end of the first session, the judges allowed Semira to introduce a new personal information form, one that reflected her actual story. The panel members said the change in forms would not reflect badly on her. However, there was now a mark on her file that would take years to erase.

The hearing was adjourned and resumed for a second session. A new RHO had been assigned to the case as the first one had taken on a new job. She was a woman whom Semira would soon call "the Cat Lady." The RHO wanted to call the former lawyer, Mr. Smith, to testify. For whatever reason, he said he was not available, although she indicated that she had talked with him.

The hearing was adjourned again, and by the time of the third session Jamal had arrived in the city. He then became the key witness in Semira's hearing since her claim and that of her children rested on the persecution they would face because of his political involvement. Jamal himself was to have a separate hearing.

We were all quite confident that things would go well. Belva had amassed a considerable amount of information about the various political factions in Eritrea and about the ongoing conflict between the ELF and the EPLF. She had written statements from the offices of the ELF about Jamal's committed and high-profile involvement in the ELF. She had also sent Jamal to the Canadian Centre for Victims of Torture for a medical assessment. He had been interviewed by an internationally recognized expert on torture and post-traumatic stress disorder.

The doctor had written a report which read in part:

He continues to suffer from marked symptoms of difficulty sleeping with bad dreams and nightmares; frequent intrusive memories of his experiences during the day; nervousness with headaches, stomach pain and increased startle response; depression with crying and brooding; and difficulty with his concentration.

Belva had attached the doctor's article on the difficulties faced by victims of torture during refugee hearings.

At times the emotional aspects of the memories of the torture will be repressed, resulting in the individual talking about the torture in a very mechanical detached manner; this marked lack of emotional response should not be taken as an indication that the torture did not occur. . . . In their country of detention, the government officials were the enemy who degraded them, who did not believe what they were saying and who had the ability to control their life completely and to kill them at any time. Although they may be aware at an intellectual level that they are secure in Canada, at an emotional level there is usually some conditioned fear and distrust of authorities.

The report and the article clearly indicated that Jamal would not be able to endure prolonged or aggressive questioning.

In preparing for the third sitting of the hearing, Semira was learning a lot more about her husband than she had known before. He had actually told her very little about his political involvement in order to protect her and the children.

He had gone to Khartoum in the Sudan from Saudi Arabia, where he was to meet the people who would take the Eritreans into the liberated zones because he wanted to see what the political climate of the country was and what chances existed for his party to make a comeback. He went to the house of some ELF activists who were living in Khartoum. The second night he was there, a group of armed men entered the house, took him, blindfolded, at gunpoint into a car, and drove him for more than a day. He was initially taken to a desert prison camp in the Sahel area of Eritrea and then moved from camp to camp in the desert area where he was held in solitary confinement for two and a half years and repeatedly beaten and threatened if he did not provide information about the activities of the ELF. Several times his head was held under water until he passed out. The EPLF wanted him to convince other members of his tribe, the Giuberti tribe, to join the EPLF. He was kept in solitary confinement for the entire time and not allowed to speak to the other prisoners. "I thought I was finished," he said simply.

As the third session began, Belva asked Jamal the questions that drew out the details of his story. She also presented the documentation about the factions in Eritrea and the medical report.

Then the Cat Lady began to scratch away at his story. She would continue her questioning for three more full days. She was also the refugee hearing officer assigned to Jamal's separate hearing and she would question him again for another three days. In all, he endured, but only barely, six full days of questioning.

Several times Belva tried to intervene, saying that this kind of questioning was clearly difficult for him and reminding the RHO and the panel members of the medical report. The panel members made no attempt to rein in the questioning.

PANEL MEMBER: And since you never gave them the answers, then what? They beat you up every week?

JAMAL: Well, when I say physical abuse, for example, it's not the way you take it. They slap you or sometimes they threaten you in words that if you don't tell us, we'll kill you, we'll do this. So, this kind of mistreat that they were abusing me.

PANEL MEMBER: I thought you stated earlier that you had been beaten?

JAMAL: Yes, when they ask you, they beat you.

PANEL MEMBER: And when you don't give a response that they like, they beat you?

JAMAL: Well, for example, one of them asks you certain questions and beats you and then the other one comes up and starts to console you that you get mollified, for example, to give them what they want. In every interrogation there is a kind of beating. Say, for example, some of them, they come for verbal interrogation, some of them they come and threaten you, some of them they beat you. This is the kind of different people. They come and do different things.

PANEL MEMBER: I see. And that was during the interrogation periods?

JAMAL: Yes, there are some days they don't threaten you, they don't trick or they don't beat you. They just try to brainwash you and go.

PANEL MEMBER: So when you were left alone between interrogations, they didn't bother you at all. They just left you on your own, is that it?

JAMAL: Yes, sir.*

Jamal was starting to slump in his chair. He started holding one hand to the side of his head. As the questions rained down, he began to flinch physically each time a panel member or the RHO delivered the blows. It had become an interrogation.

RHO: And when you say they locked you in, were these permanent structures that you were locked in?

---

* All quotations from this IRB hearing are taken from the transcript filed with the Federal Court and are a matter of public record.

JAMAL: When I say locked, it doesn't mean we were locked in like in a building in Asmara or some other place where they lock you in a house. No, this is just an area where there is a guard there to watch you and you don't make any movement.

RHO: Okay, when you say, just locked you in, and you say, no one, was this an indoor space?

JAMAL: Can I explain? For example, if you are imprisoned in Asmara [the capital of Eritrea], we have prisons built by the British. There is a door there and they lock the door. But, where we were, it was just an open area. They just put you there and they put a guard on you and they watch you.

PANEL MEMBER: So you were not in a cell? You were in an open field?

JAMAL: Yes, a desert. Just an open field. With thorny bushes around.

PANEL MEMBER: And how high were these?

JAMAL: A metre and a half. Something of that nature.

PANEL MEMBER: So, there were entrances through these thorny bushes for people to go in and out of the compound?

JAMAL: Don't say doors because doors are made, are constructed. Just an open area.

RHO: I said entrances.

JAMAL: Well, of course, they must have some entrances. Otherwise how could we go in?

RHO: That's what I'm trying to find out. How many entrances or places were open for people to go in and out?

PANEL MEMBER: Do you want to take a rest?

JAMAL: No. Let's go ahead.

PANEL MEMBER: You're all right. Okay. You just seemed to be . . .

JAMAL: Even a murderer wouldn't be interrogated like this.

I began to wonder why the RHO and the panel members seemed so intent on destroying Jamal's testimony. There was something almost compulsive about it. Then it dawned on me that these panel members and the RHO had been refusing Eritrean refugees for months. If Jamal was right, then they had got it terribly wrong—at least in some cases.

"Why do they keep hitting me?" asked Jamal as we walked home from the subway station.

"Maybe because if you're right, it means they don't know everything about Eritrea."

"They seem to think they know more about the desert camps than me. I was there. . . . How much longer?"

"Maybe another day."

"I don't know if I can do it. I will try—for the sake of the children."

By then I knew that, in order to change the drift of the proceedings, we needed some absolutely incontrovertible evidence about the EPLF, its persecution of the ELF and the desert prison camps. I phoned Fay Sims, the coordinator of Amnesty International in Toronto and asked her if Amnesty in London, England, had anyone whom they considered to be an authority on Eritrea. She said she would fax London. A few days later she phoned and said that there was such a person. He was the former head of the BBC World Service and the BBC Africa Service. He had written several books and articles on Ethiopia and Eritrea, had lived there for years, and had lectured at Oxford.

I called Patrick Gilkes at his home in Oxford.

"Can you tell me your assessment about the relationship between the ELF and the EPLF?" I asked. "Are there any reports about desert prisons camps, about kidnappings and torture?"

"The EPLF is a brutal and repressive regime," he said. "They would not have won if they hadn't been so tough. They see the ELF as their mortal enemy and chief competition for the minds and hearts of the people. There are several eyewitness reports about kidnappings of ELF leaders, about camps in the Sahel region where they keep high-profile prisoners."

This was what we needed. I asked him if he could send a fax giving his analysis of the situation and a copy of his CV. Two days later a tightly reasoned six-page analysis arrived together with an impressive list of credentials. I drove down to Belva's office with it and together we celebrated with margueritas at the local restaurant. Patrick Gilkes had independently confirmed Jamal's story almost point for point.

In the next and last session of the hearing, the documentation of Patrick Gilkes was introduced. The Cat Lady suggested it couldn't be taken very seriously because it seemed to contradict all the other information they had received about Eritrea—about how the government had promised to hold open and honest elections.

She had relied on the information provided by the provisional government of Eritrea because that was all that was available. I began to see that there would always be an information gap for refugees coming from repressive regimes. By definition, the most brutal regimes are also those that exercise extreme censorship of any critical information. It takes some time to get an accurate assessment of a shifting situation, and the refugees from an oppressive political situation will probably arrive before any accurate information is available. Patrick Gilkes was able to get that information only because of his long and deep contacts inside Eritrea. His report would eventually be accepted as substantial and crucial by IRB panel members a few months later. In the meantime, Eritrean refugees were being refused on the basis of incomplete information.

I realized that the information provided by Patrick Gilkes could be very important for some of the Eritrean refugees who were being deported. But where could it make a difference and to whom? An appeal to the Federal Court could be launched only on questions of law and procedure, not on the basis of new information. There was something called a "humanitarian and compassionate request" in which new information could supposedly be presented. We would soon discover that the procedure had become virtually meaningless in Ontario.

The hearing was over for Semira and Jamal and the panel members said that their decision would be sent in the mail. On paper to the file number. Never face to face.

"Now we wait," I said to them as we sipped a cup of tea in the kitchen.

"It's important for the children that we keep everything normal," said Jamal. "We don't want to take their childhood from them with these problems."

And that is what they did. Every morning Jamal took his children to school and every evening they were picked up. He and Semira went to every activity that was open and accessible for their children: swimming lessons, Arabic lessons, ballet for the girls and, of course, Shakespeare in the Park.

"But Jamal, he no sleep," Semira told me.

Every morning, in the spring and summer of 1992 , we went to the mailbox to look for the brown legal-sized envelope that would contain the decision of the Immigration and Refugee Board. I kept telling Semira and Jamal that I was sure the decision would be positive. The recent information from Amnesty International's expert had confirmed Jamal's story and the medical reports about his situation were more than persuasive. The panel members had accepted her word (and mine) against that of the lawyer who was producing boiler-plate personal information forms. It was just a question of time, or so I thought.

Something different was happening though. It was as if a great machine had started to grind people up and spit them out. A steady stream of refugees started appearing at our door. I would go out to get the morning papers only to find a man or woman or couple sitting on the steps at seven in the morning. Apparently, word had spread through the city about the woman whose deportation had been stopped with twenty minutes to spare. The myth about "The Lady" grew in proportion to the helpless desperation which hung about their lives. Each refugee would bring a single white piece of paper that was their order to appear for removal from Canada. They were bewildered. I saw how fear looked, the reign of terror in a face.

I listened carefully to the stories of the people who started to fill the hallway and front room of our house. Some were completely disoriented by the thought of returning to a country they had fled as teenagers. Others felt they were being ripped up by all the roots they had set down in Canada: friends, lovers, a job in which they had excelled and made a difference. Many said they would be killed or tortured if they were returned.

"There is nothing more we can do. I am so sorry." Those were always the most difficult words to say. I remembered how my father had described his experience of doing triage as a surgeon in Europe during the Second World War. He always felt guilty, he said, having to decide whom to operate on first and who was beyond his help. In the great and grinding systems of the world then, as now, those who make decisions on paper, from above and far away, never have to see the fear and suffering those decisions wreak on the face of one human being.

I took out some of the tools of my trade as an investigative journalist and began to double-check the information that had been given to me in the course of these daily visitations. I did not doubt the weight of human suffering each person was carrying but I needed to check the seriousness of the potential risk. After double- and triple-checking the sources and documents, I moved on to the most reliable sources—my contacts in the various ethnic communities in the city. In each community, I would ask three or four people for an assessment of specific pieces of information.

Gradually, it became clear to me that 80 to 90 percent of the people who had asked for our help were more in need of humanitarian assistance than the protection of the state. I referred many to other agencies who could help them sell their furniture or obtain transcripts from their children's schools. Sometimes we would drive them to the airport or store their furniture for someone else to use. They needed help but not because their lives were in danger.

That summer of 1992 I learned that the immigration system, like so many other systems, is designed to deface everyone who participates in

it. I began to see how files and numbers and pieces of paper and procedures and acronyms all served to muffle the relationship between one
human being and another. Immigration officers became faceless
bureaucrats and refugees were reduced to numbers. The only time a
decision maker ever had to face a refugee with the results of that decision was when a positive decision was given orally at the end of a
refugee hearing. If the members of the Immigration and Refugee Board
had to issue a negative decision, it was sent in the mail. If a single judge
from Federal Court refused or accepted a request for a leave to appeal,
the decision was sent in the mail—and it was not necessary for the
signer to give a reason for the decision. If a humanitarian and compassionate request was made, the submissions were done on paper and the
decision was a simple yes or no sent in the mail. The removals orders,
the deportation orders, were all sent in the mail with the always indis-
cernible initials scrawled at the bottom of the page.

Our burden and blessing at Romero House was that we were still
able to see the faces of the refugees and to know they were human
beings very much like ourselves. And there were some refugees who
looked at me, who faced me, and said, "You must help me."

I knew I could not turn away and say, "There is nothing more I can
do. I am so sorry." I knew the lives of these refugees were in danger.

There was the thin, wiry Eritrean journalist with very thick glasses
who had spent most of his life writing editorials against the man who
was now the leader of the government in Eritrea. He had shown me
one of his editorials against "The Mad Dog of Eritrea." He had a wife
and five children.

There was another Eritrean who had been a key organizer and fund-
raiser for an opposition group. He too had a wife and five children.

Both of the Eritreans had had their refugee hearings in the fall of
1991 and they, like so many other Eritreans, had been refused on the
grounds that there would be no more difficulties for them now that
the Ethiopians had been ousted from power.

There was a young Iranian man who had already been living illegally for a year. Although he had once owned a fashionable boutique

in Iran, he now survived by selling hot dogs on Yonge Street. He had just received a copy of the death warrant which had been issued against him and wondered whether it would make a difference to anyone.

There was a short, slight young Kurdish man from Turkey who had already been in Canada for four years. He had been drafted into the Turkish army and told he would be sent to fight the Kurds in the eastern part of the country. The Immigration and Refugee Board had refused his claim, saying that he could always go to another part of Turkey and hide the fact that he was a Kurd. "But the minute I open my mouth anyone would know I was a Kurd," laughed Sami. He was feisty, with a terrific sense of humour. "Don't you think the English would know someone was a Scot even if he could speak the language?" Sami had also taken part in peaceful demonstrations outside the Turkish Embassy in Ottawa and had been photographed by a Canadian television station in one of their news broadcasts. Sami had a copy of the tape to prove it. "The Turkish security people know I oppose their policies. I would never make it past the airport if I was sent back."

When I first committed myself to trying to help these people, I had assumed that something could be done. I was so sure that a well-documented case with ample evidence that a person's life was in danger would be persuasive to any reasonable person. It was only a matter of doing the necessary research and finding out at which doorstep the documentation should land.

In this state of conviction, I contacted the two groups who had a great deal of experience in advocating for refugees whose lives would be at risk if they were deported. Amnesty International and Vigil had a well-deserved reputation for carefully documenting refugee cases and then advocating for them with the minister of immigration.

However, by the spring of 1992, both of these groups were growing increasingly frustrated and confused. "We had a very respectful relationship with Barbara McDougall when she was minister of immigration," said Gwen Smith, a Sister of St. Joseph who had been working as a volunteer with Vigil for some time. "We did our research carefully and then sent a few cases every year to her office with the request that she exercise her ministerial prerogative to grant these refugees a permit to stay in Canada. She personally read the files and made the decisions. It wasn't always positive but we could expect her to be fair."

Gwen went on to explain that, in her opinion, under the new minister of immigration, Bernard Valcourt, such fairness was no longer possible. "We can't even get through to the minister," she said. "We are being told that all these decisions are now being made by local immigration officers from the enforcement branch. But when we go to the local offices, they say they have no authority to make these decisions and that we will have to go to the minister."

I had already experienced a similar runaround when I had tried to find out where to send the recent documentation on the risks faced by leaders of opposition groups in Eritrea, by people such as the journalist and the fund-raiser who had come to our door. No one seemed able, or willing, to consider this important and new information that was a matter of life and death to the people I had grown concerned about. This mounting frustration brought together a group of seasoned refugee advocates such as Nancy Pocock. We began meeting at the Quaker House on Lowther Avenue. "It has never been this bad," said Nancy. "Most of the time I feel there's nothing I can do but cry with the person."

A Time of Conscience

It was clearly a time of conscience. No one was willing to let another person be sent back to his or her death or destruction. Very early on in the meetings we began to talk about sanctuary as a last resort. We all knew enough of our Christian tradition to know that there had been many significant times when the church protected innocent people within its buildings when they were endangered by the powers that be in this world. We did a mental tour of the various Christian congregations in the city and decided that the Church of the Holy Trinity beside the Eaton Centre would be a possible place of sanctuary. I was to call someone to invite people from the congregation to our meetings.

In these early discussions, we had a spontaneous image of what sanctuary would mean—both from our knowledge of the sanctuary movement in the United States and of its history in the tradition in the churches. It would mean, or so we thought at that time, placing refugees at risk in a church so that they would be protected by the church. One of the lawyers in our group had explained that, under the new immigration bill C-86, the penalty for anyone engaging in offering sanctuary could be time in jail and/or a fine of several thousand dollars.

It was this briefly considered possibility that I discussed with Michael Creal, one of the most active members of the Church of the Holy Trinity. Michael, an engaging and articulate man, was a seasoned veteran of university and church politics. He was an Anglican priest, although he had spent most of his time and energy in leadership positions at York University from the moment of its audacious beginnings through to its rapid expansion and impressive consolidation. He was also the husband of my literary agent, Lee Davis Creal, and I knew that they were both committed to social justice with an unusual zest and humour.

"Would you come to one of our meetings?"

"Of course," Michael answered. "And then I'll talk to some of the others in the congregation."

Our discussion group widened and the conversation had barely begun when a series of events forced us to take action and to make a number of quick decisions. Sami, the Eritrean journalist, and the fundraiser received deportation notices. Sami was to be flown directly back to Ankara where he was sure he would be taken directly from the airport to a prison. The Eritreans were to be sent back to the United States through Niagara Falls because they had entered Canada via the U.S.A.

When our "Sanctuary Group"—for that was what we called ourselves by that time—discussed the situation, we felt that the decision must be left up to the refugees. However, the group asked me to tell them that we would try to protect them should they choose to ignore the deportation order and stay in Canada illegally.

I talked with each of the refugees. They were exhausted, afraid, yet amazingly resilient. This was not the first struggle they had known—nor would it be their last. They all decided that their only hope was that of remaining in Canada. For Sami, it was out of the question to go on a flight back to Turkey, where the persecution of the Kurds was even worse than when he had left it. The two Eritreans had already checked out their chances of being granted refugee status in the United States and had concluded that they were almost nil. "There was a chance when the Eritreans were fighting against the Soviet-sponsored regime of the Ethiopian dictator. But now that the Russians are gone, the U.S. doesn't really care. And now that Canada has refused us, we will have three strikes against us."

Sami said he would look after himself. "I'll just go on a little vacation and visit some Kurdish friends around the city," he winked. "How you call it—a mini-vacation. But it's too bad I'll have to quit my job." However, the situation of the two Eritrean families was far more difficult. In each case, there were five children—a large family to shelter and support financially.

I called some of the religious communities in the city who were known for their humane and generous spirit. The families were taken in almost immediately by different communities over the course of the summer while the Sanctuary Group tried to find something more permanent and to sort out a long-term strategy and solution for these people. Each of these religious communities was fully aware of the potential legal consequences of their hospitality to these families who were now classified as "illegals."

Money became a clear and pressing necessity. Fortunately, I had been invited to speak to a union group in the middle of that summer.

Putting aside my prepared speech on social justice, I spoke about the situation of these families and made a very reasoned and calm appeal for help.

There was no discussion. As soon as I had finished speaking, one of the union leaders, a massive man in jeans with a pack of cigarettes folded up into one of the sleeves of his black T-shirt, stood up and gave his assessment of the situation. "Those poor little shits are getting screwed by the motherfuckers. Let's give them a couple of thousand!" The vote was unanimous.

By the end of the summer, the two families were in a stable living situation. A parish in Hamilton had taken on the family of the Eritrean fund-raiser and had raised enough money to get them a lease on a modest apartment. The principal of a Catholic school, one of the members of the parish, enrolled the children in his school without requiring some of the usual immigration forms and a doctor, also a member of the parish, was looking after their medical needs. The father of the family would phone from time to time to see if there were any developments. "But don't worry about us here," he said. "We are in heaven here. These are good people. No one has ever welcomed us in this way."

The family of the Eritrean journalist found a home right in the middle of the city, near the corner of Yonge and Bloor. Their landlord and man for all seasons was John Masterson, the director of the nearby Jesuit Refugee House. A no-nonsense kind of guy from the Ottawa Valley, John's actions gave weight to his few words. He had been rather wary of the Sanctuary Group at first because he just didn't like meetings that were all talk. He didn't like meetings, period. But he had heard what was happening from the refugees in his house. He had read the letters which arrived from Immigration. "You don't have to be a rocket scientist to understand this," he said. "This is evil."

John eventually attended the meetings. At the end of one of them in the early fall, he walked with me to the subway station. "I think I've got a house for that Eritrean family," he said.

"A house? A whole house? That's great. How did you do that?"

"Well, I heard the Jesuits were moving out of this house near Yonge and Bloor and were going to rent it. So I went to the provincial and said, 'Eric, you know that house that's going to be free. I want to use it. But don't ask me what for and I won't have to tell you what for.' And Eric said that was fine and to go ahead and use it."

So John went and moved the family in and arranged for the kids, most of them teenagers, to attend a public high school through a teacher who was an old friend of his. He also took the father to a clinic to have his eyes checked, for the journalist was finding it more difficult to read.

In the many months to come, John and I developed a rather unusual working relationship. I became the front woman, as it were—writing and speaking about Sanctuary and about the needs of the refugees who were in hiding. I would collect the money and bring it with me to the time of prayer which we held every morning for fifteen minutes in the little garage-turned-meditation-room behind Romero House. John had also begun to join the Romero House volunteers for this time of prayer—for his own spiritual sustenance, for mutual moral support— and to collect the money for his family. We called him the bagman. He would pocket the envelope and deliver the money to the family, often pausing to sit and have tea with them, listening once more to their anxieties and concerns.

As our Sanctuary Group expanded, it began to snowball into a movement. We had issued no public statement and we were even unsure about how to do what we were already doing but we had a movement on our hands. We made contact or were contacted by groups in London, Hamilton, Fort Erie and Niagara Falls who had also concluded that they were being forced to take more radical action to protect the lives of refugees they knew were at risk. Once or twice, all of the sanctuary supporters from southern Ontario met when there was a large event or issue to deal with. However, our communications and decisions were usually done by fax or phone. For the group in Toronto, the meetings were now more regular and

frequent, a weekly event in the parish offices of the
Holy Trinity. Gradually the membership in the group
assumed the official title of the Southern Onta
Coalition.

The strength of the local Holy Trinity group lay in its simplicity. We
met every Wednesday morning at nine o'clock, unless we decided
otherwise. Our prayer was a moment of silence at the beginning of
each meeting. Then a one-hour meeting was directed by Michael
Creal. If there was nothing to discuss, we went home. We were
accountable to no one but ourselves, although we all shared the same
responsibility.

Driven by nothing but a sense of conscience and justice, endowed
with a remarkable range of experience and savvy and sustained by an
unusual sense of discipline, this was a group that would persist.

Quite simply, it is one of the most remarkable groups of people I
have ever worked with. In addition to Michael Creal, John Masterson
and Gwen Smith, there was Wilber Sutherland, the gifted director of
Imago and a man with a thousand connections, Floyd Honey, a
veteran of United Church politics, Ian Sowton, referred to by many
English students at York as the best teacher they ever had, and Alice
and Dan Heap, the unusual couple who worked as a team. She was
one of the wardens of the Church of the Holy Trinity and Dan had
recently retired as the member of Parliament for Spadina riding. Alvin
Wagner always made the coffee and never missed a meeting. Finally,
there was Joan Birkhoff who would take minutes of the meeting in
spite of her crippling arthritis.

Our goal was quite focused: we were committed to protecting the
lives of innocent refugees who would be in acute danger if they were
deported from Canada. We stuck to that goal; for four years we have
kept that one goal in sight. And we have been led along paths and in
directions that we could not have imagined in our worst nightmares or
wildest dreams.

In the beginning, one of our greatest problems was in our own
understanding of what *sanctuary* should mean. It should mean, we

..iagined, doing what American Christians had done: i.e., place refugees at risk within a church building. We banged the questions around the tabletop in the basement of the old building which housed the parish offices. But what if immigration officers came into the church and picked up the refugees? How did we know they would respect the sanctuary of the church? Someone informed us that officers had respected the sanctuary of a church in some instances but had intruded on it in other places. What if Immigration did nothing and the refugees were forced to live in the church for months, if not years? It began to dawn on us that the American model, which developed in the Southwest during the early 1980s, had depended on the possibility of moving Central American refugees from church to church up through the States until they reached the Canadian border and could claim refugee status here. But where would we, or could we, move refugees from Canada? To Greenland?

The imaginative breakthrough came when we remembered that there was another model of sanctuary in the history of the church, the model used by small Christian communities during the period when the enveloping shadow of Hitler was cast over Europe. At that time, some Jews were simply hidden in homes, in convents and monasteries until the war was over. That's what we realized we were doing. However, we also knew that although this was a time of struggle, it was not a time of war. We felt we owed it to the refugees to ensure that they could work and raise their families legally in a country which recognized their genuine need of protection.

The Sanctuary Movement in Tucson offered an important insight which seemed to fit our situation, and we made it our own. The Tucson group had come to the position that what they were doing was not civil disobedience, was not breaking the law. Instead, they were taking a civil initiative, which citizens are obliged and encouraged to do when their country is not following the law. We had become convinced that Canada was not honouring its international commitments to protect genuine refugees and so we had to take the civil initiative to protect these refugees until Canada's practice became more consistent with the international charters and conventions it had signed. This was the argument we were prepared to put forth in a court of law.

By October of 1992, the significance of sanctuary had taken on a new and compelling reality for me. Semira and Jamal had each received the brown legal-sized envelope, on the same day, with the decision of the Immigration and Refugee Board. They had been refused. "Therefore, the Refugee Division determines the claimant . . . and, perforce, the minor claimants . . . not to be Convention refugees."

Winkie Simpson, one of our board members, and I went over to be with them that evening. They bore their disappointment silently, moving around the kitchen in tandem as if to find some familiar and surer ground. I tried to offer some words of hope.

"We will appeal the decision immediately to the Federal Court. And if that doesn't work, we will make a humanitarian and compassionate application to the minister of immigration." Semira put some cloves and cinnamon into the pot on the stove and watched the water boil.

"We will not let you go. We will work until you are safe." Jamal watched the tunnels form in his curried rice in the pot on the other side of the stove.

"Why they say no?" asked Semira as she sat down wearily. "I no understand."

"They said they didn't believe Jamal," I replied. "They didn't believe there was a problem in Eritrea. They ignored the medical evidence which explained why it would be so hard for him to testify. They dismissed the information we had received from Amnesty International in London as being merely the opinion of a journalist and traveller rather than that of an international expert."

"But why?"

Once again Semira faced me and I had to confront what had happened. "I don't know why. Except . . . Maybe . . . They had to prove he was wrong, because if he was right about what happened to him in Eritrea, then many of their decisions since May 1991 have been wrong. He was really the first one to have direct experience of what was happening under the new regime."

"But why?"

There was nothing more to say and everything to do. Their lawyer, Belva Spiel, immediately launched an application for leave to appeal the decisions at the Federal Court. Since the appeal could only be made on questions of law and procedure, she could only refer to the way the panel members had ignored the medical evidence and the important report from Amnesty International. No new information could be directed to the court. It was a perplexing situation because, almost weekly, new information arrived about Eritrea which continued to confirm Jamal's story.

Belva prepared two separate but almost identical appeals which would be handled by two different judges in the Federal Court. A few weeks later we received the legal-sized brown envelopes from the court. Jamal's case had been rejected and Semira's had been accepted. No reasons were given for either decision. It meant that only Semira and the children could have their case taken to the Federal Court.

What had been unthinkable was now possible. Jamal could be deported even though the case of Semira and his children was still before the courts. I prepared a humanitarian and compassionate request and contacted the minister's office only to be told that all such decisions had been delegated to local officers in Niagara Falls. When I contacted the director of the hearings and appeals office in Niagara Falls, he said that he had no authority to stop deportation.

I contacted Rob Adamson at the office of the United Nations High Commission for Refugees (UNHCR) to ask if it would make an appeal to the minister on behalf of the Eritreans who had not received a full and fair hearing because so little information about their country's situation had been available. Rob said that the UNHCR representative could go to the minister with only three or four requests a year and that this limit had already been passed. I wrote Gordon Fairweather, the chairperson of the Immigration and Refugee Board, asking if a hearing could be reopened when new and significant information became available. No, he replied, there was no way.

I phoned Dorothy Davey, the deputy director of the Immigration and Refugee Board and the wife of Senator Keith Davey, and asked her if we could get together to talk about the dilemma posed by the new information about Eritrea. Over the next months, she and I would have breakfast together regularly at the Royal York Hotel. She was as frank and as fair as I had hoped she would be.

"The case of the Eritreans is classic," she said. "The system has no way of handling new and important information which arrives after a hearing. It's a shortcoming of the system and it distresses me greatly. We've got to find a way of addressing this injustice."

"Yes," I replied. "It's supposed to be handled through humanitarian and compassionate requests but the acceptance rate in that process is almost zero." I gave Dorothy my frank assessment of the situation. "For about a year the system has been in gridlock. No one seems willing or able to make a decision. The whole process is really just a make-work project for civil servants because it certainly doesn't do anything for the refugees."

Later, in 1993, I would see the statistics for post-claim reviews in Ontario. The acceptance rate was zero—absolute rejection. During that time all such decisions were being handled by the enforcement division of Immigration.

I asked Dorothy whether there was any possible course of action. "I can't see any way under the present legislation. The Immigration and Refugee Board can't reopen the case on the basis of new information. That's what I mean. It's a shortcoming."

The Great Wall—solid as it was stupid. A wall that seemed unconscious of what it was walling in and what it was walling out. I looked at that wall for a long time, searching for one small crack, a crack big enough for a person to slide through. But the system seemed immutable, shockproof. I needed to talk to someone who could walk through walls. I called June Callwood and outlined the situation of the refugees who were at risk. Is there someone, somewhere, I asked, who would listen to information that was a matter of life and death for a few people?

June didn't pause even for a moment. "I will call the prime minister. I have his personal phone number. I think he can be trusted on this kind of thing." She talked to Brian Mulroney that evening and called me back.

"He said it sounded serious and that he had some concerns about what was going on in the department. Marian Dewar, the mayor of Ottawa, had come to him about a refugee woman who was to be deported and he couldn't understand why the department had made that decision. He suggested that you send all of the documentation about the people you are concerned about to his office, to his executive assistant. He gave me his assurance that there would be a speedy and serious review of the files.

"I told him you people were getting desperate and were seriously talking about publicly declaring sanctuary." June went on to say that the prime minister had concluded the conversation by saying, "You see, the system works." To which she replied, "Sir, with respect, this isn't the way the system should work, that the person should need to call the prime minister to save lives."

The next evening Bernard Valcourt, the minister of employment and immigration, called me at Romero House during a break in an evening debate in the House of Commons to tell me that the prime minister had asked him to do a serious review of these cases and he would see to it that this was done. I phoned June to tell her that something indeed seemed to have happened and that there was now reason to hope. June was at that time taking a lot of public knocks for being the local "racist" at Nellie's Hostel for Women.

For the next few days I worked around the clock, assembling all the documentation about the Eritreans and Sami and the young Iranian man. In the midst of this, I realized that this was an unusual opportunity which would not come this way again, and so I called Vigil and Amnesty International to ask if they had any urgent situations which they wanted to piggyback onto our requests. Within a few days we had a package of twenty-three files, twenty-three human beings and their families, who were desperately in need of both justice and mercy.

I packed the files into a large black purse Semira had given me as a present and gave it to a friend who was going to Ottawa. He delivered it to my sister who was working in the offices of the Canadian Bishops and she personally delivered the files to the prime minister's executive assistant on November 26.

Throughout December and January we waited anxiously with the refugees. They knew, or thought, that their fate was being decided by the prime minister. Every day someone would phone. "Have you heard from His Excellency yet?" Throughout the informal network that refugees have, word got out that there was a list of names that had been sent to the prime minister. They had heard about it in their English classes, in lawyers' offices, at the Centre for Victims of Torture. People came to our office and to the offices of Vigil and Amnesty International, begging to be put on "the list." Again and again, we tried to explain that there was a difference between *difficulties* and *danger* and that the list was only for lives of those who were at risk. Of all the people who came in supplication, we found that we could only add one or two more names. The list itself varied only slightly from time to time as someone's appeal to the court was accepted, as someone was deported or as the case of someone in extreme danger was brought to our attention.

Although we had not yet heard from the Prime Minister's Office, we were hearing from local immigration officials at the removals units. They had sent removal orders to some of the refugees who were on the list. When I phoned one of these officials to suggest that it was improper to remove people when their files were being reviewed in the Prime Minister's Office, his only response was, "So what?" Only a flurry of phone calls to the office of the minister of immigration stopped these deportations.

As we discussed these incidents at our Wednesday morning Sanctuary meetings, a sea change began to happen in our perspective on the situation. Our original assumption, one which was widely shared by refugee advocates, was that the problem with the immigration system had everything to do with the Tory government. Bernard

Valcourt's evident stereotyping of refugees as gate-crashers and frauds had helped to consolidate this view. However, our experience was teaching us that the views of the political masters seemed relatively unimportant to the civil servants who, seeing refugee matters as their turf, resented any interference. As one civil servant at Immigration explained to me, "We own this place, the pols are just renters." The civil servants also seemed determined to undercut the Immigration and Refugee Board—a group of appointed civilians who had taken an important part of the refugee determination process away from the bureaucrats.

On February 26, there was a letter from Pauline Browse, a Scarborough MP who was the minister of state for employment and immigration, stating that thirteen of the people had been refused. She gave no reasons for these decisions, invoking the Privacy Act and the refugees' right to confidentiality. In fact, release of information forms, in which the refugees gave us permission to access all their information, had been included in all the files we had sent to Ottawa.

Although we did not know it at the time, Annette Gauthier, a senior official in the Case Management Division in the national headquarters in Hull, sent a copy of this letter of refusal to the removals unit in Niagara Falls. In her covering memo, dated March 16, 1993, she scrawled this large bold note: "Here is the letter we've all been waiting for. We *finally* managed to get a copy for our files. ENJOY."*

It seemed as if Pauline Browse had become the person we were now forced to bargain with. On March 26, Sister Mary Power and I met with her at the plush offices of cabinet ministers in downtown Toronto. It was the first time I had met Pauline Browse, a short, trim, blonde woman who had a number of stock political phrases to cover any and all situations: "At the end of the day a decision has to be made." Also present was Reinhard Mantzel, the director of Hearings and Appeals, or Enforcement, in Ontario.

---

* Obtained under Personal Information Request and Access to Information Request, August 1996.

Rather quickly, it became clear that Mantzel knew what was going on and Pauline Browse did not. Mantzel, a tall man with short-cropped hair, exuded cynicism. We explained to Pauline Browse that the prime minister had promised a serious review of the situation of twenty-three refugees. We elaborated on some of the information we had sent to the prime minister—information which she seemed to be hearing for the first time. We also expressed a particular concern over the fate of two families on the list who were scheduled to be deported on April 29. We objected to a deportation before their cases were reviewed. In addition, we made an appeal on behalf of the family of an Eritrean actor who were to be deported even though the husband's case was still before the Federal Court.

Pauline Browse seemed genuinely shocked when we told her that a family was to be separated. "But that's not our policy, is it?" she asked Mantzel. He did not reply. She instructed him to look into the matter.

After this meeting we tried desperately to contact the prime minister to stop these deportations, but he was in Europe. We phoned the office of Reinhard Mantzel to ask that the deportations be stopped until the prime minister returned from Europe. He did not return our calls but Kevin Sack, spokesperson for the Ontario Region, called us back to say all the deportations would proceed as planned.

TRIPS TO THE BORDER

Mary Power and I drove two families who had been on "the list" to the removals unit in Niagara Falls. It was a silent trip down to the border. The parents had tears in their eyes but tried not to show what they were feeling for the sake of their children. I tried to keep my eyes on the road.

Each family was loaded into a security van with bars on the windows and then driven across the Rainbow Bridge to American

Immigration on the other side. Very few people have seen the faces of refugees as they are being pushed into a security van—not the lawyers, not the panel members, not the politicians and not the bureaucrats in Immigration.

The picture on the cover of this book is a photograph I took as one of the women stepped into the security van with her son—who had been born in Canada and was a citizen. I will never forget her eyes. The husband of this woman and the father of this child was already inside the van with their other child. He was a leader in an Eritrean opposition group. He already knew that he had little, if any, chance of being granted asylum in the United States after he had been rejected by Canada. His plan was a risky one: to try to return to Saudi Arabia where he had been working before the Gulf War. However, he had no sponsor and no work permit to stay there and there was a good chance that he would be sent away from there too. I asked him to phone me from the airport in Riyadh. I never heard from them again.

One week later, a third Eritrean family was driven to the border. However, this family could neither stay in Canada together nor leave the country together. They had received a letter that Tzegha, the wife, would be removed with the two children even though her husband's appeal at the Federal Court was still under way and had every hope of success.

The family had been separated by the Eritrean-Ethiopian war and consequently the wife had arrived first with the two little girls, Dina and Lulu. Her claim was compromised by the combination of negligent lawyers and lack of information about the situation in the country, just as the claims of many other Eritrean women had been. The husband, Ytabarek, had arrived a little later by another route. He was a very well-known actor in Eritrea and a vocal and effective opponent of both the Ethiopian occupation and the new provisional government of Eritrea. By the time his hearing took place, the members of the Immigration and Refugee Board were willing to accept that an opponent of the provisional government of Eritrea would be at risk. However, the panel members wrote a negative judgement saying that the claimant "could probably seek safety in Ethiopia." Even before the judgement was written, the government of Ethiopia had said it would not automatically grant citizenship to Eritreans. Ytabarek's lawyer was confident that the appeal to the Federal Court would be accepted and that his wife and children would be allowed to stay.

Under the leadership of publisher Louise Dennys and writer Sandra Martin, PEN (the writers' organization that lobbies governments for freedom of expression and the release of political prisoners) had made a personal appeal to the minister of immigration on Ytabarek's behalf. However, the machinery of the enforcement section of Immigration had been set in motion and the facts seemed irrelevant to whoever was answering the phone or writing the orders. It seemed there was no alternative but to proceed with the removal in the hopes that Tzegha would be able to stay in Buffalo until the results of Ytabarek's appeal at the Federal Court were known. Mary Power and John Masterson offered to take the family to the bridge at Niagara Falls—where they would be separated.

At the end of a gruelling day, Mary Power struggled to tell me what had happened. Their journey to the border had been a quiet one. The heat of the car had eventually lulled the two girls to sleep—Dina in the arms of her mother, Lulu in her father's. No one broke the silence in the car except for rare whispers between man and wife. The tears quietly shed by Ytabarek and Tzegha said all there was to say. As for the two Canadians in the front seat, there was wordless shame, astonishment, disbelief that our country would treat people in this senseless manner.

Because Tzegha and her two small children were being deported, rejected as Convention refugees, they were to be at the office euphemistically called "hearings and appeals" at 9:00 a.m. on Lundy's Lane, Niagara Falls.

The group reached a low building in a small mall on Lundy's Lane. The children awakened, thirsty. Their father took them to buy something to drink. Their mother approached the door and entered. It was 9:30 a.m.

Tzegha spontaneously began to plead with the immigration officer behind the counter: "Why do you separate us? We came to Canada just to live in peace. Everybody said Canada was a good country. Why do you do this?"

Everyone sat down to wait for the security van which would take Tzegha, Lulu and Dina across the Rainbow Bridge to the American Immigration checkpoint. The children found games to play in the waiting room. It took them a while to discover the button that automatically opens the door for wheelchairs. Their parents sat stunned, silent. They quieted the children when their playful chattering grew too loud.

Lulu and Dina remembered some songs they had learned in school and began to sing, "I love you. You love me, we're a happy fa-mi-ly." Their father cried and hugged them. Sometimes he urged his wife to be brave, to be hopeful. They knew each other's heart was utterly burdened with despair, disillusionment, anger and fear . . . a great deal of fear.

From behind the desk came the announcement: "The van is ready." It was ten o'clock. Outside, Tzegha's luggage was being moved. No longer quiet tears. Ytabarek crushed the suddenly bewildered children in his arms. They went from mother to father to mother. "Daddy, what's wrong? Mommy, why are you crying? Where are we going, Daddy?" They tugged his coat, hugged his legs. They were lifted into the van by their mother, their father couldn't look, his face buried in his hands. But he couldn't help being drawn back to the van to embrace them again. To touch his wife—just to touch her.

The van moved away. The terrified look of the children, the realization: Daddy's not coming.

Ytabarek fell on his knees, his face again buried in his hands. He groaned aloud, "Oh God, where are you?" Shoppers coming out of the mall looked curiously and then with great gentleness at the man kneeling in the parking lot. The immigration officer looked down at the ground for a long time and then walked back into the office.

A few days after the removal of his family, Ytabarek began to write for the first time in years. He came to me with the pages he had written in Tigrinya and a translator. This is what he wrote:

My first book, *Who Will Rescue Us?*, was written in another time and place—in the midst of the Eritrean struggle for independence from Ethiopian dictators.

That was in 1972. Now, twenty years later, in Canada, the same question has welled up within me: Who will rescue my wife and children?

For the first time in years I have felt impelled to write—in a language not my own, with the help of friends who understand how words are born as the heart begins to die.

Many years ago, I fled a dictatorship but where can I go to escape the decision of Immigration Canada?

For people like myself, sometimes there is little difference between a dictatorship and a democracy: one system separates families by bombs and bullets and the other with computers and papers.

When they took my wife and children from my hands I felt my future had been taken. I lost all control. When the van disappeared over the bridge, I began to freeze and stood like a statue on the road. I wished it was a nightmare but it was not. It was real. They were gone.

When I returned to our apartment in the afternoon, I saw my daughter's toy lying on the floor. I picked up the toy and kissed it.

I went to the fridge to get a glass of water and saw my other daughter's bracelets lying on the counter. I went to the cupboard in the bedroom and saw the clothes my family had left behind. I wanted to talk to the clothes.

The furniture began to talk to me. Everything was talking in the silence.

My legs would no longer hold me up. I went into my daughters' bedroom and curled up on Lulu's bed with her toy. I became very small and curled up as people do when they are being born, or when they are dying.

Hours later, my wife phoned from the shelter in Buffalo. She had been kept waiting hours at American Immigration. I tried to encourage my wife, saying that we were working to get her a minister's permit so she could return to Canada while my case is pending. I am not sure how long they can live on hope.

I am forty-one years old. The best years of my life have been lost in political turmoil that was not of my making. I have seen too much of death and destruction, my body and spirit have been touched by terror and cruelty. I have wanted only a place to be, a place of peace in which to love my family and the world.

THE RESOLUTION TO RESIST

After what we had seen and heard during our journey with these three families, neither Mary Power nor John Masterson nor I felt we could participate in such a deportation again. We had crossed some kind of boundary within ourselves.

We phoned the constituency office of Pauline Browse and informed her assistants that immigration officers had deported two families on our list and had separated the other family—in spite of the promise of serious review. We said that we would go to her office on Friday, May 7, to talk about the remaining refugee cases that had been sent to the prime minister. We said we would not leave until we heard from Pauline Browse.

Mary, John and I arrived at the constituency office, on the second floor of a small shopping mall in Scarborough, as soon as it opened. We had brought food and coffee for the day, as well as a bundle of correspondence with Immigration which we needed to sort through. At first the two secretaries were rather polite and they even became quite friendly as the day progressed. We told them simply that we were waiting to see Pauline Browse. By five o'clock they told us that the minister was busy in Ottawa and would not be here and so we had better go. We said we would wait. The secretaries became more snarly. "Oh, for God's sake, this is ridiculous. We're going home."

"We're sorry to inconvenience you," said Mary politely, "but we did say we wanted to see Pauline Browse. We will wait."

One of the secretaries slammed the door to one of the office rooms and started shouting on the phone. A few minutes later two police officers arrived and told us to leave or we would be ticketed for trespassing. One of them looked at Mary and John and said, "You're not some of those Grey Panthers, are you?"

Mary said she wasn't but that she liked the Raging Grannies.

We received our tickets and decided to call it a day. Just as we were leaving, a fax arrived from Pauline Browse saying that yet more refugees on our list had been refused. No reason was given except to state that, in Canada's opinion, there were no human rights abuses in Eritrea.

When Brian Mulroney returned from Europe, June Callwood called him again to inform him of the situation regarding the people who had been referred to him. Once again he intervened personally and promised June that there would be a one-month delay in all deportations until a serious review could take place.

I had to address the Catholic Health Association of Canada in Ottawa on May 17, and I took advantage of the occasion to arrange to meet with officials in the Case Management Division regarding the situation of "the files." Bishop Remi De Roo offered to go with me out of concern for the people who were being so profoundly affected by the system. We took a taxi over to the large cavernous building called Place du Portage which housed the national headquarters of Immigration Canada across the river in Hull. You can see the Parliament Buildings from there.

The meeting was, to say the least, disconcerting. It was clear to Bishop De Roo and me that these men had not read the files we had come to discuss—and they were not even sure where they were. They seemed to disagree over how long a review of the files would take: one said it would take only a few days and could be done "over the phone" and the other said it could take a few months. We noted that the prime minister himself had asked that it be done within the month.

Hallam Johnston, acting director of Enforcement, admitted that there had been no clear mechanism for reviewing claims over the past year. However, he said that a new system would be in place soon.

"No clear mechanism for the past year." This was not news to us but we were shocked to think of the many people whose lives had been so profoundly affected by this situation.

The spring of 1993 edged towards summer and in spite of some correspondence with the acting director of Case Management Division, a man called Rob Vineberg, nothing had happened. There was, however, one important exchange with Immigration which was significant. I had faxed Rob Vineberg to ask for a list of documents that the department had received regarding the files we had forwarded to the prime minister. It had occurred to me that some of them may have been misplaced or lost.

On June 11, 1993, Rob Vineberg faxed a seven-page, single-spaced memo detailing every document we had ever sent to any department in the Canadian government: to the prime minister, the ministers, the minister of state, local immigration officers, etc. Nothing we had sent was lost or missing.

We were told by Case Management that a decision would be made after June 25, certainly by the end of July. By early August nothing had happened. Throughout this time I kept in friendly, courteous and consistent contact with Rob Vineberg. He explained the stress he was under, the time he had to spend with his wife who had just given birth to a new baby.

The anxiety of the refugees on the list had become almost unbearable for them and for us. Sami, the young Kurdish man, was covered with eczema and Jamal was now not sleeping at all. They saw it before I did. "But soon His Excellency Mulroney will be gone."

The Sanctuary Group began to think what had previously been unthinkable: the civil servants were trying to wait out Brian Mulroney. And indeed they did. He resigned and there was a new prime minister by the name of Kim Campbell. There was also another complete reorganization of Immigration. It was now transferred into a new ministry of public security to be headed by the Honourable Doug Lewis. The twenty-three files were in limbo.

It was as if we had walked out over the Ottawa River, desperately holding on to these twenty-three files, and the bridge between the Parliament Buildings and the headquarters of Immigration in Hull had suddenly disappeared beneath us. As we hung there, suspended in uncertainty, a hand was extended from another direction.

Archbishop Michael Peers, the Primate of the Anglican Church in Canada, had been quoted in the *Toronto Star* as saying that he was very concerned about some of the things that were happening in Immigration and was supportive of the efforts of the Sanctuary Group.

When Doug Lewis read the article, he was so upset by it that he personally called the Primate. The upshot of the conversation was that Michael Peers offered to host a meeting between the Sanctuary Group and Doug Lewis regarding the files.

Michael Peers' comments in the *Toronto Star* had not simply dropped from the sky—although they seemed almost heaven-sent. He himself had grown up in British Columbia and he remembered looking at a half-empty classroom when several of his Japanese school friends were interned in camps during the Second World War. He had also been kept fully apprised of the reasons for the Sanctuary Coalition's actions by the members of our group who had made every effort to keep ongoing communications with church leaders who were interested.

The meeting was to take place on August 4 at the national office of the Anglican church on Jarvis Street near Bloor. We had invited June Callwood to the meeting, as well as staff members of Amnesty International and Vigil.

The evening before the meeting Semira brought over a piece of *kitcha* bread and said, "God bless you." I had already folded a copy of one of her daughter's drawings into my purse: a small face with the tiniest of smiles with the words "I Live" written above it.

Rob Vineberg was one of the first to arrive at the meeting. We talked and he showed me the pictures of his new baby. Then the minister arrived with several other people accompanying him: officials from Ontario Immigration and his executive assistant, a young woman called Blair Dickerson. We introduced ourselves. I was, at that point, calm and confident.

Doug Lewis opened with some rather impressive statements about his desire and willingness to work with church groups such as ours. Then he said he would get to the point. He was, he said, happy to announce that he would accept one of the persons we had referred to the prime minister—a young woman who had refused to wear the chador in Iran. Nobody said anything. I thought I should say something. I opened my mouth and burst into tears. I just sat there and cried in front of those officials. I had never done that in my life in any public setting.

The faces of refugees came into focus. I remembered the names. I heard the echo of their voices, the stories they had told me. The mirror started to blur as I tried to catch sight of my neighbours.

But there were other voices speaking now. June and Michael Creal spoke eloquently about the purpose of ministerial discretion, about the minister's authority to administer justice when it was no longer possible within the limitations of the law. Alex Neve gave a thorough and reasoned explanation of the kind of background research which had gone into the decision to take these files most seriously.

Doug Lewis paused and then asked us to leave the room.

We waited in the corridor, shaken but still standing.

We would later learn more about what happened on the other side of the door from Brian McInnis, the director of communications for Doug Lewis. He had been one of the officials sitting silent and slouched down beside the minister and would later become the whistle-blower about the member of the Heritage Front who was employed by CSIS. Apparently, Doug Lewis looked at his officials and said, "These people are not crazy. We have to listen to what they are saying." The minister had been well briefed by his officials to be prepared for a bunch of crazies. It would not be the last time that there was a serious attempt to discredit legitimate concerns.

After a few minutes we were asked to return from the corridor and the minister said that he had instructed his officials to review the files again and to meet with us to give us reasons for their decisions. He also said that he would put a hold on all deportations until that was done. Blair Dickerson was to be our contact. He left with his people and we made a lot of noise in the hallowed halls of the Anglican Church House. I hurried home to tell Semira and Jamal and Sami, who was waiting in the office, his eczema spreading by the hour.

However, the next day, Rob Vineberg called to say that, unfortunately, the deportation letters had been sent out *before* our meeting with the minister. The letters arrived that day with crushing consequence. Two of the refugee families went into hiding and have not been heard of since. Jamal arrived at the Romero office with the letter in his hand, carrying it like a knife that had been pulled from his side.

I managed to contact Doug Lewis early the next morning, Saturday, at his constituency office. When I explained the situation to him, he was furious. He gave his personal assurance that there would be absolutely no deportations until the review was completed.

Over the next week or so, there was a series of negotiations regarding the shape and scope of the forthcoming meeting. Immigration officials seemed to think that the only purpose was to give us their reasons for their negative decision. Blair Dickerson, the political assistant, was of the opinion that a complete review would take place at the meeting.

In early September, two full days of meetings took place at the Toronto Diocesan offices of the Anglican Church. Members of our coalition were there, together with representatives of Amnesty and Vigil. Blair Dickerson, Brian Davis, the new director of Case Management, Reinhard Mantzel and Louis Rivietz of Enforcement Ontario attended.

We sat in square-table formation in a large room in the older wing of the church house. The meeting was the first time we would hear the reasons for the decisions made by Immigration.

The immigration officials appeared to be very well prepared. There was a new, colour-coded binder for each "case." However, once they launched into their reasons for rejecting each file, we realized that it was nothing more than a rewording of the original IRB decision. When we, in return, referred to documents we had sent in, we were told again and again, "We have no record of that document." No record of death warrants, medical reports, affidavits of identity, new information from news sources, photographs, the videotape of Sami in front of the Turkish Embassy.

No one apologized. No one wondered where the materials were. No one said it would have made any difference. Blair Dickerson was clearly appalled.

Yet, we all went out for a sandwich together at the local deli.

As we were sitting there eating and I was half-listening to Reinhard's asking if I knew about any fraud, the questions started to batter at the door of my mind. It was clear from Rob Vineberg's seven-page fax in May that all of these materials had been on file in May. Where had they gone by September? If they were only lost, could they ever be found again?

During these two-day discussions, the reasons given for the rejection of Sami would have bordered on the absurd if they were not so appalling. He had originally been rejected by the IRB because they felt he could return to Turkey and hide the fact that he was a Kurd; i.e., the Scot could speak like an Englishman. The immigration officials repeated this reason but added another reason which had been "filed" but which had never been disclosed to Sami or his lawyers. The officials said that it was obvious that he could return to Turkey because he had twelve brothers there.

I pointed out that there must be a typo because all of his documents clearly indicated that he had two, not twelve, brothers. I also noted that they had been sent documents showing that these two brothers had also fled Turkey and were now refugees in Bulgaria. What was even more disconcerting was that there seemed to be no record of the letters from Kurdish organizations, recent information from Turkey, photographs and the videotape of Sami's peaceful efforts to protest the Turkish cruelty towards his people.

We gave the officials copies of the materials they seemed to be missing.

As the meeting concluded, Blair Dickerson instructed the officials to take the files back to Immigration for yet another review. "I could do it myself," she explained to me, "but they've got to be brought along or there will be no long-term change." It seemed like a good idea at the time.

That was early September. The weeks dragged on. It was getting close to election day. Once again Sanctuary Group began to think the unthinkable. Was it possible that these officials were trying to, going to, outwait yet another minister? We asked June Callwood to call Blair Dickerson regarding the state of the files. What June learned was this: the immigration officials had just informed Ms. Dickerson that they had again said no to *all* the requests. She phoned me and said to me what she had said to June: "I was really shocked. I've asked that all the files be sent over so I can review them personally."

For Blair Dickerson, this was clearly an effort of conscience. Her boss was fighting for his political life and she was an important member of his campaign staff; she was going to be married the week after the election and would be leaving to live in France with her new husband. And she was tired.

In the final few days before the election, I talked daily with Blair Dickerson. She said she had been completely persuaded by the information regarding the Eritreans and that all of them would be accepted. And Sami, and several others. However, she said there were some others that she simply had not been able to resolve because the immigration officials had not sent them over from the department. They had run out of time.

They were not the only ones. Even as these refugees were getting a new lease on life, June Callwood's son Barney was fighting for his life in the hospital. An unexpected stroke on the operating table had placed her only remaining son in as dangerous a situation as any of the refugees she had so consistently tried to help.

I put down the phone from my conversation with Blair Dickerson, which had taken place just after suppertime, and ran down the street to the other Romero House where Semira and Jamal were living. The door was open in the fresh fall air and I ran in and hugged them both. "Welcome to Canada." The children looked at the three of us and the curious conversation we were having.

"What's the big deal? We're Canadians. So what's new?"

"Some day I will tell," said Semira, kissing her children one by one.

There were many celebrations, big and small, in Hamilton and Toronto in the following days as we managed to contact the fourteen individuals and/or their families who had been accepted.

When we met, as usual on Wednesday morning, the members of the local Sanctuary Group all felt that, together, we had done something good. Something very good.

LEGAL LIMBO

We weren't quite sure we would need to meet as often any more. But there was a nagging question as to what "acceptance" meant and what it would mean now that question had once again fallen back into the Immigration department. And there was that nagging little fact that there were still some people whose files were sitting unresolved on someone's desk in the department.

Each of the refugees who had been accepted received a letter, dated

October 27, 1993, from Brian Davis, the director of Case Management, saying, "It is the Minister's intention that you be landed provided you meet all the statutory requirements such as the security check and medical examination." That seemed clear enough.

We began to phone around to various immigration offices, trying to find out how those who had been accepted would get this minister's permit which would allow them to stay in Canada. As yet, none of these offices had any official document permitting them to stay. This meant it would become impossible for them to keep their children in school, to apply for a work permit so that they could work, to get medical care, etc. They had no legal document protecting them from deportation.

After many futile attempts, we finally heard from Tim Seburn, the senior immigration officer in Niagara Falls. It seemed possible that all the Eritreans would be processed through his office because they had entered Canada from that border area. He said that he had been instructed by Reinhard Mantzel at the end of October that he should not make any move on the granting of minister's permits. Perplexed, we called Brian Davis in Ottawa who promised that he would immediately write local immigration officers, instructing them to begin the process of granting minister's permits which would give people legal status in Canada until they received their landed papers. Tim Seburn said that he had received the letter but that the process of issuing the permits could take several months.

Sami, however, had decided that nothing ventured, nothing gained. One month after he received the letter from Brian Davis, Sami walked up to a wicket at the Etobicoke Immigration Centre, presented the letter and asked for a minister's permit. The document, allowing him to stay in Canada for one year, was issued in fifteen minutes.

"What's your secret strategy, Sami?" I asked.

"I guess I'm a very handsome guy. Or maybe they think I am rich and famous. You know, the young and the restless." He blushed with the thought of his own audacity.

Everyone else waited. The letter from Brian Davis was their only evidence of any assurance that they would not, could not, be deported. It seemed enough to go on. However, shortly before Christmas, three of the families that had been promised minister's permits were told that they had been cut off welfare. When we contacted the regional welfare office we were told that Immigration Ontario had stated that the families were on a removals list and would soon be deported.

We contacted Brian Davis and Hallam Johnston, the new head of Enforcement in Ottawa, and threatened to go to the press. In the next few days, the refugees received letters saying their permits would be processed at the beginning of January. They were also told that each family would have to pay approximately fifteen hundred dollars, a fee similar to that paid by those in the immigrant stream. This was our first indication of the scale of the new immigration fees, though it was only some months later that the "head tax" was announced. This fee was an impossible economic burden for either the refugees or the Sanctuary Group to carry.*

They would be removed to the United States, it was explained, and then let back in again with a minister's permit. In "immigration circles" this is usually called the "shuffle." It allows the department to save face by saying that there were never any mistakes and so the person can be removed. However, they will be let in again because of the compassion of the government. It usually means a ride in a security van across a bridge and back again.

Jamal received a letter saying that he could obtain a permit, if he paid, but that they could not issue one for Semira and the children because the department "had no record of their existence." I phoned the officer and said that they certainly existed and that they had been mentioned in every document sent to Immigration. The issue was resolved but not without another day of distress for Jamal. Semira and I joked about this one. "I will put you all in a big box marked File and

---

* This policy was criticized by the United Nations High Commission for Refugees in late 1995. Canada is the only country in the world to impose a head tax on refugees. The fee is the same as that for investor immigrants.

take it in a truck to the immigration office. I will bring it to the officer at the wicket and you can all jump out of the file and say, 'Surprise. Here we are!'"

We had to cancel the January appointments because no one had the money to pay for these additional fees—especially since they had not been able to get work permits. The next two months were spent in a desperate effort to raise this seemingly impossible amount of money.

Finally, the great day arrived. It was spring, it was April and more than the usual seemed possible. We loaded all the Eritrean families into the Romero van and two cars. The immigration officials had informed us that all the children had to come and be taken over the bridge in the security vans. Members of the Sanctuary Coalition had volunteered to go in order to assure the refugees that they would be quite safe. We believed there was no cause for concern.

We had to leave one family, that of the Eritrean journalist, behind because immigration simply could not find their files.

It was a very quiet drive down to Niagara Falls. Although the children did not really know what was going on, they seemed apprehensive. I drove into the shopping mall, thinking that this would be a more happy occasion than usual.

The paperwork in the office took about an hour as each family presented its papers and paid the required fees. The adults were serious and formal as they counted out their money with the female immigration officer who had been placed in charge of this shuffle. Then they were told to proceed outside and wait for the security vans.

Four dark-coloured vans, with their bars and grates seeming more noticeable than usual, pulled up into the parking lot. Everyone shrank. Some of the children clung to their mothers' legs. I could see what they saw. How could they know for sure that this wasn't a trick.

"Don't worry," I said. "We will be right behind you in our van. Here, let me help you get in and here's some peanuts for the kids." Slowly they began to move into the seats.

"You know," I said to the immigration officer, "we could just drive them over and you could follow us."

"No," she replied. "I understand what you're saying but it's against regulations."

The van doors snapped shut and the children pressed their faces against the window. The caravan moved slowly towards the bridge past all the bars and boutiques in Niagara Falls which catered to the enduring belief in romance and happy endings. Finally we reached the other side and the kids poured out.

The American officials started the paperwork to verify that these people had been removed to the U.S.A. and the Canadian officer proceeded to fill out the papers saying they would be let into Canada because of the compassion of the government. However, shortly after they had started, we were informed that we would have to wait a few hours as the mainframe of the Canadian immigration computer system was down. We were told that it happens all the time, we would just have to wait a while.

There was a billboard just outside the office. "Niagara Falls, U.S.A. Once you've been here you'll never really leave."

Everyone tried to make the best of it. Michael Creal and Dan Heap took the kids to see the falls. Joan Birkhoff chatted with the women about some of her overseas experiences. I went to get a lot of hamburgers—for the families, for the immigration officers, for anyone who was hungry.

Jamal had withdrawn completely into a corner and into himself. He held one of his daughters on his lap and counted her fingers again and again. We all wondered. I looked across the river at Canada and saw it for the first time as it must seem to many refugees—within reach. The border called hope.

At the end of the afternoon we were told that the computer was up and operating. A Canadian immigration officer came to the desk and called out the name of each family and gave them the brown pieces of paper which were the minister's permits they had been promised six months earlier.

"Let's get out of here," said Michael. It seemed as if everyone raced for the security vans and we were off and we were over the bridge and we were out in the parking lot and they were all running towards our vehicles.

"Thanks," I said to the officer who had seen us through.

"Well," she said as she shook her head. "I've just never seen anything like it." And she smiled.

On the ride home the kids sang "O Canada" about fifty or sixty times and then launched into "Ninety-nine bottles of beer on the wall." But Jamal didn't sing. He was still some place very far away.

The assumption of the Sanctuary Group and the refugees it was working with was that the permits were to serve as an interim bridge until the papers for landing could be issued. However, one year after Blair Dickerson had phoned to say that fourteen people had been accepted, seven people had still not received any permit at all, there had been no action from the department on those who had and Sami's permit was close to running out. He walked into the office in Etobicoke again and paid another five hundred dollars to have the permit renewed.

In January 1994 we had arranged to meet with the new minister of citizenship and immigration, Sergio Marchi. We had remained concerned about the files that had been withheld from Blair Dickerson, about those who had not yet received permits. And, after a great deal of serious reflection, and discussion with immigration researchers, we were beginning to conclude that Immigration was essentially beyond the control and direction of any political or civilian accountability. Unlike any other government department, it had been run for years by "lifers," by civil servants who had not moved laterally or up in any other department. We were also concerned about the persistent perplexities of both the importance and irrelevance of "files" to immigration decision-making. At times, it seemed that all the absurdities and cruelties that had resulted from lost or incomplete files could be chalked up to an ineffective information system. At other times, the chaos seemd like deliberate obfuscation.

Sergio Marchi had a well-deserved reputation as a hard-working and feisty advocate on immigration and refugee questions. We had looked forward to the meeting which was to take place in his constituency offices in the far end of North York. From the very outset of the meeting he seemed aggressive, but as a defensive stance. Perhaps we had brought too many people to the meeting. Perhaps it was the issues we were raising. We had asked for a public inquiry into Immigration Canada.

"There's no way I'm going to have a public inquiry and have my officials paraded in public," he said. "I'm not going to open that can of worms."

He gave us a lecture on the weaknesses of every institution. "Look, I'm a Catholic. Just because there are problems with some priests doesn't mean I'm not loyal to the institution." He promised to check on the situation of the refugees who had not been referred to Blair Dickerson. He talked a lot and reminded us of his track record.*

The coalition decided to write the deputy minister, saying that court action would be taken unless some attempt was made to honour the minister's intention. The deputy minister, Peter Harder, then appointed Michael Malloy, the new director of the Ontario Region to see that the matter was resolved as soon as possible. The Sanctuary Group had a meeting at York University with Malloy and some of his assistants. There was, as they say, a frank exchange of views. However, no one in our group doubted the integrity of Malloy and his sincere desire to settle the whole matter.

The phone calls and faxes continued, this time to an assistant at the office of Michael Malloy. By April 1995, a year after the cavalcade to Niagara Falls, there was not a landing paper in sight. A few days before the minister's permits were to expire, the six Eritrean families

---

* In a May 4, 1994, letter to the Sanctuary Group, Sergio Marchi attempted to address some of the concerns that had been expressed in the January 1994 meeting. The letter obviously reflected the perspective of senior officials in Immigration and it raised more questions for the group than it answered. There were no further meetings with Sergio Marchi.

were told to renew their medical, get new photos and take all of this to the immigration office in Scarborough. For some of the families this meant a few hundred dollars. Again.

Our little Wednesday Sanctuary Group had become more, not less, concerned about the situation of refugees in Canada since its haphazard beginning. Consistent reflection and fidelity to particular human beings had sharpened its analysis of the state of the country. It seemed increasingly obvious that "outsiders" were becoming scapegoats for the economic and social upheavals being generated by vast global forces that only certain people seemed to control and benefit from. Forces that were generating real fear among many people who felt increasingly powerless. Transnational economic corporations and global communications networks seemed to move beyond any national borders with ease, obliterating familiar boundaries. Yet, many national borders were becoming increasingly closed to any human beings who were seen as strangers and aliens. Refugees were becoming the scapegoats in the new global order.

In addition, we had been led slowly but inexorably to the conclusion that the immigration system in Canada was functioning like a state within a state. Within this separate state, a form of segregation or legal homeland for non-citizens, "refugees have few of the legal protections enjoyed by Canadian citizens: the police and immigration officials serve as enforcement, trial judge and appeal. Reasons need not be given for decisions. Equal and consistent treatment is not required. The outcome of many procedures is uncertain. Legal safeguards may not be there when a person needs them."*

It seemed important for the various faith communities to speak out in the name of the only values which can and should hold human beings and nations together. It seemed appropriate on the fiftieth anniversary of the end of the Second World War.

* cf. The Interchurch Church Committee for Refugees, "It's Time to Extend Canadian Justice to Uprooted People: A Discussion Paper," (Toronto: October, 1995).

Largely through the gentle pushing and finesse of Wilber Sutherland, a member of the Holy Trinity Sanctuary Group, representatives of every major faith community in Canada came together to sign "A Call to Conscience"* in which they committed their various communities to a process of education and action on behalf of refugees. It was an historic event. For those gathered at the Church of the Holy Trinity on that day, it was a time of reclaiming dignity and integrity in a mean and ugly time.

By June 1995, another difficulty had surfaced and it related directly to Semira and Jamal. She had won the right to appeal to the Federal Court and that right had remained a possibility as long as the family was not landed, but now the court had set a trial date for the beginning of September. Belva Spiel, their lawyer, had delayed the appeal as long as possible by not filing certain documents, thinking that it would be a complete waste to go through an entire appeal process involving three Federal Court judges and lawyers from the Department of Justice if Jamal had been promised landing papers.

Both Belva and I called Malloy's office to inform them of the impending court date and to ask that the matter be resolved over the summer to avoid the unnecessary time and expenditure. By mid-August the matter was not resolved and the lawyers for the Justice Department (representing the minister of immigration) decided that the case was to proceed. Belva proceeded to complete her arguments which had already been filed: that expert medical evidence had been ignored and insufficient weight had been given to the expert testimony from Amnesty International.

Three days before the court date, the lawyer from the Justice department called Belva to say "Justice has conceded"—meaning that their lawyers would not defend the case against the Justice Department because they knew they could not and/or should not win. Then the lawyer said to Belva, "What can I say? We read all the

*The text of "A Call to Conscience" is appended to this book.

documents and the transcript of Semira's hearing and saw what happened. It was a travesty of justice."

It was a small but important victory, an independent confirmation of what we had been arguing for years. It enabled Semira and Jamal to continue to hope that justice would prevail in Canada.

CATCH-22

Months rolled by and the negotiations continued regarding the landed status of Semira, Jamal and the other families. The prolonged delay was affecting the refugees in many ways: for most it meant that it was virtually impossible for them to get a job because every employer who examined their documents saw that they had been classified as "temporarily in Canada." It was a continual struggle for them to get even basic medical coverage and they had to pay an annual fee of fifty dollars to send each child to school. It meant that they could not enrol in any significant job-training program. Sami, who had partially finished a business logistics course and had a job waiting upon completion, was told that he had to pay a foreign student's fee of nine thousand dollars or he would be unable to complete the program. Most important, it meant that some would be unable to sponsor children who were in desperate conditions.

They had all been living in legal limbo for three years. Now a new wrinkle surfaced that threatened to develop into an insurmountable hurdle. The immigration official handling their process had said that they had to meet all the requirements that "regular" immigrants did. They had passed all the requirements except that of being self-supporting. It was a catch-22 situation: they needed to be landed to get a job but they could not be landed until they got a job. The officer designated to handle the process for the Ontario Region had consulted national headquarters on the issue and Michael Malloy had replied to us that, although they had tried to be flexible, they were bound by the Immigration Act to proceed in this way.

Sami began to consider a hunger strike to protest the delays which were preventing him from completing his training and going to work. The Eritrean journalist had still not received any official documents whatever—not even a minister's permit. His two oldest children had been accepted at universities and had been unable to attend for two years.

It was at this point that the Sanctuary Group began to discuss seriously the possibility of challenging the policies and procedures of Immigration Canada in the light of the Constitution, Charter of Rights and international law. It was becoming clearer that while there may be problems within the department, there were also problems with the Immigration Act if there was no reasonable way for the department to address mistakes it had made in handling the cases of particular refugees. While we kept our eyes on this long-term project, we did not lose sight of the needs of the individuals we were trying to help get on with their lives.

We noticed that one of the refugees who had received his landed papers rather quickly had been on welfare at the time and that two others who were landed had been only partially self-supporting. This inconsistency was noted in a letter to the office of Michael Malloy. By this time, both Jamal and Semira were working at part-time jobs.

This may have been the crack that became a doorway. In an e-mail dated July 2, 1996, Julie Wassif-Suleiman, assistant to Michael Malloy, wrote to P. McCann, C. Smith and G. Edkertt (managers at various immigration centres), "Leddy had raised the issue of whether we applied the usual rules to the three persons we have landed—a point I was hoping she wouldn't make."*

Semira and Jamal received a letter to go to the immigration office in Etobicoke on August 27 with their children to pick up their landed papers. Neither of them was sure what to expect or hope for anymore, but they dressed their children especially for the event. Amir wore his

---

* Obtained under an Access to Information Request and Personal Information Request.

T-shirt with the Canadian flag. I wanted to let them take this last step on their own.

The interview was not what they had expected. The female immigration officer scowled at them when they entered. "Are all of these your children?"

"Yes," Semira said proudly.

"That's a lot of children."

Then she scowled at Jamal. "You are a big man. You should be ashamed of yourself. You should be working." The four oldest children looked down and Muzit started to giggle.

"And you boys," she pointed to Amir and Nesredin, ages eleven and twelve, "you should be working too."

Semira interrupted. "If you could tell us where there is a job, I would work at two jobs morning and night and so would my husband."

"You listen to me. The taxes my husband and I pay are supporting you."

This was their welcome to Canada. However, it dimmed their joy only slightly. They held a party in their little house for all the friends who had helped them during their long five-and-a-half-year struggle to stay in this country. Lorne Howcroft made a moving speech for all of us: "You have brought so much to this community and to this country and we have all admired you greatly as human beings and as parents."

Jamal smiled and wiped away the tears. Semira struggled for some words. "We are rich with our friends in Canada. Money is not important but friends are. They are everything. When I left Saudi Arabia I thought I was going to the end of the world and I wondered who I would meet. . . . My friends are my Lotto 649."

As I walked with Semira to the porch she said, "You know, the immigration lady was very tough. Why she have to say this in front of children?"

I was determined not to let this so-called representative of Canada diminish this moment of hope and joy. "Semira, you have already made an enormous contribution to this country. You have brought five wonderful children. You must never forget that and never let this country forget that children are its most priceless resource, its greatest hope. And you have brought hope and courage. These are priceless."

THE PAPERWEIGHT

For Natan and Svetlana, our family from Minsk, obtaining a work permit was the essential first step in applying for landed status. They had obtained the expert medical opinion that they needed a climate such as Canada's in order to remain healthy because of their exposure to radiation. They had valid identity documents and had a good grasp of English. In addition, Natan was a highly skilled craftsperson. What happened to them is but one example of how people can be crushed by paper.

In November 1993, Natan applied for a work permit even though it was still government policy that refugee claimants could not work. He had received three job offers from companies which specialized in the restoration of historic buildings and did not want to stay on welfare. The application form did not ask for a medical or a fee. At the end of the month, Natan received a letter from Canada Immigration Centre (CIC), in Toronto on University Avenue, saying that he was not eligible for a work permit "until you have a hearing."

In January 1994, the government policy changed to allow refugee claimants to work if a work permit was paid for. At the beginning of that month, Natan again applied for a work permit at CIC Toronto. No money was requested in the application form. Natan indicated that he had taken a medical on May 7, 1993.

In February Natan received a response from CIC Toronto saying that the work permit could not be issued until "you and your dependents in

Canada have been medically examined." He sent a copy of his medical examination to CIC Toronto with another application form.

On March 3, 1994, Natan received a reply from CIC Toronto saying that the permit could not be issued until he sent a fee of two hundred dollars by certified cheque (to cover cost of work permit for him and his wife) and until the "results of the medical examination had been received by the immigration officer." The response indicated that there was no problem with photographs and fingerprints.

Natan went immediately to the University Avenue CIC office and asked where the medicals should be sent. He was given an address in Ottawa and told that it would take two months to process the medical and that he could apply again at that time. He sent the originals of the medicals to the Ottawa address.

In May 1994, Natan received a letter from the office for immigration medicals in Ottawa saying that the X-rays were missing. Natan immediately sent the X-rays to Ottawa. He also contacted his doctor to see if there was any problem and the doctor said the X-rays were completely clear. Natan phoned the immigration telecentre in Toronto several times to try to find out if the medicals had been processed yet.

In early July 1994, Natan sent a new application form for a work permit to CIC Toronto. He included in this application: a copy of the registered letter certificate indicating that the X-rays had been sent to Ottawa in May 1994 and a certified cheque for one hundred dollars. At this time, his wife was studying and wanted to complete her courses before working.

In the latter part of July 1994, Natan received a memo from Immigration Canada, Vegreville, Alberta, indicating that his application for a work permit had been received there on July 19, 1994. The memo said he would hear in four weeks.

On August 12, 1994, Natan received all of his application package back from Vegreville—except for the certified cheque. The memo from CIC Vegreville said that he had not sent in the correct amount of money. "The correct fee for your application is $125. You submitted $100 . . . an additional $25 is required." Apparently, the fee structure had changed since Natan's original application. That same day Natan immediately sent a certified cheque for twenty-five dollars to CIC Vegreville—in addition to his entire application package, which was sent once again.

On August 15 and August 22, faxes were sent from Romero House to the client service unit at CIC Vegreville, urging some action on the request for a work permit. One of his employers was still holding a job open for him.

On August 23, a woman from CIC Vegreville called Romero House to say that, according to the computer, the work permit had been delayed because of an incomplete medical. A fax was sent to CIC Vegreville that same day, indicating that the medicals of Natan and his family and the X-rays had been sent to Ottawa in March and May of 1994 and that proof of postage was included. The name of the examining doctor was included in this fax. The next day Natan had a fax sent to CIC Vegreville stating that he had contacted his doctor regarding the medicals. She said that she had never received any notification from Ottawa indicating that there was a problem with the medicals.

On September 13, 1994, Natan received a memo from CIC Vegreville indicating that the "application for employment authorization" had been received on August 29. Presumably this was the application sent with the cheque for twenty-five dollars. The memo indicated that he would be receiving a response within four weeks.

Then, on October 20, 1994, Natan received a form memo from CIC Vegreville indicating that the work permit could not be issued until "you have been fingerprinted" and "you and your dependents in Canada have been medically examined." A handwritten note on the form read: "Advised by immigration medical assessment unit in Ottawa that your medical expired before you completed the requirements."

Over the next few days Natan's wife phoned the immigration tele-centre in Toronto and tried to find out where to get forms for the new medical examination. After several phone calls, the receptionist said the medical forms would be sent in the mail. They did not arrive. At that point, the couple sought the assistance of their local member of Parliament, Jesse Flis (High Park). Flis and his assistant said they would fax Vegreville immediately. Two months passed and the medical forms had still not arrived.

On January 2, 1995, Natan called immigration telecentre again and asked that the medical forms be sent. The receptionist said that she would see a request form was sent to obtain the medical form. On January 5, 1995, the request form arrived and Natan filled it out the same day. That same day, Romero House faxed Etobicoke Immigration to ask the program specialist there to ensure that a medical package was sent to Natan. Four days later, Svetlana and Natan went to the immigration office in Etobicoke to see if they could obtain the medical forms. They explained their situation to the immigration officer. The matter was discussed for two hours. The officer did not want to give them the medical forms. The couple kept showing her the letter from Vegreville. The officer said the medical couldn't possibly be expired. Finally, the couple got the forms and were fingerprinted. The officer said that they would have to wait at least two months for the medicals to be processed in Ottawa.

The couple and their son had their medicals again on January 18, 1995, paying $260.00. The medicals were sent by the doctor on January 25, 1995.

During the month, David Walsh, the president of Wharfside Properties Ltd., who had wanted to hire Natan, sent faxes to the immigration offices in Vegreville and in Toronto. He stressed that his job offer still held and that it was a matter of urgency. Mr. Walsh also contacted two members of Parliament about the situation. He expressed his view that such delays were a waste of taxpayer dollars as the family could have been off welfare months ago. At the same time, Father Massey Lombardi and I contacted Father Kevin Lynch in Edmonton to ask him to see Judy Bethel, the member of Parliament for the Vegreville area, to try to get something done. Father Lynch did so. Judy Bethel was astounded when she saw the chronology of Natan's attempts to get a work permit and promised to do what she could.

On January 23, 1995, I went to CIC Toronto. I had tried to get through to the office by phone for several days but to no avail. When I reached the wicket, I asked to speak to a manager. Finally, a young woman came to the desk and I asked if Natan could have an appointment to get a work permit. She, in turn, asked the manager. The manager said that appointments could only be made by telephone, and that they did not issue work permits for emergencies.

On January 25, 1995, David Walsh got through on the telephone to CIC Toronto and said that this work permit was a matter of urgency. The officer he talked to said her number was 6104. He was told that only Natan could make an appointment and that he should call himself and ask for worker 6104. Natan and Svetlana called the immigration telecentre that day and asked for worker 6104. Natan was told that he could not ask for specific workers and he had to take whoever answered the phone. The person who answered the phone said he would have to wait another two months and would have to fill out another form and that there was no faster way.

On February 18, 1995, David Walsh sent a letter to the auditor general complaining about the wastage of taxpayer money in this whole process. Four days later, Natan received a letter from Immigration Canada with a sealed envelope inside. The letter said that the sealed envelope must be given to his doctor. Natan then went to the doctor with the envelope. The letter inside was a simple request for a TB skin test. On February 27 the results of the TB skin test were positive and the results were sent to Ottawa. The doctor explained to Natan that everyone from the former Soviet Union tested positive because everyone there had been immunized against TB and thus had been exposed to the germ. "Everyone in immigration medicals knows this," he said. The doctor said that Svetlana and their son, Sasha, would also test positive if the test was taken. The doctor pointed out that Natan's chest X-rays in January were completely clear.

On April 3, Svetlana sent in an application for a work permit together with a money order for $125.

On April 10, David Walsh received a reply from the office of the auditor general, L. Denis Desautels, saying:

> I am very concerned about the particular case of [Natan/Svetlana] as described in your letter. This situation raises serious questions on the procedures followed by the Department in processing work permits. . . . Since receipt of your letter the audit team responsible for Citizenship and Immigration has undertaken a review of this particular case with officials of the Department, as well as the systems and practices in place to ensure timely processing of work permits.

Natan received a letter from Vegreville, dated April 18, saying that his medical was incomplete. The letter also said: "Please note that you will also have to submit $125 cost recovery as the money orders you submitted in 1994 are non-refundable as your application for an employment authorization was refused at that time."

Svetlana's kit was returned together with the $125. The letter said:

> We are unable to process your application for an employment authorization because you are required to provide a letter of offer of employment in order to be eligible for an employment authorization. . . . Also in your application you state your son [Sasha] is ten years old. If [Sasha] is planning on attending school you must apply for a student authorization for him to do so."

This would mean an additional fifty dollars. The letter was unusual in that it was not another form letter but one composed distinctly for Svetlana.

On April 24, the doctor sent a note to the immigration medical assessment unit indicating that the results of the TB skin test had been sent by UPS courier to Ottawa on March 1. The doctor explained that all members of the family would certainly test positive, as did all people from the former Soviet Union.

The next day, Natan received another letter instructing him to take the sealed envelope inside to his doctor. Inside was a directive for Natan to take a sputum smear for TB to be incubated for six to eight weeks and to repeat a chest X-ray before and after the sputum test. At this point, Svetlana "lost it." She threw up her hands and began screaming. "By the time we get accepted in this country we're both going to be mentally retired."

Natan went to have the sputum test that day but the doctor told him that he could not take any more X-rays. People who had been exposed to high levels of radiation during the Chernobyl disaster, he said, were not to have more than one X-ray a year. That same day, Svetlana sent her application back to Vegreville together with the letter of a job offer. Two months later, she received the permit. Fortunately, the employer had been willing to wait for her services.

However, on April 25, there had also been a letter from an immigration officer who had reviewed their request to stay in Canada as members of the post-determination refugee claimants in Canada class. The request had been refused. The officer referred to the medical report of Dr. Bertell and wrote: "I do not question her credentials in that field. . . . I accept that the family were exposed to radiation. . . . In Dr. Bertell's letter, she indicates that 'the effect of thermal sensitivity after radiation exposure is well documented in the literature. . . .' I accept her statement in this regard." But, the officer gave this as the reason for rejecting the request: "There is no objective evidence before me to indicate that the family sought medical attention in Israel for their ailments related to their exposure to radiation."

I immediately wrote the officer who had written the negative judgement and said that there were, in fact, boxes of medical reports regarding the family's condition in Israel and that these had been available to Dr. Bertell. I offered to send these medical records on immediately. The officer never replied to this offer.

Natan did not have a work permit and the family was running out of time. They had to apply as immigrants on humanitarian and compassionate grounds or they would be removed from the country. In desperation, I made an appointment in late May to see Member of Parliament Mary Clancy who was then the parliamentary secretary to the minister of Citizenship and Immigration. I had sent her a chronology of Natan's efforts to get a work permit and of the impasse which had been reached because of the request for three X-rays in one year. I told her that Natan still had a job offer if he could ever get the work permit.

Generous and direct, Mary levelled with me. "When I received this package of information, I called over to the department and asked why they had not accepted this family on humanitarian and compassionate grounds. You know what they said? They said this man had shown no evidence of having made a serious effort to get a job." Her conclusion was: "Something stinks."

Through the diligent efforts of the staff in Mary Clancy's office, Natan and Svetlana did receive acceptance, in principle, to stay in Canada on humanitarian and compassionate grounds. The date was September 6, 1995. They are still waiting for their landed immigrant papers. In October 1995, Natan received a work permit for two years. By that time, his job at Wharfside Properties had been completed by others. However, he has been able to find work with several other companies.

THE PAPER CURTAIN

Joseph and Adèle and their three children were literally dumped on our doorstep. A "scooper" at the border had promised them the sky—and a place to live—if they would just let their refugee claim be handled by a certain lawyer. One of our volunteers arrived home to find the family waiting with their baggage on the front porch. The scooper was long gone.

Fortunately, we had some room at the time and we soon persuaded the family that the scooper was doing them no favours. Joseph and

Adèle got the picture quickly. He was perceptive, even savvy, and she had a quiet wisdom about her. Tall and almost regal, they were Tutsis who had fled the conflict between the Hutus and Tutsis which had engulfed Rwanda and had already claimed the lives of over 100,000 people in Burundi.

Their three children soon reigned over the old house on Keele Street. There were days when I was startled by the fresh energy and innocence of the children and I would blink with the realization that had they stayed in Burundi they could have been hacked to death with machetes.

The genocide in Rwanda had been widely reported in the media during April 1994. Less well known was the ongoing conflict within Burundi. However, the Immigration and Refugee Board members seemed well-informed about every aspect of the tensions which were tearing apart all the countries in the region. The lawyers representing claimants from Rwanda and Burundi said that the IRB panel members had been careful, considerate and even respectful in their handling of such cases. I assumed that the refugee determination process would proceed rapidly and positively for Joseph and Adèle.

Although they spoke French fluently, they began to learn English and were at the heart of the warm community which developed that year in the house. Their laughter became more frequent and their eyes lifted and smiled. Joseph began to limp more but said it was "no problem." He said he would get his knees fixed after the hearing. Apparently Joseph had been a superb athlete, the star of the national soccer team in Burundi, until his motorcycle accident. He had swerved to avoid hitting two children and the cartilege in his knees had been severely damaged. "No problem."

But Adèle had a problem. "Only one," she said. "Her name is Antoinette." She was Adèle's younger sister and had lived with Joseph and Adèle after they were married. "She is like our daughter," explained Joseph. "We want to get her away from danger."

As far as I knew they could only sponsor their own children. "But she has a sponsorship already," said Adèle. She went on to explain that a small parish in Quebec City had applied two years earlier to sponsor Adèle and some of her brothers and sisters. Adèle's brother, a member of the parish, had been living in Quebec City for some time and was already a Canadian citizen. The parish had agreed to cover the living expenses of the family members until they found jobs.

When the situation in Burundi began to disintegrate, Adèle had made an appointment with a Canadian immigration officer who had come to Burundi from the Canadian High Commission in Nairobi. When Adèle explained that there had been a sponsorship filed by the parish in Quebec City in 1992, the immigration officer told Adèle that she would not be classified as a refugee (and therefore would not be eligible for a sponsorship) because Canada did not need French teachers and there was no persecution in Burundi. The officer said that, although Adèle had Rwandan citizenship, she had permanently settled in Burundi.

"And the other reason," fumed the officer, "is that your brother tricked us."

"Tricked you?"

"Yes. He applied for a student visa but he didn't come back. He stayed and claimed refugee status." Adèle wondered why the officer expected her brother to come back to an inferno.

The interview took place in February 1994. That same day, the diplomats in the American Embassy and most other Western embassies, left Burundi because of the precarious situation. In April 1994, hundreds of thousands of Rwandan Tutsis were slaughtered.

It was then that Joseph and Adèle knew they had to rely on their own resources. Joseph had developed a business as a trader in precious stones, buying amethysts in Zaire and selling them in New York City, Montreal and elsewhere, so he had a multiple-entry visa to the United States. He applied for visitors' visas from the American Embassy, saying he wanted to take his wife and children there on a vacation after Adèle finished her school year. This route would mean waiting out the terror in the capital another three months.

During that time, their neighbourhood was attacked and their house burned to the ground. Adèle, who was pregnant at the time, was afraid she would miscarry. She fled to her mother's house in another neighbourhood and there gave birth to their daughter.

At the end of June, Joseph and Adèle sold everything to pay for their tickets. But they had to leave Antoinette behind.

As she told me this story, Adèle's eyes filled with tears but she turned away to brush her face. She seemed to feel it was impolite to cry, an imposition to talk too much about her concerns.

Joseph was a more easygoing kind of person, except when he talked about Antoinette. "If anything happens to her, I will hold that immigration officer personally responsible. She shut the door in Antoinette's face."

Two days before their hearing, the couple's new lawyer called and asked if Joseph and I could come to his office. We wondered why. Alex Neve, a lawyer with a background in refugee law, explained that the person who was to be the refugee hearing officer had given him a copy of two telexes which had been sent to the immigration offices at all border points, to national headquarters, to the national security service, etc. Alex summed the telexes up as "an all-points bulletin."

The first telex was as follows:

SUBJ REFUSED AS CR3 BY VO LETTER OF 16 FEB 94 AS CONSIDERED PERMANENTLY RESETTLED IN BURUNDI. ALTHO SUBJ BORN AND RAISED IN BURUNDI, SHE MAINTAINS RWANDAN CITIZENSHIP . . . SUBJS BROTHER ALSO BORN IN BUJUMBURA WAS STUDENT IN USA AND MADE REF CLAIM AT CIC WINDSOR ON 25 MAY 94.

The second telex, dated September 27, 1994, read:

HAVE RECD REPLY FROM USEMB BUJUMBURA CONFIRMING NIV ISSUED TO SUBJ TO VACATION IN NY FOR TWO WEEKS FROM 19 JUN. US VISA OFFICER INDICATES SUBJ WAS TEACHER IN PRESTIGIOUS JESUIT SECONDARY SCHOOL IN BUJUMBURA FOR FIVE YEARS; HAD SUFFICIENT FUNDS FOR VISIT; HAD BEEN IN USA IN 1992; LIVED IN AREA OF BUJUMBURA THAT HAS REMAINED

QUOTE RELATIVELY FREE FROM ETHNIC VIOLENCE UNQUOTE;
MADE NO MENTION OF GOING TO CANADA; AND QUOTE HAVING
MET AND SPOKEN WITH BOTH HUSBAND AND WIFE, MY PERCEP-
TION WOULD BE THAT THIS APPLICANT IS USING CURRENT POLIT-
ICAL CIRCUMSTANCES TO EFFECT ECONOMIC IMMIGRATION
UNQUOTE.

Adèle had been reduced to "SUBJ" by an immigration officer from
the Canadian High Commission in Nairobi. Alex was perplexed. "I've
never seen anything like it."

"She seems mad that Adèle and her brother managed to escape the
tragedy," Joseph commented. "And this is the person who is inter-
viewing refugees in Rwanda, Burundi, and for the whole of East
Africa. Canadians watch the news about the slaughter in our countries
and they want to help. They would be shocked to know what is really
going on."

Joseph and Adèle were extremely worried that the telexes would
jeopardize their refugee hearing. However, the panel members at the
Immigration and Refugee Board seemed quite accustomed to such
missives and dismissed them as neither an accurate assessment of the
country nor of the persons.

One of the panel members was a woman called Jeanette Goldman.
Considered tough but fair, she was the child of a man who had been
placed on "Schindler's List" and rescued from the Nazi inferno. She
listened intently as Joseph explained why the army could not protect
its own citizens. Joseph was visibly nervous and he had to shield his
eyes as the sun started glancing off the corner window. Ms. Goldman
got up and lowered the blind so he could see more clearly. It was a
simple gesture of courtesy between human beings. They were accepted
into Canada just before Christmas in 1994.

In the months that followed, we sent numerous faxes to the
Canadian High Commission in Nairobi trying to expedite the parish
sponsorship of Antoinette. As the paper blizzard cleared, it became
obvious that the immigration officers overseas didn't think Canada

needed young female students such as Antoinette. Now that the situation in Burundi was disintegrating, Antoinette was told that she could go back to Rwanda. Only a year earlier, she and Adèle were told that they could not seek protection from the genocide in Rwanda because they were permanently resettled in Burundi.

The paper curtain had been drawn around Canada. Adèle tried to file her own sorrow away but she could not contain it neatly and efficiently. On Thanksgiving Day in 1995, while she was trying to cook a turkey for the Romero House celebration, she was immobilized by pain. A few weeks later she was diagnosed as having lupus.

In spite of her physical pain, Adèle was able to get a job as a teacher's assistant in a French-language school in Toronto. Meanwhile, in Burundi, Antoinette valiantly tried to finish high school and, in spite of the fighting in the capital, finally succeeded in spite of a year's delay. Joseph enrolled at Glendon College of York University, determined to become a writer. "I want to fight with words. I want to perfect my English so I can become a journalist. I want to speak about these things, about injustice and the stupidity of war."

In Search of the Paper Trail

We knew that paper had weighed people down and walled them out. We knew that people had been written out and written off. There were the visible papers which we had seen but we knew there were invisible papers. We wanted to unlock the files.

Victoria Watts coordinated the efforts of the Sanctuary Coalition and Romero House to gain access to the files of ten cases: some of those who had been granted minister's permits, together with the files of Natan and Adèle. Each refugee signed a consent form which allowed someone from the Romero House volunteer team to access all of his or her immigration files.

Under the Privacy Act, any requests for information should be answered in thirty days. If there are reasons for a delay, a person should be notified in writing about those reasons. If there is no correspondence within this time frame, a complaint can be made to the privacy commissioner. The Privacy Act specifically mentions that a person has a right to see any and all of his or her files except where issues of national security are involved.

There was only one response within that thirty-day time frame and that was to the request to see the file of Natan and Svetlana. The remark by Mary Clancy, that "something stinks," had led us to wonder whether there may be something in this file which would indicate the reasons for the extraordinary delay in Natan's application for a work permit.

Our volunteer Shawn Beck set off to search for the paper traces. He sauntered into the immigration office on University Avenue, looking every bit like a know-nothing kid from Willowbrook, Saskatchewan. He said he was just trying to help a friend and had never done this kind of thing before. The woman who said she was the librarian handed over Natan and Svetlana's file.

There were no traces of any of Natan's numerous letters and applications for a work permit. Was this why Mary Clancy had been told that "there was no evidence that he had made a serious attempt to get a job"?

In the file was a startling array of e-mail messages between immigration officers in Ottawa and Vegreville, the office that handles work permits and humanitarian and compassionate applications:

> *6/1/95 11:00 a.m.*
> As of tomorrow this will be deemed deportation case. Subject recently submitted 114(2)—see below—Minister's office would like this considered asap. Could you kindly have someone advise me if the 114(2) has been received/actioned? Also, if decision is to be made by Vegreville, could you advise us of decision before it is released to subject?

6/1/95 11:47 a.m.

B. had suggested we request a search by CPC Vegreville for the H&C application submitted by Mary Jo Leddy on behalf of family (covering ltr was dated 18May95 and cc'd to Mary Clancy's office—but as of yesterday at 17:13 no record on FOSS-WP screen) If H&C appl. confirmed in receipt, B. would like to see it considered immediately.

We would like to avoid intervention at this stage, as the process may just work out on its own—however, in the absence of assurances, it is feared that the reppers might step up the pressure, in that (as you pointed out in your last e-mail J.) the departure order will be deemed deport this week (2nd or 3rd this week).

Then Shawn saw an important and disturbing memo that read: "(Jun 2) . . . Appears attempts being made by 9718 and NHQ (Ruth Hubter) to avoid Ministerial intervention . . ." Shawn knew that NHQ meant the National Headquarters of Citizenship and Immigration. When he asked the librarian if he could copy the memo, she replied that he couldn't because it probably belonged in a second file which he shouldn't see. However, she relented and said that he could copy the memo by hand and then even offered to let him see the second file. It contained a few more e-mail messages sent back and forth between various immigration offices.

When Shawn returned with these documents, we were quite shaken. It seemed as if Natan and Svetlana had almost been deported before Mary Clancy could intervene. It also seemed that there was no record of Natan's attempts to work. It may have been that the documentation relating to this effort was elsewhere but, if that were the case, there would have been some record of it in the immigration computer system and, under the Privacy Act, Shawn should have been informed in writing of the whereabouts of this documentation. And if there was a second inaccessible file in this case, how much more information was being withheld?

However, it was much more difficult to access the files of those who had been part of the Sanctuary Coalition's efforts. In late September 1995, a request was submitted by Victoria Watts from Romero House to see any and all of Semira and Jamal's files. There was no response for months and then Victoria received a phone call saying that all of the children had to sign a personal information request in order for the file to be released. The officer also said Semira had to submit another request. Victoria informed the officer that the children were under the age of eighteen, but the officer said it was necessary. Another request to see the file was sent on June 26, 1996, but there has been no response since then.

In response to some other requests, Victoria received phone calls from local immigration officers asking why she wanted to see the file. She was told that there was no point in seeing a file if a person would soon be landed. In one case, she was told, over the phone, that she had to specify exactly what document she wanted and that she could not see the whole file.

Victoria was able to access only one file, that of an Eritrean activist, in a local Scarborough office. It was there that she discovered the infamous memo expressing glee at the deportation of thirteen people: "Here is the memo we have all been waiting for . . . ENJOY." In that file she also saw some extensive handwritten notes between a local Scarborough immigration officer and someone from the Ontario regional office. In these notes, the local officer has described Victoria's attempts to get information and notes that she works at Romero House.

For weeks, Victoria called various government offices, trying to clarify the procedure for personal information requests. She finally contacted an investigator for the privacy commissioner in Ottawa. He assured her that all requests filed should be answered in thirty days and that the response should be by letter and not by phone. He emphasized that the response should have come from the privacy coordinator from Immigration Canada in Ottawa and not from local immigration officers in Toronto who were not employees of the privacy commission. The investigator said that asking children under eighteen to sign a consent to release information form is a violation of the Privacy Act. He also said that if *all* a person's files are requested then *all* should be released. When Victoria described the notes in a file detailing her attempts to get information, the investigator said that this was improper procedure under the Privacy Act because the requester's name should not be in the file.

These comments led Victoria to conclude that the attempts by Romero House and the Sanctuary Coalition to discover how and where people had been filed away had not been treated as normal requests. The investigator concurred: the requests were being processed outside guidelines of the Privacy Act.

We also tried to access the file of Adèle's sister at the Canadian High Commission in Nairobi in order to see how the paper curtain had been drawn. To date, we have received no reply to that request.

ERASE DISTRESS

In Mainframe, nobody dies. They're erased.
—Advertisement for a TV program on a Toronto subway car

He used to have a large house and a car and a very good job in his own country. Then his friend told him that he was on the death list for the speech he had given. He had to take out all his savings to purchase the plane fares and false visas for Canada.

He has a wife and five lovely children who are doing well in school. He has applied for jobs everywhere. Employers all ask for "Canadian experience" and his social insurance card has a nine on it which signals to them that he is "temporary." He could get Canadian experience by participating in a co-op program run by Welfare but he must be a landed immigrant to attend the program.

He has been accepted as a refugee in Canada and is in the process of applying to be a landed immigrant. To become landed he must find $4121.

He makes a ledger of his life:

He had been receiving a cheque from welfare every month for $1495. The cheapest three-bedroom apartment he can find in Toronto rents at $850. The hydro bill is about $85 a month. The gas costs about $129 a month.

He has $431 left for the rest of the month for himself, his wife and his five growing children. He gets a TTC pass so that he can go and look for jobs. This costs $80.25 a month. He gets a work permit because all prospective employers ask to see this. This costs $125 a year. He puts aside $11 a month to ensure he has at least this.

His wife would love to study computers but together they decide that they cannot afford the $125 for her student authorization. They have moved near an elementary school. His wife and children must think twice about any time they take the TTC. They try to walk every-where but still the tokens come to about $60 a month for medical and other appointments.

The telephone costs $49 a month. He comes to Romero House to get used furniture, sheets, kitchen utensils and clothing for the family. Still he has to buy shoes for the children. If he is careful, he can keep this to $30 a month.

This leaves $200.75 per month for medicine, household supplies and food for him, his wife and five children. His wife is a genius at stretching a dollar. She goes to food banks and shops in the basement of Knob Hill and at Miss Rita's vegetable market on Roncesvalles. He goes to the doughnut shop to scan the papers for jobs. He wonders where he will get the stamps for application letters. He hopes none of the children will get sick and that there will not be another classroom excursion for a while.

Now he must pay for landed status.

He must pay for the medicals: $250 per adult and $30 per child. A total of $650. These must be renewed every year.

He must pay for the photos: $21 every time he gets a permit of any kind. He must pay $975 per adult for right of landing and $500 per adult for processing fee. And $100 per child.

The total cost of landing is $4121.

He received a letter from Immigration saying that this must be paid in sixty days. Another letter said he had six months to pay. The letter said he could apply for a loan program. He did and was refused "because you do not have a job and you do not have the means to repay the loan."

The minister of immigration said that the landing fee was "only the cost of a colour TV."

He finds it hard to sleep at night. He watches an old black and white TV he found at the local flea market. In the morning he washes the dishes twice. Then he gets on the streetcar and rides it for a few hours so his children will think he has gone to work.

The silent shuffle of papers, and of sorrows, continues.

VI

NEIGHBOURS

Semira's Dream

The news that Semira and Jamal had received their landed papers was announced that Sunday at the Church of the Holy Trinity. The applause rippled through the congregation for the dedicated group of people who had remained faithful to this family, and several other families, since the spring of 1992. At the coffee hour after the mass, Michael and Lee Creal began to canvass the people at the back of the church regarding an appropriate celebration.

Two weeks later, Semira and Jamal brought their children to the church just as the service was ending. They sat shyly in the pew along the side of the nave until Michael introduced them. The congregation parted to allow them to walk towards the centre. The children were dressed in their finest and looked quite comfortable there among these people they hardly knew. Michael welcomed the family to Canada and then Lee presented them with a set of small coffee cups as a symbol of the great hospitality which this family had shown towards so many.

As we sat and ate the carrot cake that Michael had cooked especially for the event, Semira recalled a dream that she had had in Saudi Arabia—several years before she made the journey to Canada.

"I dream there was big flood and I escape with the children just before the flood begins. We lived in tents. Moving around. There was water between us and Jamal. I keep looking back to the other side and think of the people there.

"Then we took a van and drive until we come to big city. There is a big wall around city. We walk around wall until we see a big door. There is a big man beside the big door and he say you cannot come in. I look inside the door and the city looks grey and dirty.

"Then we keep walking until we find another little door. No man is there. I look through the door and see a very beautiful city with streets clean like polish floor. I say to the others, 'Let's go in.' And we went in and Jamal too.

"I dream this many years ago. Before the flood."

TEAM OF DREAMERS

Abdi Mohammed was the tallest refugee I had ever met. He was almost seven feet and had large graceful hands with what seemed like the longest fingers in the world.

"You'd make a great basketball player," I joked when I first met him.

"I *am* a basketball player," he grinned. "A very good basketball player." He went on to tell me that he had been the coach of the Somali national basketball team and that they had competed internationally before . . . He could not finish the sentence.

Before . . . his country and his world collapsed. Even high school teachers and basketball coaches were in danger. He had escaped to Italy where he scrounged for an existence. Finally, after two years of living hand to mouth, he was sponsored by the Christian Brothers in Toronto.

His first experience of Canada was traumatic, to say the least. Brother George Morgan, who had sponsored over a hundred refugees, had gone to the airport to pick him up. As Brother George was turning onto the ramp for highway 401, he had a slight heart attack and the car went out of control, barrelling into a post. Abdi and George were whisked off to the hospital in two separate ambulances. For the next few days, Abdi kept vigil beside Brother George until he began to recover.

After this eventful introduction to Canada, Abdi soon settled in and found a job in a factory which manufactured kitchen cabinets. It was not what he wished to do, having spent most of his former life trying to challenge his students to learn, but it was better than the streets in Italy.

Abdi would often drop in to our house—especially after I had told him that I had played basketball and had also coached high school teams. At that time he was working nights in the factory so he couldn't join one of the teams in the city.

One day he rushed in, waving his big hands, his eyes glistening. "Two more members of our national team in Somalia are here," he gasped. "And Said Ali-Korshell, the one who was the manager, has just arrived in Ottawa." He was thrilled that the core of their national team had survived and would soon be together in Toronto.

"But it's sad too," he went on to say. "They stayed as long as they could but they were being forced to take sides. They weren't interested in political competition, they just wanted to compete for the joy of it."

A few months later, Abdi was placed on the day shift and the world seemed to open up before him. He phoned me, great excitement in his voice. "I have a dream. We want to come over tonight and tell you about it."

That evening four Somali gentlemen appeared at the door with a delicately decorated chocolate cake. "We are celebrating the birth of the Somali-Canadian Sports and Arts Centre," they said, placing the cake on the table. "Please cut a piece of cake."

Which I did and served each one in turn. I made spiced tea for everyone and waited until they were ready to go on with their announcement.

Said took the lead. He was clearly already well versed in the way things work in Canada. "We have applied to be incorporated as a non-profit organization," he said. "We will then be able to receive donations. We are going to form a team to compete in the city league and we want to create little-league basketball teams for the young people. First we need to get a place to practise, or a couple of places, and then we need to get some uniforms. And we want you to be on our board of directors."

I felt quite flattered and, of course, I accepted.

Abdi then went on to explain the genesis of the dream. "We know the Somalis in the city have a bad reputation. People don't know us. One of the ways we can get to meet other Canadians is through sports. It's a way of bridging the gaps even when language or cultures are different. Some of our people keep waiting for the government to do something about our problems but it is we who have to help ourselves. If we don't help ourselves, who will? We have to show that we can be responsible, that we can be good at sports and that we have a lot to contribute. And sports is a way that people from the different tribes in the city can get together. Each little group is in its little corner with its little centre. We don't want to repeat what's going on in Somalia here. We need new projects, a new beginning.

"Our young people are getting into trouble because they are bored. They live in these big tall prisons in Dixon. They need to get out of these prisons and learn how to cooperate. Many of them have lost one or both parents and our teams will help them with this."

"'Big tall prisons'?"

"You know. Those apartment blocks."

I understood. Dixon is the code word for the area around Dixon Road near the airport where thousands of Somalis live.

I believed in their dream and still do. We mapped out a modest strategy for beginning.

My main contribution was to phone Ted Schmidt, a teacher at Bishop Marrocco-Thomas Merton High School. Ted and I had worked for years together on the editorial board of *Catholic New Times* and I knew he remained a sports enthusiast even though he had rather vocally denounced the crass economic interests which had hijacked major league sports. I arranged for Ted to meet Abdi and Said at the local coffee shop, across from the high school and just around the corner from one of our houses near the Dundas West subway stop.

Ted immediately recognized a good dream when he saw it. Within days he had arranged for the team to have practice time at the Swansea Community Centre. He raised money to get the city team uniforms and running shoes. He corralled his friends to attend some of the practice sessions and then got an old acquaintance to begin teaching some of the Somalis baseball. Ted also arranged for the Somali team to have the use of a fourth-floor court at the high school where they could hold soccer games on Friday nights.

By then the team was flying. They had played several exhibition games—one of them against the police team. It was an excellent opportunity, Abdi said, to have better relationships with the police. They entered city competition and did very well. They set up their own tournaments, inviting other Somali teams from Europe and the United States. They had almost eight hundred kids coming out for the little-league tournaments and practice sessions. When they announced the Friday night soccer session at the high school, five hundred people showed up.

It was soon clear that they needed an office where people could contact them and they could use as a base for their operations. As yet, the organization did not have a cent to its name—other than what it raised through small contributions from the Somali community. We were a bit stumped by this, because renting an office was more money than the centre could manage. Said had put in several applications to the city, to the Ontario Ministry of Multiculturalism and to the Ministry of Recreation. Everything seemed mired in red tape. Officials were enthusiastic. No one doubted that the organization deserved government support but each one mentioned the spectre of cutbacks.

At this point we contacted Father Massey Lombardi, an affable and generous priest who had worked on social justice projects for years.

He began setting up further contacts in government circles and even arranged a meeting with Minister of Multiculturalism Elaine Ziemba. She was very impressed at what had been done with nothing and sent the team to her staff to arrange for interim funding for a feasibility study. Then the provincial election got into gear and the requests of the Somali team sat waiting in the dust.

It occurred to me one day that we had a free room in the basement of one of our houses. I would never have considered it as an office for the team but the situation was becoming urgent. The team had taken wing but it had no place to come home to roost.

The room could not be used for living space because it was too low to meet the ceiling requirements. And there was a crack in the wall which resulted in a regular flooding of the basement. Until this was repaired, the room could not be used in any way by the usual residents.

So this room became the Somali-Canadian Sports and Arts Centre. The team found an old xerox machine which occupied about half the room, and then installed a phone and fax machine. A small table with eight chairs completed the decor. Everything was three inches off the floor—in anticipation of the regular flooding. The members of the team walked around the room hunched to keep their heads from touching the roof. They never complained, they never ceased to thank us for this little hole in the wall.

It was easy to help them, to want to help them. As Ted Schmidt said, "They are such a class act. Everywhere they practise or play, people remark on how polite and sportsmanlike they are."

Everyone—except for one neighbour. The team had put a small sign on the front of the house with an arrow pointing to the back door: Somali-Canadian Sports and Arts Centre. The neighbour watched. She phoned the city councillor and complained about people "coming and going at all hours," about "taxis driving up and letting people off," and how "one of the taxis tried to run over my child." And she complained about garbage on the front yard and the back yard.

We attempted to talk with her. We explained to the councillor how ridiculous the charges were. There were always new complaints. She called the police. It was clear that she saw the Somalis as trouble, as dirty, as even criminal. It was painful to hear. She did not know them. They were strangers and she kept them that way.

Finally, we wrote to her and to the city councillor saying that we would charge harassment if there were any further complaints. That ended the matter, sort of.

Nevertheless, she would always be sitting on her porch, watching, judging, protecting. The Somali team had become her nightmare. She never saw their dream.

THE BAG LADY OF BRAMPTON

It is called the Romero Boutique, a small space for secondhand hope, hand-me-downs hope. It is a shop for those who cannot afford to go shopping—not for winter clothes when they first arrive from a warm climate, not for shoes for growing children, not for the furniture they will need when they eventually move out of Romero House. It is a very small storeroom in the basement of one of our houses and its constantly changing merchandise is an inventory of the generosity and ingenuity in the city.

It began in an informal way when Lynn Haley came over to the house a few days after Semira and her five children arrived. Lynn walked into the one room which Semira had called the "Ritz" and was shaken, indeed summoned, by the sight of another woman intent on creating a home out of almost nothing.

A teacher at a Brampton separate high school, Lynn had taught teenagers religion for years. She believed in the idea of social justice and she had always taught about justice but she had remained wary of "social justice types" who seemed more concerned about legislation than committed to life.

And she didn't like having to apologize for being middle class.

Call it an awakening, call it being turned inside out, Lynn reached out that day she walked out of Semira's room and down the stairs. "Listen," she said to me, "I can get some things for these kids."

And she did. She took Semira shopping over at Zellers for five pairs of socks, five pairs of shoes and five sets of underwear. It did not end there. In the months to come, she kept bringing over bags of clothes that she had gathered up from the highways and bi-ways of Brampton. Lynn began to meet the other refugee families in the house and during each encounter she made a mental note of their various sizes and shapes. Black garbage bags began appearing at the doorstep almost weekly. They contained washed and wonderful clothing, neatly folded and sorted according to age and sex.

Thus, she became known as "the Bag Lady of Brampton" to each new group of refugees at Romero House. The sources of this lady's bountiful-ness were to be found in Notre Dame High School in Brampton. One by one, she had talked to each staff member about the various people at Romero House, where they came from, what they couldn't bring with them and what they needed now. That's all she said, but it was a quiet war against the garage sales that had once seemed so easy and automatic in the suburbs. Eventually, she had vans of furniture driving down high-way 427 towards the centre of Toronto. Each fall she organized a winter clothing drive for the refugees who would soon have nothing to shield them from the cold except the care of those who saw them as neighbours.

"Don't tell me people aren't generous," she said to me one day. "They're just waiting for someone to tell them how they can give in a way that makes a real difference."

"Well, it makes all the difference in the world here," I said. "The difference between dignity and destitution."

"But it is the difference in my life too. I have a community in a city of strangers."

Sorting the bags from Brampton was another kind of challenge and soon became the responsibility of some remarkable people such as

Rosemary Broughton. She had been a teacher of theology in the United States and had quite recently come into a substantial inheritance. In pondering her good fortune, she decided to tithe a year of her time to working with what she then called "the poor." Although she was a professional academic, she was also eminently practical. As soon as she got to know her neighbours at Romero House, she realized that what they needed most urgently was some of the basic necessities of life. She set about organizing the Romero Boutique, folding the clothes and placing them neatly on shelves in easily identifiable ways. She refused to put any dirty or spoiled clothes in the boutique because she felt it would be an insult. Rosemary designated certain times when the boutique was open and she pointed out the various merchandise as if she were working in a high class department store.

The generosity of Notre Dame High School emboldened us when we received phone calls from other high schools with the offer to help. Well, yes, it would be nice to have some Christmas gifts for the families. Even if they aren't Christian, we know it is a time of giving. And thus it was that Joan of Arc, Marrocco-Merton and Monsignor McGivney high schools and then other schools, began their annual Christmas hamper effort. Each classroom received the name of a family with all the details about sizes and shapes and interests. A few days before Christmas, our van would travel around to the schools and pick up what seemed like a mountain of boxes—each with a name and a note from the students of a particular classroom. The volunteers would sort out the boxes into little mounds on the porch, on the sidewalk, in the office, in the front room and up the stairs of the various Romero houses. The day before Christmas, another group of volunteers would pick up the mounds of joy and deliver them personally to the various refugee families who had now moved out of Romero House and were living in various parts of the city. At the end of the day, the volunteers sank happily into the debris of cardboard and wrappings that lay littered all over the houses.

Not all of the clothing in the Romero Boutique was second-hand. Some of it had never been used, was top-of-the-line designer labels—

and had never been sold. This clothing came to us through a one-of-a-kind organization called Windfall. It had begun when two friends noticed tables of unsold merchandise in clothing stores. They soon learned that many clothing distributors were simply ploughing their surplus items back into landfill. The reasoning of these distributors was that if they put their surplus or slightly damaged goods on sale, then the cost of their items would go down. The women were horrified at the sheer waste of it all, especially when so many people could no longer afford even the basic necessities.

It was Joan Clayton and Ina Andre's initiative to approach some of these companies and to make them an offer they could not resist. They said they would take the surplus and would sign an agreement saying that these items would not be resold and that they would be given to people who would never buy them in the first place. It was a win-win offer and many companies signed on.

Nevertheless, dignity is not built on clothes alone and we at Romero House have faced the almost impossible task of trying to ensure that the refugees who move out of the houses, once they have been accepted, have at least the basic necessities to begin living in their own households: a pan, a pot, some dishes, a bed or two, some sheets and blankets and maybe even a table and a few chairs.

The task would be virtually impossible were it not for a wily older Catholic nun called Sister Ann Shenk. Once the principal of a posh Catholic girls school, she has spent the last few years of her life working with refugees. She has quietly brought together the seemingly incongruous parts of her life. While keeping in touch with the refugees she knows, she had also maintained her relationships with the school graduates, some of whom are now connected to corporate executives and lawyers throughout the city. She is especially interested in lawyers who do estate work, lawyers who are charged with disposing of the contents of houses and apartments of the deceased. Sister Ann has set up an informal agreement with several of these lawyers that she will send in a team to "relieve" them of the contents and even clean up if the relatives are not interested.

When we need beds, the most precious item, we call Sister Ann. We call her genteel connivance "Beds from the Dead."

Across the Street from Africa

Barbara and Jim were some of the first neighbours to welcome us on Wanda Road. They had heard about Romero House through their involvements in social justice issues. Barbara and Jim were nearing retirement age and their two oldest children had left home, had married and were pursuing academic careers.

It was their youngest son, Paul, who was to become much of the focus of our encounters. Every day I would see Barbara walking Paul down the street, his ears covered with large earphones—the type you see on airline personnel. Barbara explained to me that Paul needed to wear these because he was very sensitive to sound.

"Paul only makes sounds," said Barbara. "He has never said a word to us." Paul was a young adult with special needs and Barbara and Jim looked for any and every way to communicate love and security to him.

Early in the fall two years ago, Barbara had met me on the street and begun talking about what seemed like a breakthrough for Paul. It was a form of interactive communication and involved a trusted person pushing against the hand of the disabled person who then would react by pushing forward. What they were finding, she said, was that a disabled person was able to direct the forward movement quite accurately. Some people were starting to use a board with the alphabet on it in the hope that the person could begin to spell and communicate.

We didn't talk too much about this new development in subsequent conversations. Our focus was rather on how they could get some assistance to help them with Paul now that they were getting older. It was really a round-the-clock job and they were finding that their energy just wasn't what it used to be.

The weeks came and went, the snow fell and then melted, and soon it was Easter. I sat outside on the porch savouring a cup of coffee in the early morning of Easter Sunday. The silence that hovered about the street was broken when I saw Barbara come running out onto the street. She ran partway up the street, turned around and ran back, and then turned again when she saw me sitting on the porch.

"He talked, he talked," she shouted as she grabbed my arm.

She explained that after a week of pushing against her son's hand, he had suddenly started to direct his finger to specific letters on the alphabet board. He had spelled out his first words: I am happy.

This was his first message to his mother in twenty-five years. Until then she had no idea that he could read, that he could write, that he could express himself more fully.

A few days later Barbara called me over and said that Paul had become a cascade of words, as if everything that had been bottled up for years had finally found an outlet. She was worried that somehow she was unconsciously suggesting things to Paul. However, she found him telling her things that she had never known and that were confirmed independently by other people.

She told me that she had pointed over to our house and had asked Paul who lives there.

"Mary Jo and Africa," he spelled out. "They work in Africa."

I told the refugee mothers in my house about Paul's first words. "I never see such a mother," said Semira.

THE TREKKIE WITH A TIE

We called him "The Dunk." Perhaps he could have been a basketball player if he had been a little more coordinated. He had the height for it but not the slightest interest in sports. An anglophile and very conservative, he was a passionate intellectual and looked the part, rarely being seen without a tie. He was a history major at the University of Saskatchewan specializing in the British House of

Lords in the nineteenth century and, for reasons which were unclear to me, he had volunteered to work at Romero House for a summer. He was also a Beatles fan and a Trekkie and booked off three days during his stay at Romero House to attend a Star Trek event in the city. Duncan, in short, was a genuine eccentric at the ripe old age of twenty-one. We could hardly imagine what he could do to assist the refugees at Romero House, but he was keen.

Life and necessity presented Duncan with a calling at Romero House. The day before he arrived for the summer, I had attended a meeting at the local school with Jamal and Semira. The teachers had said that because of his language difficulties, Amir would probably have to be slow-streamed during the next year at school. We all knew that this would greatly affect his future. Amir was a natural leader and those of us who knew him could easily detect his natural intelligence. His only problem was that English was his fourth language. When he had arrived at Romero House he had told me he wanted to be a dentist but after two years in school he had modified that dream to say he wanted to play baseball and make a lot of money. And he was good at sports, winning several trophies.

Duncan and I had our first meeting. "Your mission, should you choose to accept it," I said teasingly, "is to work with Amir so he can feel more confident in school. It may not seem very important to you but it is this young boy's whole future."

Duncan looked solemn as he considered this. "Well, I've never really taught young children but I do accept this as a very serious responsibility."

And he did. Every evening Duncan worked for hours with Amir on spelling and grammar. Soon, all of Amir's brothers and sisters wanted to join "Duncan's school." And then all the kids in the houses wanted to attend.

I was astounded. I knew from the kids and Duncan that not only was he teaching them English, he was also teaching them about Greek mythology, about Queen Victoria, about the British parliamentary system and about the prime ministers of Canada. He took them to the museum and the art gallery and explained various schools of painting to them. They wrote essays about their excursions. I could not imagine how he had wrested these kids away from the lure of the Nintendo games that some of their fellow students played.

One evening I paused by the door to listen while Duncan was teaching his students about the difference between Roman law and British common law. Suddenly I realized that, unaware of any trendy child psychology, Duncan was teaching the children the way he would teach adults. He was treating them with respect.

The day before he left to return to university he threw a big party in the backyard and blasted Beatles songs through his tape recorder. The kids jived and rocked and thought it was the greatest. Duncan didn't dance; he said he never liked dancing after some people laughed at him during a dance competition in high school.

The next day when Duncan left for the airport, he broke down crying as he said goodbye to the kids assembled on the sidewalk. The house was like a tomb for the whole day. Finally, I asked Sasha, the son of Natan and Svetlana, why he was so quiet.

"Because Duncan is gone," he said wistfully. "The bestest person in the world."

A few months later, Duncan asked me for a reference for a Rhodes Scholarship and I quoted Sasha's recommendation. I could hardly think of anything better to say.

Duncan has written all the kids regularly and remains a constant presence in their lives. He always asks how they are doing in school and they write back—with greater and greater articulation. Duncan came back this summer and stayed at Romero House while he was doing research in the Ontario archives on the House of Lords. He was invited to have supper with the families of all the children and they even cooked vegetarian meals because, as Semira said, "We know he is a vegetable person."

The Long and the Short of It

Neither Victoria Watts nor I, nor any of us, could have anticipated what would follow upon her casual phone call inquiring about the volunteer program at Romero House. She made her entrance at the end of the university year in early May, just looking for something to do over the summer. "I'll do anything," she said. "I like being with kids. I'd like to have lots of kids." Her only contact with Romero House was Lorne Howcroft, her former high school principal, her guide on a social awareness program to Jamaica and the friend of her parents who were also, like Lorne, teachers in the Dufferin-Peel Separate School Board. Later, I would learn how her parents always had room in their home for students who were in difficulty and how they always gave Victoria the space she needed to find her own way.

Yet, in the beginning, Lorne told me only that Victoria had asked to volunteer over the summer until she decided what to do next with her life. "What has she done with her life so far?" I asked.

"Well, she spent a long time in dance school training to be a ballerina and she's just finished a B.A. and she has good parents. Family means a lot to them. She has two younger sisters. One of them was born with a serious heart problem and that really pulled the family together."

And what has this to do with the price of tea in China, I wondered.

It had a lot to do with the cost of living—as I would discover during the summer and the many months that followed.

Victoria looked like a dancer and moved like one, tall and graceful, her long hair swept up on her head in a casual sort of elegance. She had the air of a prima donna but we soon discovered that she was anything but. Victoria told us she had gone to dance school for many years but had quit because of some vague sense of dissatisfaction with what she could only call "the artificiality." She decided to go to university and become a corporate lawyer so she could become rich, if not famous. She was all set to be a woman of the nineties. When an uncle asked her if she was set to be married by a rich man, she laughed and replied, "They'll be lining up to marry me because I'm so rich."

By the time she finished her undergraduate degree, that goal no longer seemed appealing. Although she had done very well academically, only a few courses in native studies and women's studies had really excited her. She had become involved in student organizations and even worked on an underground student newspaper called *The Dissident*. However, she remained unconvinced and unsatisfied with the black and white world of protest groups. "It was a lot of talk and no action. It wasn't very grounded." In short, she was a young woman in search of a purpose for her life.

A radiant seven-year-old Somali girl by the name of Sahra began to hold her hand and call her "Vit-Toria." And for Victoria, Sahra became "Bella." Through the children, Victoria began to meet the mothers and the few fathers that were there. Sensitive by nature, Victoria was soon overwhelmed by the stories of suffering she heard from the parents of the children, stories of rape and torture, indignities and disappearances.

It all started to get to her. She got tired, became sick, and then recovered. Somehow, the suffering hadn't overwhelmed her completely. She sensed that, however painful, this suffering was at least real. She took more initiatives, became decisive and focused. All the skills she had learned through her studies, the tools for research and analytical thinking, were directed in the service of the refugee who sought her help. She worked with lawyers to defend a Salvadorean teenager who had been picked up with a group of kids who were swarming in a mall. She began phoning agencies in North America and South America that could provide information for an appeal by a Colombian refugee who was being hunted by the drug dealers of that country.

Victoria's time at Romero House extended beyond the summer and into the winter and then into another summer. For Angela, a Sri Lankan woman who arrived after that summer, Victoria's decision to stay meant all the difference to her world.

Angela had become one of the many incidental victims after a series of suicide bombers had inflicted serious damage in the city of Colombo and elsewhere throughout Sri Lanka. The suicide bombers had been young Tamil men and women who had strapped bombs to their bodies in an act of "patriotism" and revenge against those who had killed members of their family. They blew themselves up in places where they would inflict the most damage on the Sinhalese majority who lived in the capital of the country. After each bombing, the Sri Lankan police would surge through the city picking up anyone suspected of being even remotely connected to the bombings.

At that time, after the peace talks between the government and the Tamil Tigers had broken down, Angela, her husband and two children were living in a middle-class suburb of Colombo. The couple had good jobs and had saved enough money to buy some land where they were planning to build a new house. After nine years in a large multi-national company, Angela had been promoted to the position of executive secretary to the son of the managing director. It was important and interesting work and Angela was encouraged to take initiatives and assume more responsibilities. The civil war which had already claimed so many victims had not yet touched them.

Then the police came for Angela and for other Sinhalese women and men. Their only crime was that they were associated with young Tamils. Angela had rented a room in her house to a young Tamil woman and had duly registered the new tenant at the local police station.

This so-called crime seemed to provide some police officers with more than enough justification for beating and raping an attractive young woman who was powerless to defend herself inside the police station. The police threatened reprisals against her relatives if anything was revealed about what had happened. The war against the Tamil Tigers had served to legitimize the injustices by the police against the people they were claiming to protect. In the end, it was this very corruption of the police force that enabled Angela's husband to secure her release through bribery.

It was only a temporary reprieve. As a condition of her release, Angela was to report weekly to the police. Each time she went to the police station, she was taken to a small windowless room and raped again by the same police officers. Finally, Angela decided she had to tell her husband about what had really happened to her while she was in detention. Shame and the fear that her husband would react by doing something foolish which would endanger the whole family had made her keep the extent of her humiliation to herself. However, the situation had become intolerable. She summed up the situation in this way: "Some things are worse than dying."

Barely intact, Angela left her country with a visa for Canada. But she had to leave half of her family, half of her life, behind. If she had tried to leave the country with a lot of money or with her entire family, the immigration officers at the Canadian High Commission in Colombo would not have issued her a visa, for she would have been suspected of trying to escape as a refugee. Angela had to provide the Canadian immigration officer with a copy of a bank statement showing that all the savings, the money which was to purchase their new house, would remain in Sri Lanka. The screening process at the Canadian High Commission meant that Angela was forced to choose which of her children she would take with her. Such a decision became like the sword of Solomon dividing her from herself. No choice could ever be right. In the end, she took her daughter and left her younger child, her son, behind with her husband.

Angela was in a state of shock when they arrived at Romero House. She walked with sadness surrounding her and her eyes filled with tears at unexpected moments. But her daughter, Debbie, was a delightful, effervescent child who charmed everyone who met her.

Debbie called her new doll Victoria, after her new friend. Hiding behind the door at Romero House, Debbie would rush forward to hug Victoria's legs as she came in. As she giggled and chirped like a little bird, Victoria would scoop her up in her arms and cover her with kisses.

"Do the Macarena! Do the Macarena!" Debbie squealed. And together they would sing and go through the movements like the most carefree dancers in the world.

Victoria began to take Angela to the tedious series of appointments related to the refugee determination process: the welfare office, the legal aid office and the medical appointments. Each visit was a trial barely endured, a reliving of the shame and indignity. Yet, on the subway trips to and from the various offices and over tea, Victoria began to hear the details of Angela's life. She learned that Angela had been abandoned by her parents when she was a young child and had been raised in a Catholic orphanage. There was one nun in particular who became almost like a mother to her.

Now and then, Victoria caught a glimpse of who Angela had been at another time and in another place. She had been confident and professional in her work and the delight of her family and friends. She had been as stylish and sophisticated as Victoria—if not more so. Now Angela seemed more timid and tentative, still bewildered by what had happened to her, unsure of what the future would hold for her in Canada. Her whole life seemed diminished. No longer in her spacious home, she was living in two little rooms on the third floor of Romero House. "But it's not the fine things I miss," she said. "It's the fine feelings."

The medical appointments were extensive and varied as the doctors attempted to deal with the side effects of multiple rape. Angela went for interviews and examinations at the Centre for Victims of Torture and the Four Villages Community Health Centre. However, she did not go alone for Victoria was there to help her.

The burden of the past was real and Victoria seemed to grow stronger the longer she carried it with Angela and many other refugees. Gone was the unbearable lightness of being she had experienced in dance school. "I know I can help carry some of their burden without totally understanding it," she told me. "It isn't too heavy because now I can always see that there is some hope in any situation. Still, it shocks me when I hear them talk about what happened in the prison. You read about such things or see it on TV. But it does happen.

You learn that from the people who become your friends here. I watch the news and I know that there will be some people from the conflict being reported who will soon be my neighbours."

Angela turned to aerobics to try to deal with the anxieties haunting her. Three times a week, she and another refugee woman would go to the low-impact aerobics at the Keele Street Community Centre. Still, the violent headaches would come and she would be immobilized for hours. Guilt consumed her. She felt she had abandoned her little son, just as her parents had abandoned her. In her own country she had had a cook and a servant to look after things in the home while she went to work. Now, she set about learning how to cook and she gradually took on cleaning parts of the house and making sure the garbage was in order and out on time. She needed to keep busy.

For a few weeks she had tried volunteering as an office helper in a service organization, something she could do as long as someone else could pick up her daughter from school. However, there were days when Debbie was sick or no one was free to pick her up at the appointed time. Angela had to let go of the work through which she had been able to contribute something, work that connected her to a sense of her former self. Nevertheless, one thing had become clear. Angela had regained some of her strength and would be ready and able to work as soon as her daughter was in school full time.

There was one hour a day when she seemed able to disconnect from it all and that was when she watched "The Young and the Restless" in the afternoon. We teased her about this and often asked for the latest updates. She could laugh as she told us about the latest tragedies and deaths and divorces of "The Young and the Restless" which were a relief from her reality.

"What do you like better Angela—romances or mysteries?" asked Victoria.

"I like them both," Angela responded with a grin.

It was great to see this grin and the flash of the imp she had been and her daughter now was. But we all knew that life, for her, was not like it is in the movies.

Angela was in regular, although infrequent, communication by telephone with her husband. The news was rarely good and often we would find her sobbing in the front entrance to the house. The police had come for her husband after she had not reported for her weekly "interview" at the station but he had evaded them by going through the back door with their son and into a neighbour's house. Since then, the husband had moved from house to house.

"It's no life for them," she said. "It's no life for a little boy."

The phone rang one day with the news that her son had to be taken to the hospital because he was suffering from an appendicitis attack. It was a risk but her husband had little option. For the next few weeks Angela didn't even enjoy "The Young and the Restless." When the boy was released from hospital she was able to relax a little. Then she learned that the police had come to her grandparents' house where her son was recuperating, threatening to take the child unless her husband gave himself up to the police. Only the abject entreaties of the grandparents and a substantial bribe had prevented the police from taking the sick child. But they said they would return. Once again, Angela's husband gathered up his son and moved to the house of another relative outside the city.

The crisis with Angela's son forced us all to think about ways of getting them to Canada. It was obvious now that Angela's husband and son could not wait for her to be accepted as a refugee, wait until she could pay the head tax, then wait another eighteen to twenty-four months until she was landed. It could be years before they could be processed for landing in Canada.

Victoria was fuming. "Her husband and son should be able to go to the Canadian High Commission in Colombo and ask for a visa because they are in so much danger. Her husband should be able to apply for refugee status there and have his claim adjudicated there. Canada has signed the Geneva Convention to protect genuine refugees. Now the only way her husband and son can come is if they get some false documents. And then they'll be under suspicion here. This is not justice! This is not what Canada is about!"

Victoria fell silent as we all did. We knew that the last reason a Sri Lankan would get a visa was because he or she was in danger. We knew about Immigration's policy of interdiction and "Operation Shortstop"* and how it was stopping not only some criminals but also many innocent people.

"It's just like prohibition," Victoria shouted. "They make it impossible for real refugees to come to Canada legally and so people must find illegal ways in order to live. It just sets up a whole illegal business run by people who traffic in human suffering."

I heard what she said but I was listening to a new Victoria. She had spoken with authority.

MR. SHINE AND THE IRANIAN SHADOW

They both came in June. One from Willowbrook, Saskatchewan, and the other from Tehran, Iran. They met at Romero House and they lived together in what would become a year of sunshine and shadows.

We had accepted Shawn Beck as a volunteer sight unseen. We knew only what he had told us in his application—and that had seemed sufficient: he was twenty-one, had completed his B.A. at the University of Saskatchewan and had taken a year off before beginning his studies in theology. Since his graduation he had worked in a coffee shop and had saved enough money to spend several months in the Christian community on the island of Iona off the Scottish coast. There he had hoped to connect with his Celtic and Christian roots. Romero House was to be his summer of service. It all sounded very earnest.

He phoned from Saskatoon to tell us when he would be arriving by bus and provided us with a description so we could recognize him among the passengers. "I'm the one with the long ponytail and a beard and a black leather jacket."

---

* See Appendix 3.

Norbert, the volunteer who took the message, put down the phone and said, "This is going to be interesting."

Thin and slight, Shawn arrived with nothing more than a knapsack and a pack of cigarettes. Over our first lunch together at the crowded table in the basement of the Romero office, he fed us intriguing tidbits about himself: he had been a New Age devotee before he became a Christian and that was after he had a vision of Jesus on the roof of his father's barn. He had never been without a girlfriend since he was eleven. He did all his reading in coffee shops. He liked Gregorian chants and the songs of Loreena McKennitt. He thought we were living in Babylon, especially in Toronto, and that the time of judgement on this culture was near. He thought TV should be banned.

"This is really going to be interesting," Norbert whispered.

Given the number of bases that needed to be covered at Romero House, we made Shawn the office manager. "You have been immediately promoted," I told him. "You will probably not make your fortune here but you will have a meteoric rise to prestige and power."

Within a week, Shawn had all the office procedures finely tuned. He kept a little notebook of lists which he checked off as each task was completed. And all the while he kept up a steady stream of conversation with the other volunteers in the office—a joke here, a quip there and the occasional pause for a long exchange on the meaning of life, the mysteries of God in general and of women in particular. At times he sounded like he was fifty-one and at other times just twenty-one.

In any case, Shawn was ready for more. He was quickly "promoted" to the position of coordinator for the house on Keele Street where he had a room on the first floor. A family from Burundi occupied the whole second floor, and there was a large room on the third floor which was ready and waiting for the next arrival.

After the phone call came from the hostel downtown, Shawn scurried around to prepare the place for the Iranian man by the name of Alireza. The worker at the hostel had said that Alireza needed a quieter place, that he didn't belong with alcoholics and drug addicts and that he needed help with his refugee application.

Alireza arrived and moved through the house like a thin, slight shadow. He stooped more than stood, his eyes dull and drained of light. He never opened his mouth except when he went outside to have a smoke with Shawn. They didn't say much at first, out there on the front steps. It was obvious that Alireza did not know a word of English but soon Shawn learned to talk with his hands, his face and his eyes. The first words Alireza said were, "You, Shine. Mister Shine." Even then, Alireza barely opened his mouth.

Shawn's conversations with Alireza gave a whole new meaning to the biblical term "the gift of tongues." Although there was no shared vocabulary, they seemed to understand each other. After each smoke on the front steps, Shawn would tell us a little more about Alireza.

"Alireza like smoke. Alireza like coffee. Alireza like beer. Alireza no like Khomeini. Alireza no sleep. Alireza hurt teeth, hurt back, hurt everywhere." Norbert, our only francophone volunteer, told Shawn he should brush up on his English grammar.

We would all learn more about Alireza when Shawn took him to a refugee lawyer to help prepare the personal information form which was to be the application for his claim to be a refugee. For the first time, an interpreter was present and Shawn discovered what had happened in Iran, and crossed the border into shadow land.

Alireza explained that he had come from an Iranian family who had grown wealthy during the reign of the Shah of Iran. Most of their property had then been lost during the fundamentalist Islamic revolution of the Ayatollah Khomeini. Never that interested in politics, Alireza watched the upheaval in his country and then got on with his life. He became a cameraman for an Iranian television studio and married an attractive and vivacious young woman by the name of Farahani. They were in love and for a few brief months Alireza knew that joy was possible.

That joy and hope and his youth were snatched from him the day he heard that his wife had been picked up from work by members of the Revolutionary Guard. Frightened, he went to the most dreaded place in Tehran, Even Prison, to find out if his wife was there. She was and because he was her husband he was also taken into custody.

He waited in a crowded cell with many other prisoners, unable to comprehend what had happened or why. The next morning he was walked blindfolded into a room where he heard another voice telling him that his wife had been a leader in the Mujahideen, an underground opposition group. The voice accused Alireza of being a member of the Mujahideen. It demanded to know what she knew, what he knew, what he knew she knew.

Alireza was stripped and hung by his arms from the ceiling. He was beaten on the soles of his feet, on his back and around his head. But there was nothing to tell, because he knew nothing. This seemed to infuriate the voice even further.

The next day Alireza saw his wife for the last time. He was bound hand and foot, his blindfold was taken off and he saw five soldiers bring his wife into the cell. He was forced to watch as she was stripped and repeatedly raped in a brutal frenzy. That was when he felt that he had died. That was when God died.

He was blindfolded again and the voice came back into the room. It said that his wife had confessed to her crimes and that she would be executed the next day unless Alireza confessed. But there was nothing to tell.

An eternity later, Alireza received a note from his wife. She had been allowed to send one last message to him before her execution: "I am sorry I did not tell you about my political involvement but I didn't want to put you in danger. I had to do this for my country. Please try to forget what happened the other day. Goodbye. I leave you in the hands of God." He kept the note in his pocket until one of the guards took it from him and, holding the piece of paper in front of his face, lit it with a match. That night in the cell Alireza found an old can and cut his wrists. For some unexplainable reason, the guards would not let him die. He was taken to the medical ward where he received excellent care from the prison doctor.

For the next eight years, Alireza was a political prisoner. He was tortured with electric shocks, placed in solitary confinement and then forced into a crowded cell block where the corridors echoed with howls of pain and terror. It seemed as though he had been forgotten until three guards burst into the cell and rammed his head repeatedly against the wall. The madness of his situation was once again apparent when the guards hauled his body over to the medical ward and issued the order that he was to be kept alive. Complicated brain surgery saved his life but he suffered partial loss of memory and concentration.

Ironically, his head wounds provided the opening for one small shaft of light during those years in the prison. The doctor was a compassionate man who seemed to be trying his best to remain human in a dehumanized place. He touched Alireza gently, talked to him about the weather and read him poetry.

After his release, Alireza spent almost a year under the supervision of a psychiatrist who tried various forms of medication to ease the effects of the psychological and physical trauma in prison. He was incapacitated by depression but became more motivated when he discovered that there had been many changes in video technology since his imprisonment. He decided to borrow some money from his family to start a video and camera shop. He also tried to read a book lent to him by the doctor he had met in prison. The book was *The Satanic Verses* by Salman Rushdie. Perceived as blasphemous to Islam, it had been banned from the country and a *fatwa*, or death sentence, had been issued against the author.

Alireza's decision to read this book was his first, last and only act of sabotage against the Iranian government of Ayatollah Khomeini.

Alireza hid the book in his apartment and would take it out every night and try to read it with an English dictionary, but he had no knowledge of English grammar and found it impossible to follow. His act of rebellion seemed of no consequence until he received the news that the doctor had been picked up by the Revolutionary Guard for possession of idolatrous literature.

Alireza knew it was only a question of time before the sophisticated and brutal forms of torture in Even Prison would force the doctor to tell all. An uncle arranged for his train passage to the western part of the country where he was to contact Kurdish rebels who would take him by mule over the mountains to Turkey. His uncle had provided him with a false passport which enabled him to go through Europe to Holland where he had a brother. He would have stayed there but his brother told him that the Dutch government was refusing almost all refugees from Iran because it was trying to set up diplomatic and trading relationships between the two countries. The brother paid fifteen thousand dollars to a courier so that Alireza could get on a plane to Canada.

Alireza's first night in Canada was spent in a hostel where he heard howls of pain and terror filling the corridors at night.

"And that's the story or most of it," explained Shawn. "That's why he hardly opens his mouth. His jaw is broken. His teeth are broken."

Shawn took Alireza to a dentist only to discover that dental surgery was not covered by the new Federal Interim Health Program. Ontario had backed away from covering the health costs of refugee claimants and the federal government had agreed to pay the medical bills only for procedures that were deemed essential. To find out what an "essential procedure" was and whether the federal government would cover it, a person had to write to Ottawa. The answer was that easing the pain from Alireza's broken jaw and teeth was "not considered an essential procedure."

"People are worried that we are heading to a two-tier medical system," said Shawn after he read the letter of response from Ottawa. "But we've already got a three-tier system."

Daunted but not defeated, Shawn took Alireza to a doctor to see if something could be done about his headaches and the pain in his lower back. The doctor wrote a report about the scars on Alireza's head "consistent with brain surgery" and the pain in his lower back due to kidney damage "consistent with beating." A prescription for painkillers was given.

Mr. Shine began spending time with the Iranian shadow on the weekends. They would walk in the park, go for coffee at the Country Style doughnut shop on Bloor Street and out for a beer at Joe

Mercury's on Dundas West. On Sunday mornings Alireza asked to go to church with Shawn at Bloor Street United. Shawn had no desire to "convert" Alireza but he didn't want him to feel unwelcome. Alireza would sit in the pew, uncomprehending, staring at the large plain cross at the front of the church.

By the end of the summer, Alireza did open his mouth, apparently less concerned about how his teeth looked. Words jumbled out in an almost charming mix of English and Farsi. And Mr. Shine decided to stay for the year.

As the fall colours sharpened, Alireza seemed to emerge from his withdrawn space. He was initially dignified and polite and then an endearing clown. It may have been that he felt safe enough to let go of the chains which had not only held him captive but which had also bound him together. But by the first snowfall, Alireza began to unravel.

Alireza talked incessantly and stayed up all night watching TV or reading his Farsi translation of the Bible. He had taken to drinking alcohol and eating little. His room became littered with beer bottles and cheap whisky as he became more glassy-eyed and unsteady on his feet. His jokes became darkly obscene. The other people in the house avoided Alireza when he was drunk. Shawn tried to explain that Alireza was drinking to get rid of the pain and then he told Alireza that drinking was unacceptable in the house. Soon Alireza was treating Shawn as just another prison guard to be scorned.

One night the police appeared at the door of the house, looking for Alireza. They told Shawn that he had been caught shoplifting at a local drugstore. The manager said that it had been easy to catch him because he was just walking along the aisle stuffing his pockets with bottles. The police found Alireza had taken nearly two hundred dollars worth of Tylenol. Shawn tried to explain that he was probably hallucinating at the time. The police later decided that there had been some problem with the paperwork in Alireza's case and the charge would be dropped.

In the midst of this, Shawn was organizing Christmas hampers for the members of the Romero community. The office had been turned into a wonderful warehouse of generosity, crammed full of donations from various church groups and high schools. Shawn's monumental task was to ensure that each gift reached the right person of the right age and sex and shape and size.

The radio was playing some old familiar carols as Shawn worked with some of the refugees and volunteers in the process of sorting the donations. Alireza walked into the room holding a fistful of empty prescription containers in front of Shawn's face.

"Need more. Go store but me no speak English. They say no. Help me." Many of the people in the room looked down or away.

Shawn looked at the labels on the containers and called the pharmacy where the medication had been purchased. The pharmacist told him that he couldn't fill the prescription until the doctor made out another directive. "You know that medication is enough to kill a horse."

Shawn asked him what would happen if it was taken with alcohol.

"If it didn't kill him, he would hallucinate, become delusional."

It was an unusual Christmas for Mr. Shine, one in which his family had been replaced by the delightful children he had been tutoring in English, by the volunteers who had become his good friends and by his constant companion and shadow, Alireza.

Immediately after the holidays, Shawn and I took Alireza to the Centre for Victims of Torture. After a thorough assessment he was referred to a doctor who specialized in the treatment of torture, so that his medication could be monitored and stabilized. Alireza was more than willing to see a therapist and to join the special English classes offered at the centre.

As we talked about what had happened to Alireza over the Christmas holidays, Shawn seemed to feel that he had failed badly.

"Mr. Shine," I said, for by that time that was also my term of endearment for him. "Neither you nor I can make up for what happened for eight years in an Iranian prison. We just do what we can and usually it's not enough but it's better than nothing."

"But I think I started to identify with him."

"It's hard not to do that when you don't set up clinical walls. When you're neighbours, you cross over a certain boundary but you also have to come back again. It's not helpful for him or for you to stay in the shadow land."

Little by little, Alireza emerged from the pain he had been living with. He met some people at the English class and he found an evangelical church where some members of the congregation and the preacher spoke Farsi. At the same time, Shawn was becoming more and more engaged by the questions that had been raised by the "Common Sense Revolution" in Ontario. He went to every relevant talk and seminar possible in order to try to understand the issues.

Around Easter time, Alireza announced to us that he had asked to be baptized at Pentecost in the evangelical temple. We weren't sure how to react to this news or how to interpret it. By then, all Shawn and I could say was that we knew Alireza felt the need to be saved.

Alireza came to talk the day before the ceremony. "Need new name," he said. "Me need Christian name. Give me name."

I understood that he was looking for a baptismal name and discussed the matter with Shawn. We decided that perhaps Peter would be a good name because it was the name of the apostle who was impulsive, who denied Christ, who was weak and who had messed up, and it hadn't seemed to make any difference to Jesus.

On the evening of Pentecost, Shawn and I and two other volunteers went to the temple where we were escorted to the front row as members of Alireza's family. Ahead of us was a large wall with a fresco of downtown Toronto painted on it. Shawn was familiar with such evangelical proceedings but the rest of us got more nervous as the service became more emotional. After many songs and teachings, two panels in the upper section of the fresco were flung open to reveal pink and blue clouds above the city scene. From above the panels, the baptismal candidates walked down the stairway from heaven until they could face the assembly and make their testimony. Then they disappeared below the panels with a splash and emerged soaking as Christians.

We held our breaths waiting for Alireza. In a white robe, he came down the stairs and stood at the doorway to heaven. The translator said Alireza thanked his friends and that he wished there would be missionaries to Persia. He disappeared and came up soaking.

To commemorate the event, Shawn gave Alireza a Celtic cross from Iona. "My name is Peter," said Alireza as he put it on.

Alireza-Peter's refugee hearing took place a few weeks later. He was so nervous that he had taken several antidepressants beforehand. He rambled and mumbled and blanked out at certain points in the hearing. In spite of a sheaf of medical reports about his condition, one of the judges was visibly irritated with Alireza-Peter's lack of precision. The panel members questioned him for a full day. It was clear that they thought he was lying. By the end of the day the translator told them that she couldn't understand Alireza. "It's not the language. I just can't make out what he's saying. It's so slurred."

Shawn was sitting beside me. We both were horrified when a panel member asked him to repeat what was in the note his wife had written him in prison. "'I am sorry I didn't tell you about my political involvement. . . . I had to do it for my country. . . . Please try to forget . . .'"

"Get on with it," the member said.

"'I leave you in the hands of God.'"

"Is that all?"

"Yes."

It seems that Alireza was left in the hands of God. In what seemed like a miraculous decision, he was accepted by the Immigration and Refugee Board. After that, he seemed to enter into a state of grace. He held down two jobs and began to help other refugees. "Me Peter," he said. "Me new."

THE REACH OF MERCY

She looked as if she could have been related to Anne of Green Gables with her long strawberry-coloured hair and, indeed, Darlene O'Leary was from Little York, Prince Edward Island. There were times too when she was just as impish and then equally as bookish. And Darlene had also experienced some sense of being orphaned. She could not have imagined that she would one day be adopted by an Eritrean woman.

Darlene had left the island and had come to Toronto to do graduate studies in theology. During her undergraduate years at St. Thomas University in New Brunswick she had been deeply influenced by the important Catholic thinker Bernard Lonergan and knew that the Lonergan Centre at Regis College in Toronto was the place to pursue her interests. Lonergan's insights into the significance of value, meaning and community had become part of her way of living and moving in the world.

During her first year in Toronto, however, she lost some of her sense of the meaning and purpose of theology. Her own self-worth was seriously shaken by her inability to engage in some of the academic games or to navigate the reefs and shoals of church politics. The pain of her own past, coming from a broken family, surged to the surface.

Sensing her sadness, two of her friends, who had been volunteering part time at Romero House, invited her to a barbecue for one of the refugees who had just been accepted. As the people began to dance in a circle to an African rhythm, Darlene caught a brief glimpse of the faces of joy and of hope. She remembers thinking she needed that kind of feeling in her own life. After a few more visits to the house she decided to spend the next year away from university so she could volunteer at Romero House.

Darlene was quieter, more introverted than many of the other volunteers. She started slowly, answering the telephone, folding and sorting the clothes that had been donated to the Romero Boutique, doing what she could. Often she sat looking sad but nobody asked her a lot of questions about herself. Discretion with newcomers has become almost a habit of being at Romero House.

Then she said she would take the new woman from Eritrea to the welfare office. All Darlene knew was that the woman's name was Gabriela and that she had two or maybe four children.

When they returned, I sensed that something had changed in Darlene. She began having tea with Gabriela while she waited for her two daughters to come home from school. Gabriela had tried to make a home for the children in the two plain rooms which had become their temporary place of refuge. Washed as they had never been before, the walls seemed to give off a light of their own. They were adorned with pictures of flowers that Gabriela had found in the Romero Boutique and posters of pick-me-up sayings: "Prayer makes a little Easter as you go along."

Darlene began to write down what she was learning as her heart was being schooled:

I took Gabriela to get her welfare. I was in the room with her. She was noticeably tired and strained, but she smiled at me and trusted me to be with her. She was just so tired of it all, going from country to country, from office to office, but she seemed more concerned about whether I was tired. I kept thinking, why do these people have to suffer so much? How do we keep humanity in all this? The welfare worker was mechanical and distant.

Yesterday I went with Gabriela and some of the other women to the food bank. I hated the place. It looked dingy and smelled. It made people feel guilty for being poor. There wasn't enough food and people started to push and shove and the workers behind the counter became rude and vulgar. Victoria and I stayed at the back of the room with our women. There was desperation and fear in the air. It felt like a riot could have started. Our women seemed so dignified. I wish I did not have to take these women there. They were uncomfortable and humiliated. I wanted to say: These are people with names and lives and histories. But with the welfare cuts, their children don't have enough to eat. They have to go and they will go for the sake of their children.

Gabriela told Darlene about her two other children: "My husband was killed by the Ethiopians. I walked through desert with my kids. The two boys were teenagers. There were fighters in the desert [the rebel army of the EPLF]. They say we will drive you to Sudan with two little kids but no room for the big boys. I went but my boys do not come. The fighters keep them to make them fighters.

"I cannot go to my country now. The fighters have the power now. I never forget what they do. If I go to my country now, the first thing I do is to go to the government and ask where is my kids. I never stop asking where is my kids. If they are dead, I will find the fighters who take them. The government knows this."

Darlene began to realize just how strong Gabriela was. And she learned how lonely Gabriela was. "It doesn't mean when you are a refugee you don't know nothing. We understand. We had a country, home, friends. This makes you. It's easy when you have a home. You can think in your home. You know who you are and people know who you are. When you don't have a home, you don't have identity. Nobody can understand you. Nobody knows who you are. It's not easy like this. I cry behind doors. It's painful when you don't have home."

Darlene continued to reflect on the transformation that was taking place within her:

> There seems to be a profound compassion within me. I don't know where God fits in all of this. I feel very far away from God at times which terrifies me but I feel compassion. I value human life so much that I feel crushed by the thought that any life can be lived in pain and fear and sorrow. . . .
>
> Gabriela's smile reveals her spirit and strength and grace. I think that the human spirit can endure many things. I think that the human spirit can endure almost any pain and struggle. It is clear when I see people who have been through hell and still can remain decent, caring people. In the light of this, there is always hope. . . .

I feel the love of my friends, their goodness throughout their pain is a sign of the presence of God. I feel that my response of compassion and sadness and love and pain is a sign of the presence of God. I think that in relationships that hold very basic notions of value as true, there is the presence of God. In our questions and confessions and struggles and triumphs, there is the presence of God—grace. . . . I'm confused with all of this. . . .

I now think of Gabriela as a friend. Not many experience friendship in this culture. Particularly in the city, people have become isolated from each other and consumed by our own well-being. We forget the value of humanity. There is an immediate suspicion, mistrust. . . .

There is the continual presence of God in hardship and in joy. There is a call for and need for conversion of heart, mind and spirit. It is my responsibility to be aware of the world . . . of meaning and value and to act out of that. What else can I do? The world keeps turning.

Yesterday Gabriela said to me: "There are so many problems and so much suffering and I see these good people and I say, 'I love the world.'"

HODGEPODGE

"Let's go to Joe Mercury's," said Brian O'Halloran. It was the end of a long day that had gone in a thousand directions. The attraction of Joe Mercury's grill and bar near the subway station was that it had pool tables and Brian was a big shark, albeit the friendliest one in town. He and Peter Haeg had come to Romero House as volunteers after finishing college in Minnesota and had previously volunteered a year in Israel. Both sons of upper-middle-class families in the suburbs of Minneapolis, they had simply wanted to do something for other people.

They were known to be out late at night and often forgot their keys. However, they had perfected the art of climbing up the drainpipe to a balcony where the door was sometimes open. In the morning it was all business and they whizzed around the city in the van, picking up furniture and clothing. At every stoplight, they would point to the sign on the van, Donated by the Canadian Auto Workers, and raise their arms and yell, "Social justice!"

They weren't exactly sure about what to do about church on Sunday but they were there every morning for prayer in the meditation room. They were intelligent and diligent and easily developed warm relationships with their neighbours. Brian perfected an application form for refugees who had been in Canada for three years, had a job and spoke English. Peter cranked up our secondhand computer and was soon whizzing around the globe to various sites in search of information that would help this or that refugee's process.

On the run and by the way, Brian played soccer with some of the refugees, the best opponents he had ever met and Peter took many a refugee child skating.

And so they went to Joe Mercury's that night. Brian and Peter and Ana de Jesus, the evangelical woman from Guatemala, and Laura, the young woman from Markham who had developed a program for the children at Romero House, and Ali, the sort-of-Marxist from Iran.

"How was your evening?" I asked Peter.

"It was fine. It gives a whole new meaning to the word *hodgepodge*."

Miss Pinky and
the Women's Group

She was called Winkie by her family and friends and was also known as Winnifred on formal documents. However, "Winkie" was a bit of a verbal stretch for many of the refugees and so she was often referred to as "Win-Tee" or "Wimpy" or "Miss Pinky." Whatever her name, it was a term of endearment and respect.

During her days at Runnymede Chronic Care Hospital, Winkie Simpson worked with people who had debilitating illnesses such as Huntington's disease or multiple sclerosis. Her patients jerked with random movement and were sometimes quite violent because they were not able to communicate with others. Huntington's often struck patients in their prime of life, in their early thirties; they would usually remain in the hospital for seven years or so until they died. Patients who were seriously debilitated by MS were often paralysed from the neck down. They would stay at Runnymede for anywhere from a couple of months to many years. Many of the patients had been at Runnymede for years and for some it was the only home they could remember. For most it was their last home.

For Nurse Simpson, work at Runnymede was more of a vocation than a job. Where others would see only hopeless, terminal cases, she saw human beings who needed, and deserved, respect and the highest quality of care. "It is a mystery. My experience with people who work with chronic diseases is that they either last a day or stay there for the rest of their lives. The only care that makes any difference in their lives is real caring. Cure is not really possible so what remains is care. You try to massage out every bit of strength that they have so that they can have a better quality of life. Our patients have taught us a great deal. It's not necessarily what we would think is important for quality of life that they see as important. For example, we were trying to teach a patient to do something but what she really wanted to do was to be able to use the remote on the TV and once she learned that then everything else followed."

Winkie was familiar and comfortable with people from other cultures. In Sierra Leone, she taught nursing students to teach health care at the village level. She would go out into the villages to run clinics and would often see up to a hundred children a day. "We were really barefoot doctors."

She learned some important things in Sierra Leone that would stand her in good stead at Romero House. "It was the first non-Christian culture I had worked in. I was struck with the hospitality. Every inter-action we had was a hospitable moment. After every clinic we were exhausted and we were fed by the villagers. It was really a feast given the income they had to work with. We would eat together, all of the workers and even some of the patients. What we had to share was filtered water. The minute you thought you understood something, then would find out that you didn't and there was always something bigger that you didn't quite get."

In 1982, after about a year working as a CUSO volunteer in Sierra Leone, she was suddenly afflicted with a severe case of fulmanent hepatitis A. Survival expectancy from this form of hepatitis is less than 1 percent. She was flown out of the country to England and hovered between life and death for three days as she lay in a deep coma. When she was in the emergency room she showed no vital signs but during that time, she had what would now be called a near-death experience:

> I was up in the ceiling watching what was going on. What I was doing was watching the emergency staff do its work. They were saying there's no vein or artery and I remember saying that there's a vein in my right leg, and that's where they eventually found it. That was the only time I could remember where I was.
>
> It was the most significant spiritual experience. Up to that time I had no real faith. I was an agnostic although I had been brought up as a Christian.
>
> I was being pulled down a tunnel and it was very pleasant. There's a light at the end of the tunnel. There was a swishing sound, like the sound of air going by. I heard voices and I communicated with the voices. I couldn't tell if it was male or female. The message was that I would be okay. I was given a choice to carry on towards the tunnel, very warm or comfortable, or to go back. The choice to go back was

painful but there was the sense of an unfinished life.

I had a strong sense that it would only be for a short time. I had the strongest sense of resurrection. It was Easter season in the church. I was in England overlooking the heath. There were flowers and daffodils and kids flying kites. Sitting with me through all this was a young doctor who I had worked with in Africa. He and I had fought all the time in Africa. He brought in music, classical music. He was instrumental in helping me hang on.

It was the most significant spiritual experience in Winkie's life and left her with a strong belief in the presence of God here and now. "It hasn't changed the way I work, it's changed the way I feel."

I had first heard about Winkie from a friend in the parish who was always asking me to pray for "Winkie's hospital." Housed in an old elementary school building on St. John's Road, the hospital was always on the edge financially. Again and again it was placed on the chopping block and then granted a last-minute reprieve when politicians were informed that the Runnymede Chronic Care facility had received the highest accreditation rating in the province—and in the country.

So I was delighted when my friend brought over the woman who seemed to embody the feisty commitment of the hospital. At the end of supper, Winkie offered to help one refugee family. It was a simple, direct offer to help.

"I find God's presence in rather simple things," she said. "Mostly in a person's ability to find joy or to keep a strong commitment to a faith."

Every Monday night, Winkie would come over to Romero House and have tea with the most recent refugee family. She listened carefully and then took note of one or two very concrete things that the family needed: a bottle of vitamin pills, a calendar to keep track of events at the kid's school, a baseball glove for an aspiring player. On Monday nights, the kids in the house would start shrieking: "Win-Tee's coming. Win-Tee's here."

And Winkie's face would light up too, fresh and clear. Later she would say that she had wanted to spend time with refugees because she needed to be with people who were more in the process of living than of dying. Perhaps it was her experience of working with women that made Win-Tee particularly attentive to the needs of the women at Romero House. At any rate, the women in Romero House began to suggest to her that it might be good to have a group to talk about "women's things."

At first, the men in the house felt a little excluded. "What are the women going to talk about?"

Winkie and the women decided to hold a regular meeting once a month on a Saturday afternoon.

Initially, the women wanted to talk about women's health problems, and questions of nutrition because they were living on such a restricted budget. Then they wanted to share their concern for their children, their health and safety and discipline and on how they could all deal with winter. Every mother was worried about what their children were learning from TV. Single parents were worried about their children without a male role model.

In the winter of 1996, the central question became: how can we feed our kids? The government cutbacks meant that their children would not have enough milk or fruit.

Winkie described those meetings. "One or two of us would show up on time and the others would come later. At first it was to bridge the time gap but then it became more of a warm-up. It became sharing simple recipes. Being together, reading the recipe, learning to measure, introducing alternatives to store-bought, how to look for nutrition, how to read labels to tell quality of food. The element of being the hostess in it, a kind of shared hospitality. It was a very good way to integrate new people, it's comfortable, it's warm, it's a familiar place. You don't have to be verbal to join in."

The women's group became a sustaining group for all involved. "There was a sense of aloneness that each person brought to the group," said Winkie, "and a strength that the group support seemed to surface. When I heard how desperate they were about their kids' nutrition, I hoped that some inner resource or spirit would mobilize us."

When AIDS Came Knocking

"There is a woman from Grenada here," said the doctor at the clinic. "She is an illegal and she has a small son . . . and she has AIDS and she needs a place to die. Will you take her?"

It was a question similar to the one we had been asked when Sir George came to Romero House. The only difference was that she had AIDS. I told the doctor that I would have to consult with the other people in the house. He felt that this was not necessary at all and that I could be violating the woman's rights and her privacy. "But this is not a rooming house," I tried to explain, "this is a community. There are no locks on any of our doors. We do not live in separate apartments."

"I don't see your point," continued the doctor. "This is a dying woman. Will you look after her or not?"

"It is not my decision alone."

Over the next few days I consulted with the volunteers and with the refugees in the house where I was living. There was a free room next to mine, just as there had been when George came but it was a different group and there seemed to be another unspoken difference: I sensed that this was an important question for us.

All of the volunteers felt that we should take in the woman. However, each of them acknowledged that it was an "easy vote" as they might not be around for the long-term care the woman would require—and for the long-term responsibility the son would deserve. They were also concerned that there was a husband and father in the city who was taking no responsibility for the situation. One person reminded us that she was not a refugee, but another pointed out that she was a human being.

The next step was to talk to the refugees in the house. There was Natan and Svetlana, the couple who had been burned by Chernobyl,

Ali and his wife from Iran and a newly arrived family from Rwanda. I asked them to come to a meeting that evening and we all sat around the common room together while I explained as best as I could. Winkie, our ever-available nurse, was present during the conversation and answered some of their questions about AIDS itself. She explained that it was very difficult to become infected with it but that some of the secondary diseases which the woman would develop, such as TB, would be more infectious. We agreed to think about it for a day and then each of them would come and give me their decision.

The next morning Ali, the sort-of-Marxist Iranian, knocked on my door. In slow and ponderous words he said, "My wife and I feel we have a duty to help this poor woman."

By noon, the husband of the Rwandan family had come into the kitchen and said in French, "We understand AIDS where I come from. I had a nephew who died from it. Usually we care for these people at home. So we are not against having her here. But we are not sure who would look after her. We are all at school or at work all day and what would we do if you were away? What if there was an emergency and you were not here?"

I waited for the response of Natan and Svetlana. In the evening I knocked on their door and Natan opened it, looking very wan and white. "What's the matter?" I asked.

"Svetlana gone. Svetlana gone freedom," he said.

"Gone freedom?"

"Yes. Go outside. No come home all day. Never do this."

"Why is she upset?"

"She think Sasha get sick AIDS because not strong from Chernobyl."

We talked about the matter again as a Romero team and decided that we simply didn't have enough support to carry it off for the long haul. We also realized that Romero House was the one safe place for many of the refugees and, willingly or unwillingly, we had introduced an element of danger.

I still do not know if it was the right decision. I know it was the only one possible. Nevertheless, it was a stranger we did not welcome.

The Tuna-tin Cross

In the little village of La Broquerie in Manitoba, Norbert Piché had grown up eating chicken and mashed potatoes, hot dogs on Saturday evenings while watching Bugs Bunny, and hamburgers and french fries after mass on Sundays. On Christmas Eve his Franco-Manitoban family would sit down to a table filled with the traditional tortière, sweet peas, roast turkey and lots of homemade bread and pies. Although they were not wealthy, they always had food on the table.

Food was not the only thing that could be taken for granted. The members of the closely knit francophone community knew that they could count on each other and that they could depend on their little church for moral and spiritual support. The "outsiders" and "strangers" were the English, and Winnipeg was another world.

As it became more difficult to find priests to serve in rural Manitoba, the parishioners of Eglise St. Joachim began to take more responsibility and leadership for the life and faith of the parish. As a teenager, Norbert became involved in the parish and was a committed member in the movement to form small Christian communities.

It was assumed that Norbert would go to university and then become a teacher. He had always done well in sports and it seemed natural for him to become the physical education teacher in a rural school. Soon he had all the things that seem to be part of the life of a teacher: a new car, a house of his own and a girlfriend. He loved cooking and developed a reputation as something of a gourmet. Winter holidays in the south and a retirement savings program seemed to complete the picture.

He was twenty-five. He had everything. And he knew he wasn't happy. At the end of a day of teaching he was tired and wondered what he was doing with his life. Norbert talked to his pastor who suggested that he pray for guidance.

Norbert tried to pray but he felt alone. In a moment of insight, he decided that he couldn't hear what God was saying because there was too much noise in his life. He resolved to unplug his radio, stereo set and

TV for three months. At the end of that time, he had little clarity about what he should do but he knew he could not remain where he was.

With a speed that surprised his family and friends, he took a leave of absence from his job at the school and put his house up for rent. Though he wanted to serve others, he didn't know how or where. His pastor provided him with information on many volunteer programs but Norbert didn't receive any reply to his inquiries. He spent the summer in limbo and wondered whether God had played some big joke on him.

His doubts dissipated when he received a phone call from the director of the Jesuit volunteer program who said that there was still room for Norbert even though the deadline for applications had long been past. The director told him that the placements with the Jesuit projects had been filled but that there were other organizations who could probably use his help. Norbert immediately packed a single bag, got on the earliest plane and hitched a ride to Toronto, to another country and another world.

He landed at Romero House where the first refugee he ever met in his life greeted him in elegant French. Norbert was astounded. He had assumed that all of his work in Toronto would be conducted in English but some great providence had ensured that his coming to Romero House coincided with the arrival of several refugees from French-speaking Africa: Rwanda, Burundi, Zaire.

Norbert became the great interlocutor and more—he became a brother to the adults and a godfather to their children. Each month he prepared a bilingual and multicultural Sunday liturgy which was attended by the Christian members of Romero House and people from the extended community. At the end of the service there was a time for Romero community announcements and a potluck lunch. Once again, Norbert found himself engaged in the process of building small Christian communities.

He discovered new perspectives in his own faith from the refugees who shared their reflections after the reading of the scriptural texts. One Sunday the community listened to the reading from the Scriptures in which Moses tries to pray for his people but his arms begin to flag.

In this story, Aaron goes to assist him, holding up the arms of Moses so he can continue in prayer.

Augustin from Rwanda was particularly pensive. He had barely escaped with his wife and children from the genocide in his country but many cousins, brothers and sisters had been murdered. The horror of this news had been compounded by reports that some members of the Catholic clergy had encouraged the genocide or, at least, remained silent.

"When I think about what happened in my country," he said, "I think that the Church must have got tired and stopped praying. And I am very sad. It makes me question my faith. But then I remember that I am also the Church and I must, like Aaron, help the Church to hold up its hands and pray. And so I must ask myself what I have done to help the Church pray and to become holy and just. The Church is not just the clergy, it is each of us helping each other become holy."

Norbert started an English class for the refugees who had not arrived in time to register for the regular ESL programs in the schools. Every afternoon at four o'clock, gales of laughter could be heard coming from the living room beside the Romero office as Norbert pulled out yet another rabbit from his teaching bag of tricks.

Norbert himself was laughing most of the time. He was having the time of his life teasing the other volunteers or "ripping," as they say. When Rosemary was recalling an event in the sixties, Norbert piped up, "So you were in your forties then. That was kind of old for a hippie!"

We soon found out how to get Norbert's goat by calling him "Bert" or "Peachy." He was often reminded who won at the battle of the Plains of Abraham and why. "Because we were bigger and better and smarter." The great national unity debate was conducted in a most undiplomatic fashion. "Riel will rise again!" yelled Norbert, his fist held high.

Norbert's year at Romero House extended to two and then to three. He had become as competent as anyone could be in dealing with immigration matters. Many refugees came to the door asking for his assistance in filling out various application forms. With his clear intelligence, he cut through the immigration jargon and cleared the way forward for them. On one occasion he reached back to his parish and asked them to raise money to help a young woman from Zaire bring her husband and two children from a refugee camp in Spain.

Gradually Norbert laughed a little less but a lot louder as his time at Romero House extended into years. We knew the Common Sense Revolution in Ontario was deadly serious and had started to affect the lives of the refugees. Since the 21 percent cut in the welfare budget, most of the people in the houses were hungry at least half of the month. The parents worried, not for themselves, but for their children who were not getting enough fresh fruit and vegetables. Refugees could no longer afford the cost of transit to English classes or job interviews. New shoes or winter boots were out of the question. Many could not afford the trip to the Romero Boutique to pick up used clothing. Every nickel had to be saved to pay the new immigration head tax, and all that could be saved was nickels and dimes. Refugee claimants found it almost impossible to get jobs because of the stigma of the number 9 (temporary status) on their social insurance card. Legal aid was cut so severely that the conscientious lawyers did not have enough time to prepare their cases. And we knew these cuts would do little to curtail the activities of more unscrupulous lawyers who were overbilling for minimal effort. A three-tier legal system was developing.

Norbert still loved to cook but he lost interest in expensive gourmet meals. The pressure increased on those of us working at the Romero office. Refugees phoned insistently asking us to try to speed up their process for becoming landed immigrants so that they could get a job, so that they could go to school, so that they could bring their families to safety. They kept calling, it seemed, because we were the only ones who answered the phone. If they dialled the information centre of Immigration Canada they were put on hold for half an hour or more until a machine answered and asked them to push buttons until they got another machine.

"I'm sorry." That was all we seemed able to answer. "I'm sorry we don't have enough money to help everyone pay the head tax." "I'm sorry we don't have enough food for everyone." "I'm sorry we don't have clothes for everyone." "I'm sorry we can't cover the transit costs for people to go to school."

We became sorrier and sorrier. We felt helpless in the face of the wave of suffering which was being cast up on our shores as the great ship *The Economy* went steaming by.

Norbert was alternately depressed by what he saw and then angered by the news of bank profits, salary increases for top executives and tax deferrals for corporations. Yet what galled him the most was the statement from the minister of social services, Dave Tsubouchi, that the poor could eat tuna. When someone challenged him saying that tuna was expensive, Tsubouchi replied that people could get a can of tuna for sixty-nine cents if they bargained at the counter.

"But that's just sawdust." Norbert's eyes were filled with tears as he blinked in disbelief. He took this all into his heart and he brought it with him as he prayed. There were no easy solutions, of this he was sure, but just feeling sorry led nowhere. Once again he journeyed to the border called hope.

We began meeting on Wednesday nights to pray, to reflect on our life with the refugees in the light of the revolution initiated by Jesus. Norbert spoke eloquently about the importance of not casting the government as the enemy to be fought against. He was searching for a way to construct an alternative based on love. The discussions sparked our imaginations at a deeper level and rekindled our belief that the power of love and truth was stronger than the forces of greed and indifference in the world.

Someone recalled our experience of holding a twenty-four-hour vigil outside the law society buildings during the time when the cuts to legal aid were being debated by the benchers inside. Some of the benchers had taken notice of our little group and it seemed to matter to them that we were there. And even if they hadn't noticed, we knew it had felt right and true to bring all the concerns for our neighbours in one long act of prayer.

In a matter of minutes we decided to hold another twenty-four-hour vigil outside the legislature buildings at Queen's Park on the day before the omnibus bill was to be voted upon. With the image of the sixty-nine-cent tuna can vividly in our minds, we resolved to bring a large cross with tuna cans nailed along its length and breadth. This was the cross of the poor in Ontario, the cross we were now resolved to carry with our friends and neighbours.

It was only a matter of days before the omnibus bill was to be voted upon and we moved quickly to make the necessary preparations. Winter-weather wear was begged and borrowed, containers of water and energy food were packed and the security police at Queen's Park were informed. I went shopping for cans of tuna but the cheapest I could find cost eighty cents. They were emptied out—the contents to become tasteless tuna loaves and the cans to provide the substance for our new religious symbol.

We carried that cross around Queen's Park every twenty minutes throughout the day and during the long night of intense wind and cold. People came and went, listening to the Scriptures which were read every time the cross would pause in front of the legislature buildings. The video surveillance cameras swivelled to and fro, quickly at first and then more slowly. In the early morning hours, one of the security guards came out of the side door and said, "We were worried about you guys out there in the cold."

In the long cold night each one of us faltered and then crossed some line through physical pain towards the conviction that we could be part of a human revolution.

A photographer from the *Toronto Sun* caught an image of the tuna-tin cross as it was being carried around Queen's Park by our long-haired volunteer, Shawn Beck. Following behind him, head covered with a toque, eyes lowered and hands clasped in prayer like an altar boy, was Norbert Piché.

Early in the new year, Shawn and Norbert started to brainstorm about possible ways through and around the economic brick wall that had been thrown up before the refugees. The two volunteers instinctively knew that our model of neighbourliness had to be deepened spiritually and given a stronger economic foundation. To this discussion, Norbert brought his experience in building local communities of faith and Shawn drew upon his knowledge of the models of cooperation which had helped farming communities survive the Great Depression on the prairies.

Together they drew up a plan for a Romero House cooperative, which was circulated to everyone involved in the community for discussion. They also outlined two parallel initiatives, one called the Romero House Small Loans Program and the other called the Romero Companion Program. All three programs went through several revisions before they were presented at a large meeting to which everyone interested was invited. A committed and competent group of refugees took up the challenge of doing some market research in order to develop the bulk purchasing and distribution of food.

However, Norbert also knew that every refugee, no matter what his or her qualifications were, was at the back of the line for any job. The only alternative, he reasoned, was for people to create their own jobs. He contacted the Calmeadow Foundation, which was developing alternate ways of helping small-business ventures, and invited those interested to discuss the possibility of forming collective loan agreements.

There was another twenty-four-hour vigil held at Queen's Park during the night of Holy Thursday and throughout Good Friday. Once again, those participating shared in a scriptural prayer before the cross was carried around the park every twenty minutes. Around seven in the morning, the security guards came outside the legislature buildings and quietly removed the large metal barricades that had been placed there since the riots which had taken place after the government had introduced its omnibus bill. Perhaps they thought it was the time when hardly anyone would notice that the barricades had come down. However, the small group surrounding the tuna-tin cross was there. When the security officers departed, the two volunteers, Norbert and Darlene, ran up the steps of the legislature buildings with the cross.

We have a photo on the wall of the Romero office of that glorious moment on Good Friday. Norbert and Darlene are standing beside the cross, each holding it up with one arm and with the other arm stretched up and out. They are laughing resurrection.

IN OUR BACKYARD

Behind one of the Romero houses on Wanda Road is an old two-storey garage which may have had pretentions of coach-house grandeur at some earlier point in its history. It would probably be true to say that we bought this particular house because of the garage. The two large doors on the ground level were warped beyond the point of closing, the shingles waved in the slightest wind and wires hung helplessly from the mildewed walls. But it had space, generous and ample space.

We had developed a moderate plan to renovate the dilapidated structure so we could store donated food and clothes there and have a workshop where old furniture could be repaired. In bolder moments, we even envisioned that the top floor could become a place for arts and crafts with a corner for a sewing machine and weaving loom.

It was a modest dream, one which did not seem out of the realm of possibility. Slowly, over a period of three years, we raised money from various groups and individuals for this project. Finally, we were in a position to hire an architect who was willing to do the drawings for half of his usual fee. He held a series of meetings at Romero House so the refugees could give him some input as he was preparing the designs. Someone reminded him that the workshop should be separated from the rest of the building so the children wouldn't be tempted to play with the equipment. Another suggested that a second sewing machine would be more useful than a loom. Those were exciting hours as we gathered around the long table on the porch, poring over the architect's designs. We were building something together.

All that remained, or so we thought, was to go through the committee of adjustment at city hall for the necessary building permits. We did not foresee any difficulty as we had a letter from Patrick Collins, our next-door neighbour, saying that the building had been used for storage and a workshop over fifty years ago. This meant that the garage renovations would not be hampered by the more recent city bylaws which had been designed to prevent the conversion of coach houses into rental units.

Pat Collins was an unusual Torontonian in that he had lived all of his life on this one block. He and his wife, Mary, now in their fifties, had seen many people come and go over the years. From the first day we moved in, they greeted us as a welcome and interesting change to what had been an all-white street.

Mary and I would sometimes chat on the back steps. "I listen to those kids when they're playing in the driveway," she said. "Those are happy kids."

There was a shared driveway between our house and the Collins' home and it was here that we became tested and true neighbours. When the Collins' boys left one of their reconstructed jalopies in the driveway, I would ring their doorbell and ask that it be moved so we could drive the van into the garage in our backyard. They drove or pushed the old car out of the way. When some of the kids in our house constructed a barricade of cardboard boxes across the driveway, Mary came and asked if this great architectural wonder could be relocated elsewhere. With a few swift kicks, our five-year-old architects collapsed the barricade and hauled it into the Romero House living room. It was the daily negotiations of people living side by side that made us neighbours.

Pat and Mary lived in full view of our large garage which sat as a two-storey wall along much of their backyard. They thought the plans for its renovation were sensible, long overdue. "It's going to collapse some day," Pat told me as he was watering the old grapevine that hung on a trellis near the garage. "If something isn't done, it's just going to fall down."

Barbara from across the street also liked the plan to renovate the garage. She had started working on crafts during the nights when she couldn't sleep for worrying about Paul, her disabled son. "I could teach the refugees some of the things I have learned once the craft area is set up," she said. "And we could have a big block party for everyone on the street to celebrate when the garage is finished."

Barbara and Pat and Mary were like all of the neighbours on the street we had met since we had moved in three years ago. The wife of a photographer across the street dropped off a supply of paper and crayons for the children. Jane, a teacher who was recuperating from a serious illness, created small jobs in her yard so the refugees could earn a little extra money. A young couple from around the corner dropped off some hockey sticks when they saw some of the Romero kids playing ball hockey on the road with pieces of two-by-fours.

There was only one neighbour I had not met—the man who lived down the street from us. I had never seen him, or at least never noticed him and I did not know his name.

All the neighbours within two hundred feet of the garage received notice of the date the renovation project was to be presented to the Committee of Adjustment at city hall in early September 1995. None of the neighbours we knew were planning on going to the hearing because they thought the garage was a good idea and they assumed that everyone else was of the same opinion. Little did we know that the neighbour we had never met was preparing to do battle. He contacted all his Eastern European friends from the street behind us and began to whip up a storm of protest.

The evening of the hearing at city hall, Lorne Howcroft, the chairman of our board, presented the proposed changes to the garage. Earlier that afternoon he had sensed that there would be trouble when he had gone over to the house on Wanda Road and had been accosted by the unknown neighbour on the street.

"You people over there are just ripping the country off."

"We don't get any money out of this, you know. We're all volunteers."

"Like hell you are."

Lorne tried to contact the neighbours we knew to see if they could go to city hall in the evening but they were either out of town or already committed elsewhere. Mary Collins got word of the crisis to Pat who was away on a fishing trip. Much to Lorne's surprise, Pat showed up in the hearing room at city hall just before the proceedings were about to begin. Summoning up all the skills he had honed during his years as a high school principal, Lorne launched into his presentation of the garage project, treading adroitly through the minefield of potential objections.

Then the unknown neighbour and his allies began to present their objections: the building would be raised twenty feet and it would make it easy for the peeping toms who were "over there"; there were wife beaters at that house; there were wild parties going on at that house with lots of drinking; it would bring criminal elements into the neighbourhood; there are too many children over there, like rabbits. Pat fought back saying that this was not the case, that the garage wasn't to be raised; that the parties were quieter than most on the street; that there were good people in the house and that he should know because he lived next door.

It was too late. The board sensed that much of the neighbourhood was against the project and ruled against the renovations on a technicality.

The garage sat in a state of slow deterioration all fall. We could have appealed the ruling of the Committee of Adjustment but we sensed that the unknown neighbours would make life even more difficult for the refugees. The money we had raised for the project was returned to those who had given it specifically for renovations to the garage.

I was somewhat discouraged by the turn of events on Wanda Road just as I was disheartened by the mean spirit which seemed to haunt the political landscape. As I walked along the streets near our house that autumn, I noticed a lot of people who seemed to be Eastern European. I would look at the man raking his leaves, at the woman sitting on the porch, at the two men on the sidewalk with Eastern European accents. And I wondered: Was it you? Were you the one? Were you at the meeting?

The questions built upon one another until I had constructed a wall between me and the unknown people on the next street. However, there was a crack in this wall just small enough for my soul to slip through. I realized that I had become like those I was fighting against. I had stopped thinking of these people as neighbours. I had become racist, indulging in a dangerous caricature of Eastern Europeans. I had begun to think of them as my enemies and I had constructed a border within myself to keep them out of my heart.

I prayed. Don't let me give up hope in all of us. May we meet again at the border.

A few weeks before Christmas I received a phone call from some neighbours, the Leckies, on Wanda Road whom I had met only briefly. They felt that their children would be receiving many things for Christmas and that it was important to learn that Christmas was a time for giving, a time for thinking of your neighbours and those who may have less than you do. Could their family bring presents for all the people at Romero House on Wanda Road?

I went over to the house of Keith and Mary Leckie to discuss their thoughtful inquiry. Mary and Keith had visited our house one Boxing Day but there had been little time to converse—either at the party or later in our friendly but quick hellos on the corner of Wanda and Indian roads. They were both thoroughly engaged in raising their small children and in the writing and production of television programs.

It was obvious that they were serious about their desire to share their family's Christmas with the people at Romero House. As the Leckie kids roared in and out of the living room, Mary explained that she needed to know a little bit about each family, or partial family, in the house. What were their ages, their gender, their sizes, their interests? "You know we are really fortunate to have the refugees on our street," she said.

The words did not come easily. "It means a lot to hear you say that, Mary . . . especially after what happened to the garage."

"To the garage?"

I went back over what had happened earlier in the fall. Keith was outraged and said, "That's terrible. You should have told us. We didn't know."

"Perhaps that's what I've learned," I replied. "We have been so preoccupied with trying to live as neighbours with the refugees that we haven't had enough time to get to know our other neighbours and so they don't know us."

"Well, you can't do everything," said Mary. "Let's try and do something about Christmas."

And she did. Three days before Christmas, Mary and her children arrived at the door with boxes of presents and food for everyone. Each gift, carefully wrapped and clearly named, was placed under the tree. The kids in the house circled the tree hourly, waiting for the magic morning when they could open their presents.

One of the gifts was for Debbie, the sprightly little girl from Sri Lanka who loved frilly dresses for herself and for her doll. As she tore through the wrapping paper she saw a shimmering velvet blue dress with a white lace collar and it fit her perfectly.

She clasped the dress to her chest and said, "We have such wonderful neighbours here."

The winter became spring on Wanda Road and the boys in the house spent the early evenings and weekends out on the street playing ball hockey with the other kids on the street. The hockey sticks they had received from the Leckie family were a little the worse for wear but with a little tape they remained treasured possessions that allowed the boys to enter the world of Canadian sports. When someone donated a small bicycle to Romero House, the boys and girls spent hours zigzagging along the street, trying to navigate on two wheels.

A new neighbour on the street had a ringside view of the children playing on the street as he spent hours working in his designer garden. He was concerned about what he saw and spoke to one of the volunteers living at Romero House. "The kids are so busy playing hockey that they don't notice when the cars turn the corner. And the kids on the bicycle need a helmet. Someone, not me but someone, could report them to the police for not having a helmet."

We knew his concerns were legitimate and thanked him for watching out for the kids. What to do about the situation presented a little more of a challenge because we knew that the kids needed to play somewhere and that their parents could not afford to buy them helmets for bicycle riding.

And then the garage re-emerged from the recesses of our minds as more of a solution than a problem. We purchased a simple basketball net and built a backboard for it just over the doors of what would have been the entrance to our dream. The kids in the house soon learned to dribble along the shared driveway and would shoot hoops for hours. Gradually, the other kids on the street began looking down the driveway to the basketball net hanging from the garage.

Little five-year-old Mohammed came bouncing in the front door and gasped, "Can the other kids play too?" He was excited and proud. The other kids wanted to come to his place.

"Yes. They can all play in our backyard."

LANDINGS

In the summer, the direction of hope lies north. More precisely, the signs for it can be seen along highway 400 North until it becomes 69 and then turns west to become highway 17 leading into Espanola, Ontario—the gateway to Manitoulin Island. We have followed these signs every August for five years now—a caravan of fifty-five people in an old school bus accompanied by the Romero House van and several cars.

We go north to a place where the landscape seems less marked by borders and frontiers. At Anderson Lake, about ten kilometres from Espanola, we become more aware of when day borders on night and how each morning becomes a new frontier. We see where the line between earth and sky blurs and billows. There, the fish seek refuge from the heat between the rocks and the birds fly high above any checkpoint. This is the landscape of hope and it is here that we all find a place to be.

The landscape teaches what all the information about the history and politics of Canada cannot: a sense of place, a love of this vast and mysteriously beautiful land that one can call home. We leave as a group of refugees and neighbours and we return as citizens of a place called hope.

The journey north has been the focus of preparations during the winter and spring months. As soon as one camp is finished, Jack Costello, a member of the Romero board, begins sending out appeal letters to the *Toronto Star* Fresh Air Fund, to the Office of Missions of the Catholic Bishops and to several loyal friends. Although he is extremely busy during the academic year in his capacity as president of Regis College, it would be true to say that the summer camp is his favourite project of the year. In his spare time, he browses around dollar stores and garage sales in search of supplies and pieces of equipment for the camp.

By Easter, a letter has gone out to all of those who may be interested in the camp. Priority is given to former residents who have continued to volunteer their services to the Romero community. Small committees are formed and the next few months are times of intense preparation for the children's program and the food supplies.

The greatest challenge facing everyone is how to stretch the few dollars available for the camp venture. Most of the money given in donations goes to cover the cost of transporting the whole group in the school bus. This means that the cost of feeding the entire group must be kept to what would be spent in a week on a welfare cheque.

Winkie and her committee have now perfected the fine art of finding tasty and healthy food for fifty-five people for the lowest possible price. Together with Semira, Winkie begins hunting for food bargains at all the retail hot spots: Knob Hill Farms, Maple Leaf Farms, the Price Club and, last but not least, the vegetable market of Mrs. Rita on the corner of Grenadier and Roncesvalles. All the meat, juice, margarine, rice and pasta and various other essentials are frozen and stored during the summer in Winkie's freezer and in the various freezing compartments throughout the Romero houses. The day before the departure for camp, Semira and I go down to Mrs. Rita's and purchase large cases of fruit and vegetables—enough for the entire week. This advance shopping is necessary because of the increased cost of food in the north.

The Bag Lady of Brampton inventively amasses supplies for the children's program: paper plates for masks, macaroni for glue paintings, paintbrushes, puzzles for a rainy day, popsicle sticks and plastic containers for the construction of jewellery boxes and bird feeders.

All of the food, the camping equipment and supplies for the children's program are loaded into the Romero van in the early hours of the morning of the departure. By eight in the morning, the refugees, the volunteers and some members of the Romero House board begin assembling in front of the house on Wanda Road. The school bus arrives, the group assembles for a brief prayer and the journey called hope begins.

As the bus and van make their way north, some of those who are looking out the windows are seeing the Canadian countryside for the first time. It is a different face of Canada and, as the miles go by, the walls of the city and the immigration system seem to fade away.

Six hours later, the group arrives at the Anishinawbe Spiritual Centre on Anderson Lake. A cluster of small cabins surrounding a large central log building and circular timber frame chapel seem to grow out of the rocks on the edge of a pristine northern lake. When Fadumo first saw the centre, she said, "Wow," and many other refugees and volunteers over the years have said much the same.

The Anishinawbe Centre is a place of spirituality for the native peoples of Manitoulin Island. The initiative for the centre came largely from the Jesuit priests who have served the people on the island for more than a century. It becomes, once again, a place where the native peoples and their friends welcome newcomers such as ourselves. Here we live together for a week, swim together, eat together and celebrate a great deal. Valerie Walsh, an adult educator for the City of York and a member of the Romero board, brings an abundance of know-how and gentle wisdom to the task of coordinating the camp. There are many activities: swimming, fishing, blueberry picking, mushroom walks, marshmallow roasts, trips to native art galleries, hikes and boat rides on the North Channel. The meals are prepared by rotating teams who experiment with a wide variety of national dishes and have displayed an incredible ingenuity with leftovers. It is a time of community.

As the camp draws to a close, I am writing the final pages of this book and, as mist in the morning, memory rises. The loon calls and I recall the party at Club Romero last night. It was held on the little porch off the kitchen that we turned into a cabaret for the adults so they could play cards and dance after the children had gone to bed.

Last night they danced and, for once, I just sat there and watched. It was the music of all nations in one cassette after the other, Eritrean, Somali, reggae, Russian rock. Semira began to lead the circle around the room, and then Natan and Svetlana joined hands and followed: Gabriela and Zeinib started to dance with their shoulders in the Eritrean way and Mark and his wife seemed to leap with energy off the floor. Then Joseph made his grand entrance looking like a Tutsi king. Angela watched, but only for a while. Soon they were cutting up a storm. Once the music turned to reggae, Patrick, the new man from Nigeria, entered the circle on one foot with his hand held high. Even the shy and pensive Djillali from Algeria couldn't resist.

I wanted them to dance like that forever, dance away all tears and sorrows of the world. And for those few hours, it seemed to me that they did.

When the music stopped, we talked about the ones who were not with us, about Ana de Jesus and Ghenet who were trying to get back into Canada after they had been deported to the United States, about Mama Miriam who had never written again but we remembered her sambusas, about Mon Général who couldn't come because Dan couldn't leave his job at the gas pump, and those great Kurds, Sami and Suleyman, who never seemed to take it easy.

And we started to read from the scrapbook that people had been writing in all week:

"I am not born for one corner. The whole world is my native land." Signed Gabriela.

"It is night outside and the wind blows and the rain falls. . . . Now I feel better. In this very special place God has shown me how to start over again." Signed Angela.

"So diversified a nation. Yet so united a community. Better experienced than told." Signed Patrick.

As we read the comments in the scrapbook, someone recalled the great voyage to "Amirland" at the last camp. The older boys were to go on a day-long trip, a boatride across the lake and a hike along an island. It was the first time that many of them had really been apart from their parents and some of the mothers lined up on the dock to wish them a worried goodbye.

When the boats were on the water, Amir, Semira's oldest boy, shouted that he wanted the island named after him. "I name this land Amirland," he proclaimed. Minutes later the boats arrived at the rocky coast, the boys clambered out, grabbing what bushes they could and that was when the wasps' nest fell. Twenty minutes later the boys were back at the dock at the centre crying for their mothers. Such was their first great expedition into manhood.

Their voyage of discovery was different this year. As Jack and Lorne and Maureen, a summer volunteer, were taking the older children along a strenuous path to another lake, their troops began to lag. Sasha, the child of Chernobyl, was running short of breath and had started to turn pink from the heat.

Just when it seemed wiser to go back than to proceed, the group came upon a fifteen-foot rock cliff overlooking the deep, clear water. Cool water for Sasha. The children wanted to jump but were afraid. Jack, once again the little boy from northern Quebec, told them he would jump with them if they wanted to try and he would even hold their hand if they really really wanted to do it.

He jumped with each of them into the deep and then they did it on their own, vaulting with their knees held in a crouch. Semira's sons and oldest daughter, Gabriela's daughters, Zeinib's sons, Joseph and Adèle's sons, Sasha—all of them.

Again and again and again. Bobbing up like corks in the water, swimming to the shore and then running up the ragged incline to the top. Glistening, screaming with glee.

They leaped and turned, saluting to some unseen flag, waving to the world. Shining, shining like the sun. The winged ones.

APPENDICES

APPENDIX 1

A CALL TO CONSCIENCE

A Statement on Refugees from Faith Communities of Canada

June 27, 1995

Toronto

Memories serve us well when they present us with the possibility of making choices and commitments that will make a difference now and in the future. This spring we marked the fiftieth anniversary of the end of the Second World War. We continue to remember how many lives were destroyed or diminished by a conflagration fueled by hatred and racism. This is a time to recommit ourselves as a nation to the values of freedom, tolerance and justice.

It was only after the war that we as Canadians slowly realized that while we were engaged in fighting a racist nationalism in Europe and the Far East, we were engaging in our own forms of racism here at home. We became more aware we had treated certain groups with callous injustice.

In the book *None Is Too Many*, historians Irving Abella and Harold Troper documented how Canada had the worst record in the western world in accepting Jewish refugees. Many Canadians were shocked to hear this as we hold an image of ourselves as a tolerant and generous people. Nevertheless, it is true that a senior civil servant when asked by a reporter about the number of Jewish refugees Canada would accept, replied saying, "None is too many."

That policy was effectively implemented because politicians pandered to racist groups in the country, because the vast majority of the population did not know and did not seek to find out the truth of the refugee situation and because many official church bodies did not make a vigorous effort to speak out.

We will not let this happen again. We believe it is now our moral duty to speak about the reality of Canada's treatment of refugees. We know this reality because of the people in our respective communities who are working closely with refugees. Like them, we are worried that "none is too many" could become the operative policy within Immigration Canada today. We will not let this happen.

We are profoundly concerned about the situation of refugees who have come to our country because their lives are at risk. Most of these people are decent, often courageous human beings who were forced to leave everything that they had, everything that they were, because of their political convictions, their religious beliefs or their membership in a certain social group. Under the Geneva Convention and other international covenants, we as Canadians have bound ourselves to offering protection to these people. This commitment is a measure of our decency as a country.

Unfortunately, these people are being scapegoated for many of the profound social and economic problems in our country. In the media, refugees are often portrayed as criminals or potential criminals, as welfare frauds, as gate crashers, etc. No doubt there are some people who have no right to claim refugee status but the vast majority of them are people who ask only for a second chance at life.

As people who have been shaped by the biblical tradition, we are called to welcome the stranger as we would welcome God in our midst. We reject attempts to portray refugees as problems rather than as people who bring great promise to our country. It is morally wrong to make scapegoats of these people. As a nation we have begun to feel very insecure about our national boundaries. However, it is wrong to think that those boundaries are threatened by the relatively small number of people who enter our country seeking refuge. Our boundaries have been and are being erased by vast transnational economic forces, by freer trade, by global communications.

It is tragic that while we are opening our borders for business, we are closing them to desperate people. We are profoundly disturbed by rumours of our government's plan to shut out refugees who arrive at our border via the United States. Our estimation is that any such policy would drastically reduce the number of refugees who could find safety in Canada.

We are often told, and then we think, that we have a generous and accepting refugee policy. In fact, ours is a rather modest effort. Compared with most countries in the world we accept a pitifully small number of people (less than half of one percent of the world refugee population). The vast majority of refugees are welcomed and sustained by countries in the "two thirds world."

It is almost impossible for refugees who are in danger of their lives to get a visa from a Canadian immigration officer overseas.

We also have in our communities people who work for Immigration Canada. We know most of them are decent people. We also know they are overworked and are often frustrated by conflicting and changing directives. However, our concern is that the financial resources of Immigration are increasingly directed at keeping certain people out instead of offering protection to genuine refugees.

We are particularly concerned about the "head tax" which was recently placed on refugees. Most refugees had to spend all their resources just to get to Canada. The cost of attaining landed immigrant status is virtually impossible for most of them. This makes it impossible for them to sponsor spouses and/or children who may be in situations of great danger. It also makes it very difficult for them to begin any serious job training program.

Let us reach out in mercy. Let us help these people stand on their own two feet. Let us not stand by and watch while they stoop and bend under the burden of the head tax.

We believe that we as Canadians have been, can be, much better than this. Even in difficult economic times, most Canadians know there is a difference between being out of a job and out of a life.

Never again.

We now commit ourselves to engaging in an extensive process of education within our communities regarding the real situation of refugees. We believe that most of our people will be shocked and motivated by information regarding the distress of refugees in Canada.

We commit ourselves to supporting and working with other faith communities whose members can feel extremely vulnerable at such a time.

The Second World War happened, in part, because not enough ordinary people spoke out against the racism and intolerance which was developing in the 1930s. Never again.

We will speak and act on behalf of those whose lives and human rights are threatened at this time. We owe this to those who lost their lives. We owe it to ourselves and to future generations—to become a nation we can hope in.

SIGNATORIES

Alexandra Johnson, President, Canadian Council of Churches; Archbishop Michael Peers, Primate, Anglican Church of Canada; Most Reverend Nicola De Angelis, CFIC Auxiliary Bishop of Toronto, on behalf of the Canadian Conference of Catholic Bishops and Bishop Faber MacDonald, chair of the Social Affairs Commission, CCCB; Deacon Michael Morcos, Ecumenical Officer, Coptic Orthodox Church Canada; Rev. Arie G. Van Eek, Executive Secretary, Council of Christian Reformed Churches; Pastor Henry A. Fischer, Dean of the Toronto Conference, Eastern Synod Evangelical Lutheran Church in Canada on behalf of Bishop William D. Huras; The Very Rev. Nicolas Boldireff, Archpriest of Christ the Saviour Cathedral, Toronto, on behalf of His Grace Seraphim, Bishop of Ottawa and Canada, Orthodox Church in America; The Rev. Drew D. Strickland, Moderator of the Presbytery of East Toronto of the Presbyterian Church in Canada representing the Rev. Dr. Raymond Hodgson,

Associate Secretary Justice Ministries, The Presbyterian Church in Canada; Heather MacDonald, Staff Officer, Immigration and Race Relations, United Church of Canada; Irving Abella, Past President Canadian Jewish Congress; Rabbi W. Gunther Plaut, OCO Ont, Senior Scholar, Holy Blossom Temple; Rabbi Baruch Frydman-Kohl, Beth Tzedec Congregation, represented by Cantor Tobias Gabriel of Beth Tzedec Congregation; Rabbi Daniel Komito Gottlieb, Executive Director of Canadian Council for Reform Judaism; Rabbi Mark Dratch, Shaarei Shomayim Congregation.

CO-SIGNATORIES

Dr. Mohammed Ashraf, Director, Islamic Society of North America, Canada Division, represented by Mazharful Haque Shaheen, Office Manager; Manohar Singh Bal, Secretary, Ontario Council of Sikhs; Ellen K. Campbell, Executive Director of the Canadian Unitarian Council; Dr. Budhendra Doobay, President, Vishnu Temple; Edward Hyland, S.J., Chairperson of Inter-Church Committee for Refugees; Sr. Betty Delio, Toronto Region Director of the Catholic Immigration Bureau of Toronto, on behalf of Constance Crosby Laidlaw, President of the Board of Directors, Catholic Immigration Bureau of Toronto; Jackie Kott, Integration Coordinator, Jewish Immigrant Aid Services, for Susan Davis, National Executive Director, Jewish Immigrant Aid Services; Dr. Nancy Pocock, on behalf of Mona Callin, Clerk of Canadian Friends Service Committee; Michael Kerr, Coordinator, Karuna Community Services (Buddhist Communities of Greater Toronto); Rochelle Wilner, Vice-President of B'nai Brith Canada and Ontario Chair of the League for Human Rights; Adolfo Puricelli, Co-Director of Mennonite New Life Centre of Toronto on behalf of the Mennonite Central Committee of Canada; Tony Meers, Vice-Chair, Soka Gakkai International of Canada; Gerald Vandezande, National Public Affairs Director, Citizens for Public Justice; Dr. Nancy Pocock, Coordinator of the Quaker Committee for Refugees; Sam Ifejika, Coordinator, Jesuit Refuge Services, Canada; Henriette Thompson, representing Don Posterski, Vice-President National Programs, World Vision.

APPENDIX 2

INTERNATIONAL GUARANTEES

1. THE GENEVA CONVENTION ON REFUGEES*
(Adopted on July 28, 1951 by the United Nations. Canada was a signatory.)

Chapter 1 GENERAL PROVISIONS
Article 1. A. (2) Definition of the term "Refugee"
... *Owing to a well-founded fear of being persecuted for reasons of race, religion, nationality, membership of a particular social group or political opinion, is outside the country of his nationality and is unable, or owing to such fear, is unwilling to avail himself of the protection of that country, or who, not having a nationality and being outside the country of his former habitual residence as a result of such events, is unable or, owing to such fear, is unwilling to return to it.*
Article 2 General Obligations
Every refugee has duties to the country in which he finds himself,

---

* This is not a complete text of the Convention. It has been excerpted to reflect the concerns of this book.

which require in particular that he conform to its laws and regulations as well as to measures taken for the maintenance of public order.

Article 3 Non-Discrimination

The Contracting States shall apply the provisions of this Convention to refugees without discrimination as to race, religion or country of origin.

Article 4 Religion

The Contracting States shall accord to refugees within their territories treatment at least as favourable as that accorded to their nationals with respect to freedom to practice their religion and freedom as regards the religious education of their children.

Chapter 2 JURIDICAL STATUS

Article 12 Personal Status

1. The personal status of a refugee shall be governed by the law of the country of his domicile or, if he has no domicile, by the law of his country of residence.

2. Rights previously acquired by a refugee and dependent on personal status, more particularly rights attaching to marriage, shall be respected by a Contracting State, subject to compliance, if this be necessary with the formalities required by the law of that State, provided that the right in question is one which would have been recognized by the law of that State had he not become a refugee.

Article 16 Access to Courts

1. A refugee shall have free access to the courts of law on the territory of all Contracting States.

2. A refugee shall enjoy in the Contracting State in which he has his habitual residence the same treatment as a national in matters pertaining to access to the courts, including legal assistance and exemption from cautio judicatum solvi.

3. A refugee shall be accorded in the matters referred to in paragraph 2 in countries other than that in which he has his habitual residence the treatment granted to a national of the country of his habitual residence.

Chapter 3 GAINFUL EMPLOYMENT

Article 17 Wage-Earning Employment

1. *The Contracting States shall accord to refugees lawfully staying in their territory the most favourable treatment accorded to nationals of a foreign country in the same circumstances, as regards the right to engage in wage-earning employment.*

Chapter 4 WELFARE

Article 20 Rationing

Where a rationing system exists, which applies to the population at large and regulates the general distribution of products in short supply, refugees shall be accorded the same treatment as nationals.

Article 27 Identity Papers

The Contracting States shall issue identity papers to any refugee in their territory who does not possess a valid travel document.

Article 29 Fiscal Charges

1. *The Contracting States shall not impose upon refugees duties, charges or taxes, of any description whatsoever, other or higher than those which are or may be levied on their nationals in similar situations.*

2. *Nothing in the above paragraph shall prevent the application to refugees of the laws and regulations concerning charges in respect of the issue to aliens of administrative documents including identity papers.*

Article 31 Refugees Unlawfully in the Country of Refuge

1. *The Contracting States shall not impose penalties, on account of their illegal entry or presence, on refugees who, coming directly from a territory where their life or freedom was threatened in the sense of Article 1, enter or are present in their territory without authorization, provided they present themselves without delay to the authorities and show good cause for their illegal entry or presence.*

Article 32 Expulsion

1. *The Contracting States shall not expel a refugee lawfully in their territory save on grounds of national security or public order.*

2. *The expulsion of such a refugee shall be only in pursuance of a decision reached in accordance with due process of law. Except where*

compelling reasons of national security otherwise require, the refugee shall be allowed to submit evidence to clear himself, and to appeal to and be represented for the purpose before competent authority or a person or persons specially designated by the competent authority.

3. The Contracting States shall allow such a refugee a reasonable period within which to seek legal admission into another country. The Contracting States reserve the right to apply during that period such internal measures as they may deem necessary.

Article 33 Prohibition of Expulsion or Return ("Refoulement")

1. No Contracting State shall expel or return ("refouler") a refugee in any manner whatsoever to the frontiers of territories where his life or freedom would be threatened on account of his race, religion, nationality, membership of a particular social group or political opinion.

Article 34 Naturalization

The Contracting States shall as far as possible facilitate the assimilation and naturalization of refugees. They shall in particular make every effort to expedite naturalization proceedings and to reduce as far as possible the charges and costs of such proceedings.

PROTOCOL RELATING TO THE STATUS OF REFUGEES

On October 4, 1967, the United Nations Assembly passed the "Protocol Relating to the Status of Refugees." The protocol updated the Geneva Convention to include refugees caused by events after 1951.

2. THE CONVENTION AGAINST TORTURE AND OTHER CRUEL, INHUMAN OR DEGRADING TREATMENT OR PUNISHMENT

(Passed in 1984 by the United Nations. Canada was a signatory.)

Article 3

1. No State Party shall expel, return ("refouler") or extradite a person to another State where there are substantial grounds for believing that he would be in danger of being subjected to torture.

3. THE CONVENTION ON THE RIGHTS OF THE CHILD

(Passed in 1989 by the United Nations. Canada was a signatory.)

Article 9

1. States Parties shall ensure that a child shall not be separated from his or her parents against their will, except when competent authorities subject to judicial review determine, in accordance with applicable laws and procedures, that such separation is necessary for the best interest of the child. . . .

Article 10

In accordance with the obligation of States Parties under article 9, paragraph 1, applications by a child or his or her parents to enter or leave a State Party for the purpose of family reunification shall be dealt with by States Parties in a positive, humane and expeditious manner. . . .

APPENDIX 3

FACTS ABOUT REFUGEES[*]

REFUGEE STATISTICS
- Number of Refugees world-wide who are not permanently settled: 15,337,000. (USCR World Refugee Survey, 1996)
- Number of uprooted people around the world, including all estimated displaced within their own countries: almost 50 million (United Nations High Commission on Refugees). One out of every 115 people on earth has been forced into flight.
- Top five countries unofficially hosting refugees relative to their population: Gaza Strip, West Bank, Jordan, Guinea, Lebanon.
- Top five countries of asylum: Iran (with over 2 million refugees), Zaire, Pakistan, Tanzania and F.R. Yugoslavia (with over half a million refugees).
- Total immigration to Canada in 1995 (including all refugees): 212,270
- Total number of refugees landed in 1995: 24,968
- Refugees as percentage of total landings: 11.8 percent

[*]Statistics compiled with the help of the Canadian Council for Refugees.

- Canada's population is growing at its slowest rate in 50 years. The birth rate is 1.5 percent below replacements levels. At current immigration levels, Canada's population will begin falling by the year 2000 and decline to ten million by 2075.
- Canada's official per capita rate of accepting refugees seems to be one of the highest in the west. However, many European nations accept hundreds of thousands of refugees who don't show up in the statistics. About 80 percent of people who are rejected as Convention refugees in Europe are allowed to stay under some other status.

WOMEN AT RISK

The Women at Risk program, set up in 1988, was hailed as a major achievement by Canadian feminists. However, the statistics show that women and women with children are underrepresented among refugees in Canada. The numbers admitted under the Women at Risk program have been disappointingly low.

The program was established because of the perceived need "for special resettlement assistance for those refugee women who were considered ineligible under existing resettlement processing criteria, and for whom no local solutions were feasible."

Eligibility criteria for this program specifically include: a) women in precarious situations, i.e., women who are experiencing significant difficulties in refugee camps, such as harassment by local authorities or by members of their own communities and b) women who are not in immediate peril, but are existing in permanently unstable circumstances which allow for no other remedy. Because of low level of skills, or because they are accompanied by small children, or other factors, these may be women who have been passed over by Canada or by other resettlement countries.

Prospective applicants for the Women at Risk program are identified by UNHCR branch offices, Canadian visa offices or NGOs and are supposed to be processed as quickly as possible (within a three month period) by Immigration Canada. However, by 1992 many

UNHCR branch offices had stopped referring cases to the Canadian Women at Risk program, especially if they were urgent, due to the lengthy processing time. The wait can be as long as three years.

From 1988 to 1996, 309 cases had been received, and an average of 41 women at risk were admitted to Canada annually.

OPERATION SHORTSTOP

Through Operation Shortstop, Canadian immigration officers overseas routinely prevent people whose lives are at risk from coming to this country.

By forcing all people coming from refugee-producing countries to obtain visas, the Canadian immigration system fails to take account that asylum-seekers who are refugees are in special need. Operation Shortstop does not make any distinction between refugees and other people, such as immigrants, coming to Canada.

Refugees are usually forced to leave a country because of the unpreparedness, or inability, of their own national authorities to protect their liberty and security of person. National authorities, in many instances, constitute the threat. Yet it is the national authorities who are responsible for the issue of identity and travel documents without which the required authorizations for entry into other countries cannot be obtained. Without a travel document there can be no visa. By imposing a visa requirement on refugee asylum-seekers, Operation Shortstop undermines Canada's obligations under the Geneva Convention. With the visa requirements in place, refugees are forced to face the very institutions they need to escape from. No one is allowed entry simply for the purpose of claiming refugee status.

It is very rare that an entire family would be issued a visa from a Canadian Embassy or High Commission overseas because the Embassy assumes the family will make a refugee claim. In legitimate refugee cases where only some of the family have received visas, the lives of those left behind are placed in danger.

Operation Shortstop also employs carrier sanctions to prevent refugees coming to Canada. Transport companies who have carried asylum-seekers to Canada may face stiff fines if the asylum-seekers do not have proper documents. Workers for travel companies have, in effect, become agents of interdiction.

It is estimated that at least 9000 people a year are intercepted through Operation Shortstop.

APPENDIX 4

KEY ADDRESSES

Amnesty International
440 Bloor Street West, 2nd floor
Toronto, Ontario M5S 1X5
Tel. 416-929-0496 FAX 416-929-0539

The Canadian Council for Refugees
6839 Drolet, #302
Montreal, Quebec H2S 2T1
Tel. 514-277-7223 FAX 514-277-1447

Inter-Church Committee for Refugees
129 St. Clair Avenue West
Toronto, Ontario M4V 1N6
Tel. 416-921-9967 FAX 416-921-3843

Minister of Citizenship and Immigration
Ottawa, Ontario K1A 1L1

For information on how to sponsor a refugee, contact:
The Working Group on Refugee Resettlement
1339 King Street West
Toronto, Ontario M6K 1H2
Tel. 416-588-1612 FAX 416-588-1702

ACKNOWLEDGEMENTS

I am grateful to the members of the Romero House team who made it possible for me to spend time away from the important daily life of the community in order to write this book. It is theirs as much as it is mine: Rosemary Broughton, Peter Haeg, Brian Halloran, Lorne Howcroft, Sonia Sirone, Darlene O'Leary, Maureen Lymburner, Ken Horricks, Ursula Blenke, Gabe Thirlwall and Norbert Piché.

Shawn Beck and Cathy Dunphy cheerfully took up the challenge of putting some order to the boxes of my correspondence.

Victoria Watts made a significant contribution through the generous gift of her skill as a competent and persistent researcher.

Kathleen McAlpin, Sister of Mercy, guided our team through a series of reflection evenings in the fall of 1995 and provided me with an important opportunity to gather my own thoughts in a prayerful context. She, Margaret Brennan, IHM, Mary McDevitt, IHM, and Elaine Biollo, SC, provided me with a space of welcome where I could write the final draft of this book.

Long ago, Emil Fackenheim, Hannah Arendt and Gregory Baum taught me that I had everything to learn from refugees.

As always, I am grateful to my agent, Lee Davis Creal, for her encouragement and advice. Phyllis Bruce, my editor, believed in this manuscript when it was only a collection of stories in search of a book. Bernice Eisenstein, my copyeditor, and Nicole Langlois, of HarperCollins, were most helpful in seeing the manuscript through to production. Without their practical acts of hope, I would not have risked taking the time to write.